# *Audrey Grant's*

## BETTER BRIDGE

# Play

 Prentice Hall Canada Inc.
Scarborough, Ontario

**Canadian Cataloguing in Publication Data**

Grant, Audrey
  Play

(The better bridge series)
ISBN 0-13-080121-6

1. Contract bridge – Dummy play.   I. Title.   II. Series: Grant, Audrey. The better bridge series.

GV1282.435.G73 1998        795.41'53        C98-930421-3

Prentice-Hall, Inc., Upper Saddle River, New Jersey
Prentice-Hall International (UK) Limited, London
Prentice-Hall of Australia, Pty. Limited, Sydney
Prentice-Hall Hispanoamericana, S.A., Mexico City
Prentice-Hall of India Private Limited, New Delhi
Prentice-Hall of Japan, Inc., Tokyo
Simon & Schuster Asia Private Limited, Singapore
Editora Prentice-Hall do Brasil, Ltda., Rio de Janeiro

ISBN 0-13-080121-6

Acquisitions Editor: Robert Harris
Production Editor: Kelly Dickson
Production Coordinator: Julie Preston
Cover Design and Image: Alex Li

Original edition © 1995 by Audrey Grant, published by Centennial Press, Box 82087, Lincoln, Nebraska 68501, an imprint of Cliff Notes, Inc.

1 2 3 4 5 W 02 01 00 99 98

Printed and bound in Canada

Visit the Prentice Hall Canada Web site! Send us your comments, browse our catalogues, and more at **www.phcanada.com**.

*To all the bridge players I've met over the years.*
*You've been prepared to share with me the secrets of your expertise*
*so that they can be passed on to new generations of bridge players.*

# Contents

# Preface

For many years, I've seen people of all ages and all walks of life playing bridge. These bridge players are so obviously enjoying themselves that I've made it part of my life's work to teach and write about the game.

The best theorists in the world have shared their secrets with me, and I bring these pieces of bridge wisdom to you in a manner which I hope you will find readable.

Bridge is more than a game. It's a wonderful life skill. It's given me—as it can you—friends around the world. Anywhere you travel, being able to play a hand of bridge opens the door to meeting new people.

Here's more good news about bridge. It's healthy. The days of smoke-filled rooms of bridge players are long gone. It's accepted now that bridge exercises the mind the same way that physical activity exercises your body. That's right. Research indicates that the brain actually changes in response to the stimulus which a game like bridge provides.

This book is a sure way to improve your game. You're on your own as declarer, and here you'll discover the tools you need to do a good job. It's an innovative approach, and you'll see why the order in which you play your cards is the key focus to taking more tricks.

Once you start reading this book and see its potential, you won't be able to wait until the next time you're the declarer. I've spent many years shopping around for the most practical advice on the play of the hand. I think you'll find insights which you can put to immediate use.

*Audrey Grant*

# *Acknowledgments*

To my husband, David Lindop, who works hand-in-hand with me in all my bridge endeavors. Without his talent, drive, and love, these books would still be in the conceptual stage.

To my mother, Connie, who became an expert in counting up to thirteen while making sure every card was in its place.

To my dad, Alex, who writes my bridge jokes—and that's no laughing matter.

To my children, Joanna and Jason, who get involved in so many aspects of the projects—from making crepes for the bridge students to dressing up as cards.

To my brother, Brian, who has helped test much of the material used throughout this series.

To Henry Francis, editor of the *American Contract Bridge League Bulletin,* and his staff, who have been editing my work for years and have helped turn me into a better writer.

To Jerry Helms, the true bridge professional, who has generously shared both his teaching methods and expertise.

To Pat Harrington, whose understanding of the beginner's point of view has helped me write with more clarity .

To Eric Rodwell and Zia Mahmood, world-class players, who have spent countless hours sharing their theories about the game.

To Fred Gitelman and Sheri Winestock, for showing what bridge will look like in the 21st Century.

To Michael Laughlin and Kirk Frederick, for their belief in me, together with their creative input.

To Flip Wilson, for his confidence that even my wildest promotional ideas would work out.

To Jim Borthwick and Bob Covalik, who took care of all the details to bring this series to fruition.

To Michele Spence, for the many hours spent proof-reading each page of the manuscript and her cheerful disposition throughout the project.

To John Reinhardt, for combining his bridge knowledge and design talents to make each book in the series pleasing to the eye.

And of course, I'd like to acknowledge all those students, teachers, and expert players who have constantly provided inspiration and ideas in the field of bridge.

# First Things First

"A journey of a thousand miles must first begin
with a single step."

—LAO-TZU,
*The Way of Lao-tzu*

You're the declarer, and although bridge is a partnership game, you're on your own! The guidelines you've read about and those you've been given by your friends are all running through your mind. You're supposed to stop and think, but everyone appears to be anxiously awaiting your first play from the dummy—after all, a card is meant to be played the same day it's dealt.

By sticking to a few basic principles, you can play many hands as well as the most seasoned bridge players. This book will provide you with the hints you need to become a skilled and confident declarer.

Let's start with three things to consider each time you're the declarer.

## First—Focus on the Target

The first concept is as relevant for the most straightforward hands as it is for those that have been recorded for posterity. The contract is 3NT, and the opening lead is the ♥6. It's your play from dummy to the first trick. Are you going to play the ♥A or the ♥Q?

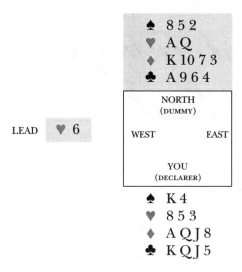

♠ 8 5 2
♥ A Q
♦ K 10 7 3
♣ A 9 6 4

NORTH
(DUMMY)

LEAD ♥ 6

WEST    EAST

YOU
(DECLARER)

♠ K 4
♥ 8 5 3
♦ A Q J 8
♣ K Q J 5

 You have to consider more than the heart suit itself before you can make a decision. The play of each suit has to be put in the context of the entire hand. Before you can decide whether to play the ♥A or ♥Q, focus on your target. How many tricks do you need to make the contract and how many do you already have?

### The Target

The target number of tricks is calculated by adding the book of six tricks to the level of the contract. A contract of 1NT requires 6 + 1 = 7 tricks. A contract of 3♦ requires 6 + 3 = 9 tricks. Does this sound too simple? Focusing on the target will improve your play immediately.

 Look at the above hand. You need to take nine tricks in a contract of 3NT. This dictates how you play the heart suit. If the contract were 4NT, you'd need to take ten tricks, and the play in the heart suit would be different. That's why that first question is so important.

## Counting Tricks

Once you've directed your attention to the number of tricks you need to take, look at the combined partnership hands to see how many tricks you already have. These are the *sure tricks*, or *winners*— the tricks you can take without giving up the lead to the opponents. This lets you know how close you are to reaching the target. If you have eight sure tricks in your contract of 3NT, you need one more to reach the goal. If you have nine winners, you're already there.

Count the sure tricks in each suit, and then add up the sure tricks for the entire hand. Let's look at some examples of counting sure tricks in a suit.

DUMMY
♥ 7 4 2

DECLARER
♥ A K Q

You can take three tricks with this combination of cards in the heart suit: one with the ♥A; one with the ♥K; and one with the ♥Q. The opponents can't stop you from taking these tricks once you have the lead.

DUMMY
♠ A Q 2

DECLARER
♠ K 7 4

The high cards don't have to be on the same side of the table. You can make use of both dummy's high cards and those in your own hand. You would have three sure tricks in this suit.

DUMMY
♦ 9 7 4 2

DECLARER
♦ K Q J 10

Although you have a lot of high cards in this suit, there are no sure tricks. A sure trick is one that you can take without giving up the lead to the opponents. Since the opponents hold the ♦A, you can't take any tricks from this suit without the opponents winning a trick first. This type of suit is a good source of tricks when you need to develop additional winners, but it shouldn't be included in your sure trick count.

DUMMY
**♣ K Q J 5**

DECLARER
**♣ A 6**

count of sure tricks.

The cards may be unevenly divided between the two hands. This suit will provide you with four winners: the ♣A, ♣K, ♣Q, and ♣J. When the last two winning tricks are led from dummy, you'll have to discard from another suit in your hand. This doesn't affect your

DUMMY
**♥ K J**

DECLARER
**♥ A Q**

There are only two sure tricks from this suit combination, even though you hold the four highest cards in the suit. When declarer plays the ♥A, a card has to be played from dummy. The high cards are all played on the first two tricks.

DUMMY
**♥ K J 5 2**

DECLARER
**♥ A Q 4 3**

What a difference the low cards can make. Now there are four sure tricks in the suit; there are four high cards and four cards on each side of the table. When the ♥A is played, a low card can be played from the dummy, rather than the ♥K or ♥J.

DUMMY
**♠ 8 6 5**

DECLARER
**♠ A K Q J 3 2**

Although the combined hands contain only the four top cards in the suit, the suit can be counted as six sure tricks. A sure trick can be taken with a card as low as a two if there are no cards in the suit left in the other hands. You have nine spades in the combined hands, leaving only four for the opponents. Even if one opponent holds all four of the missing spades, there will be none left by the time you've taken the first four tricks with the ♠A, ♠K, ♠Q, and ♠J. When you play the ♠3 and ♠2, they'll both win tricks and can be counted among your winners at the beginning of the hand.

DUMMY

♦ 7 5 4

DECLARER

♦ A K Q 3 2

This suit may provide five tricks if the five missing diamonds are divided favorably between the opponents' hands: one opponent holding three diamonds, and the other holding two. There aren't five sure tricks, however. One opponent could hold all five of the missing diamonds, and you might end up with only three sure tricks: the ♦A, ♦K, and ♦Q. Count on three winners from this suit—but be prepared to look to this suit later on if you need extra winners.

Let's return to the original hand and count the winners.

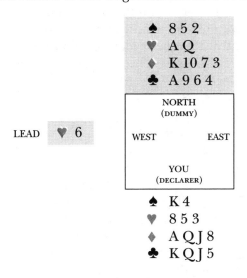

♠ 8 5 2
♥ A Q
♦ K 10 7 3
♣ A 9 6 4

NORTH
(DUMMY)

LEAD ♥ 6

WEST            EAST

YOU
(DECLARER)

♠ K 4
♥ 8 5 3
♦ A Q J 8
♣ K Q J 5

There are no sure tricks in the spade suit. The ♠K could take a trick, but you can't count on it. There's only one sure trick in the heart suit, the ♥A. You might be able to get some use out of the ♥Q, but it isn't a sure trick. In diamonds, there are four sure tricks because you have the top four cards in the suit and sufficient length in the combined hands. Similarly, there are four sure tricks you can take in the club suit. That gives you a total of nine sure tricks for the combined hands.

## Applying the Information

Focus on the number of tricks you need and the number you already have. This brings you to a critical point in planning the play of the hand. You've reached a fork in the road: you either have the number of tricks you need, or you don't. If you have the sure tricks needed to make the contract, take them. This is sometimes easier said than done, and possible complications are discussed in the final stage of the planning process.

Already, however, you can see how this first step is useful in deciding whether to play the ♥A or the ♥Q on the first trick. You need nine tricks, and you have nine sure tricks. The play of the heart suit can be put in the context of the entire hand. You need only one heart trick, the ♥A, which you win on the first trick. There's no need to consider playing the ♥Q, even if you're feeling lucky. Counting on Lady Luck doesn't make up for counting your sure tricks. You might be putting the contract at risk by playing the ♥Q if this were the complete hand:

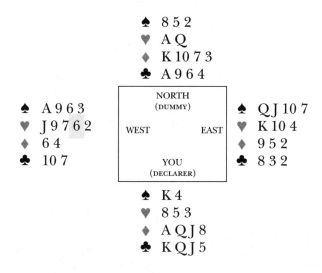

♠ 8 5 2
♥ A Q
♦ K 10 7 3
♣ A 9 6 4

NORTH (DUMMY)

♠ A 9 6 3          ♠ Q J 10 7
♥ J 9 7 6 2        ♥ K 10 4
♦ 6 4              ♦ 9 5 2
♣ 10 7             ♣ 8 3 2

WEST          EAST

YOU (DECLARER)

♠ K 4
♥ 8 5 3
♦ A Q J 8
♣ K Q J 5

If you play the ♥Q on the first trick, East will win the trick with the ♥K and might decide to lead the ♠Q. Whether or not you play your ♠K on this trick, the defenders can now take four spade tricks to go along with the ♥K. That's five tricks, enough to defeat the contract.

The situation would be different if your contract were 4NT. You'd need ten tricks but would have only nine sure tricks. You'd need to find an extra trick to make the contract. It's time to move on to the next part of the planning process.

## Second—Use the Checklist

When you don't have enough sure tricks to make the contract, you'll have to look for places to develop them. There are three basic techniques that are useful in both trump and notrump contracts: promotion, length, and finessing. There are two additional techniques that are useful when there's a trump suit: trumping losers and discarding losers. Together, they make up a little checklist you can use when planning the play of the hand. Each technique will be discussed in the upcoming chapters.

## Third—Note the Order

Have you ever played a hand that you thought you were going to make when, all of a sudden, the opponents take over, and you find yourself falling short of the target? I certainly have.

There are a number of things that can go wrong when taking your sure tricks and when attempting to develop additional tricks. Most of these have to do with the order in which you play your cards.

### Take Your Tricks and Run

In the first hand, there were nine sure tricks in a contract of 3NT. Nothing could go wrong, provided you took the nine tricks right away. This is a simple but effective principle: **if you have the tricks you need, take them**.

If you didn't take the time to count your sure tricks, or if you tried to get an extra trick by playing the ♥Q from dummy on the first trick, you could be defeated in your "sure" contract.

## Drawing Trump

Here's another hand. This time, you're playing with a trump suit. The contract is 4♠, and the opening lead is the ♣J.

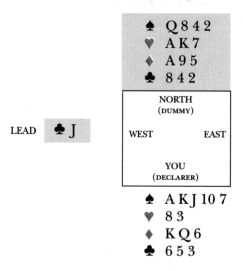

♠ Q 8 4 2
♥ A K 7
♦ A 9 5
♣ 8 4 2

NORTH
(DUMMY)

LEAD ♣ J

WEST          EAST

YOU
(DECLARER)

♠ A K J 10 7
♥ 8 3
♦ K Q 6
♣ 6 5 3

Your target is to take 6 + 4 = 10 tricks in your contract of 4♠. There are five sure tricks in the spade suit, two sure tricks in the heart suit, and three sure tricks in the diamond suit. That's ten tricks. This appears to be a straightforward case of taking your sure tricks. What can go wrong?

The order in which you take your tricks is important. Suppose the opponents take the first three club tricks, and then lead a heart. You win this trick with one of dummy's high hearts. Does it matter which suit you play next?

Suppose you decide to take your three sure tricks in the diamond suit. That will be fine if both opponents have to follow suit each time, but the complete hand might be something like this:

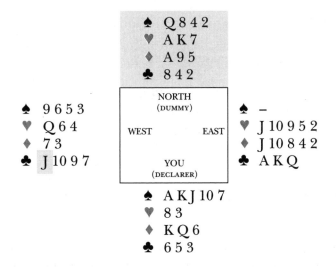

When you play the third round of diamonds, West can win the trick by trumping with a low spade. One of your sure tricks has suddenly disappeared, and you can no longer make the contract. The solution is to take your winners in a different order. Start by playing the trump suit. When neither opponent has any spades left, it's safe to take your remaining winners. Nothing can stop you now.

Removing the trump cards from the opponents' hands is referred to as *drawing trump*. In a suit contract, one of the basic principles is to **draw the opponents' trump first when you have enough sure tricks to make the contract**. We'll see later on that you don't always draw the opponents' trump right away in a suit contract. It's only when you have all the tricks you need that you get rid of the opponents' low trump cards before they can do any damage.

When drawing trump, *count* the trump cards as you see them so that you'll know when there are none left in the opponents' hands. Counting cards is something you have to get used to when playing bridge. The important thing to remember is that there are only thirteen cards in each suit. Elementary though this may appear, it's one key to improving your play. The best place to start practicing is with the trump suit.

On the last hand, you start with nine spades between your hand and the dummy. That leaves four in the opponents' hands. As you play each round of trump, watch to see whether both opponents follow suit. Some players prefer to focus on the number left in the opponents' hands; others focus on the total number they have seen so far.

You're missing four spades. When you play the first round of trump, West plays a low spade, but East discards from another suit. If you're focusing on how many trump are left in the opponents' hands, there are still three outstanding spades. Since West has all of them, you'll have to play the spade suit three more times to draw all the trump. If you're focusing on the total number of trump you've seen so far, your nine trump plus the one that appears from West on the first round of the suit brings the total to ten. The next round of spades will draw another trump from West and bring the total to eleven. It will take two more rounds until the total reaches thirteen and you're finished drawing trump.

Either way you look at it, you have to play the spade suit four times on this hand to draw the opponents' trump. Only then is it safe to take your sure tricks in hearts and diamonds.

## The Tortoise and the Hare

If you're in a contract of 3NT, you don't have to take the first nine tricks; any nine tricks will do. Here's a hand where you have the tricks you need, but you'll have to concentrate on what you're doing while the opponents are busy taking their tricks. The contract is 3NT, and the opening lead is the ♥2.

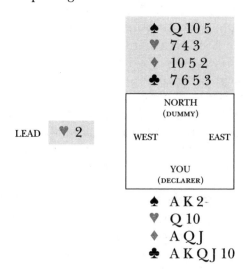

♠ Q 10 5
♥ 7 4 3
♦ 10 5 2
♣ 7 6 5 3

NORTH
(DUMMY)

LEAD    ♥ 2    WEST          EAST

YOU
(DECLARER)

♠ A K 2
♥ Q 10
♦ A Q J
♣ A K Q J 10

The opponents have attacked your weakest suit, and the hand is out of your control for now. The player on your right wins the first trick with the ♥A and leads back the ♥6. Your ♥Q is taken by the ♥K on your left, and the defenders proceed to take two more heart tricks. What have you been up to all this time?

Although things appear to be getting off to a poor start, it's still important to go through the planning process. You need nine tricks and can count nine sure winners. There are three sure tricks in spades, one sure trick in diamonds, and five sure tricks in clubs. This hand points out one of the problems with sure tricks. They're sure only if you get to take them. If the opponents take the first five tricks, it will be too late for you to take your nine winners because there's only eight tricks left to take. You'll have to hope the defenders can't take more than four heart tricks.

Even if the opponents can take only four tricks in the heart suit, you still have to be careful. As the opponents take their third and fourth tricks, you must discard two cards from your hand. Keep focused. The cards you can afford to discard are the ♦J and ♦Q. It's difficult to throw away high cards when you still have the ♠2, a low card, left in your hand to discard. Nonetheless, if you discard the ♠2, you won't make the contract. You counted three sure tricks from the spade suit, assuming there would be three spades in each hand. If you throw away your ♠2 in order to keep the ♦Q, you can no longer take your three sure spade tricks. Here's the complete hand:

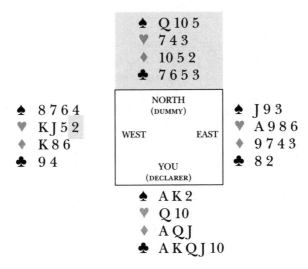

A frequently quoted guideline for choosing your discards is to "keep winners and throw away losers." It's often more important to keep a low card in your hand, rather than a high card.

## The Value of Entries

The last hand brings up an important point. A sure trick is a sure trick only if you get to it—something like counting chickens before they're hatched. Look at this layout of the heart suit:

DUMMY
♥ A K Q 5 2

DECLARER
♥ –

There are three sure heart tricks, if you can get to the dummy to take them. If you can't get to the dummy, there are no sure tricks in the suit.

A card which lets you get from one hand to the other is called an *entry*. Managing the entries between your hand and the dummy has a lot to do with playing your cards in the right order.

## Having FUN

There are three things to keep in mind when you're declarer. You can have FUN when playing the contract by **F**ocusing on the target, **U**sing the checklist, and **N**oting the order.

The game involves bidding, play, and defense. Often the focus is on bidding, but as Shakespeare once said, "The play's the thing."

## Summary

The play of a particular suit can be decided only after declarer has considered the entire hand using the following guidelines:

- **F**ocus on the target.
  - How many tricks do you need to take?
  - How many tricks do you have?

- **U**se the checklist if you need extra tricks.

| *Checklist* | |
|---|---|
| | Promotion |
| | Length |
| | Finessing |
| | Trumping Losers |
| | Discarding Losers |

- **N**ote the order.
  - If you have the tricks you need in a notrump contract, take your tricks and run.
  - If you have the tricks you need in a suit contract, draw the trump first.

Following each chapter we have included several hands for you to practice the techniques we've covered. The solution to each of the following hands appears on the first left-hand page following each hand. Good luck.

# Practice Hands

## Hand 1.1

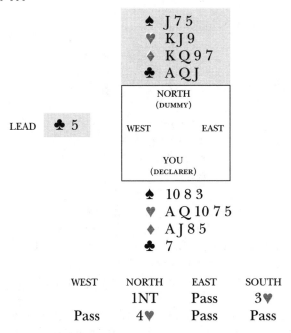

♠ J 7 5
♥ K J 9
♦ K Q 9 7
♣ A Q J

NORTH
(DUMMY)

LEAD ♣ 5

WEST                    EAST

YOU
(DECLARER)

♠ 10 8 3
♥ A Q 10 7 5
♦ A J 8 5
♣ 7

| WEST | NORTH | EAST | SOUTH |
|------|-------|------|-------|
|      | 1NT   | Pass | 3♥    |
| Pass | 4♥    | Pass | Pass  |

West leads the ♣5 against your contract of 4♥. Which card do you play from dummy on the first trick? Which suit do you plan to play after winning a trick?

**Solution 1.1**

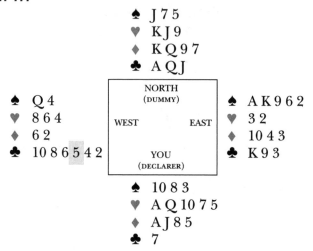

♠ J 7 5
♥ K J 9
♦ K Q 9 7
♣ A Q J

NORTH
(DUMMY)

♠ Q 4                      ♠ A K 9 6 2
♥ 8 6 4      WEST    EAST   ♥ 3 2
♦ 6 2                      ♦ 10 4 3
♣ 10 8 6 5 4 2             ♣ K 9 3

YOU
(DECLARER)

♠ 10 8 3
♥ A Q 10 7 5
♦ A J 8 5
♣ 7

You could win the first trick with dummy's ♣A, or you could try playing dummy's ♣Q or ♣J. Before deciding which card to play in a single suit, consider the entire hand. You need 6 + 4 = 10 tricks in a contract of 4♥. You have five sure tricks in hearts, four sure tricks in diamonds, and one sure trick in clubs. That's the ten tricks you need to make the contract.

There's no need to take any chances. Win the first trick with the ♣A. The next thing you have to be careful about is the order in which you take your sure tricks. Because you're in a trump suit, start by drawing trump. You need to keep playing hearts until the opponents have none left. On the actual hand, you'll have to play hearts three times before it's safe to take your four sure tricks in the diamond suit.

If you played the ♣Q or ♣J on the first trick, you're likely to go down in the contract. East wins the first trick with the ♣K and may lead spades next. After taking the ♠A and ♠K, East will see West's ♠Q fall. East can lead another spade, and West will trump it to defeat the contract. You'll also go down if you don't draw three rounds of trump after winning the first trick with the ♣A. If you start playing diamonds while West still has a heart left, West will be able to trump one of your diamond winners, and you'll end up a trick short.

Not too much to this hand. Take your tricks and run. Didn't someone write something about a bird in the hand?

## Hand 1.2

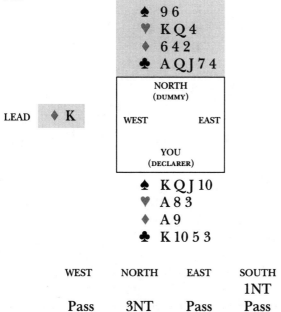

| WEST | NORTH | EAST | SOUTH |
|------|-------|------|-------|
|      |       |      | 1NT   |
| Pass | 3NT   | Pass | Pass  |

Your contract is 3NT, and the opening lead is the ♦K. What's your plan?

## Solution 1.2

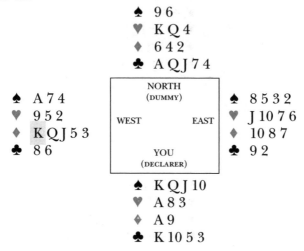

```
              ♠  9 6
              ♥  K Q 4
              ♦  6 4 2
              ♣  A Q J 7 4
                  NORTH
♠  A 7 4          (DUMMY)         ♠  8 5 3 2
♥  9 5 2                          ♥  J 10 7 6
♦  K Q J 5 3   WEST      EAST     ♦  10 8 7
♣  8 6                            ♣  9 2
                  YOU
                (DECLARER)
              ♠  K Q J 10
              ♥  A 8 3
              ♦  A 9
              ♣  K 10 5 3
```

After winning a trick with the ♦A, you might be tempted to look toward your fine spade suit as a potential source of tricks. If you do lead a spade, West will win the ♠A and take four diamond tricks to defeat the contract.

There's no need to put your contract at risk. You need nine tricks to make your 3NT contract. You can count three sure tricks from the heart suit, one from the diamond suit, and five from the club suit. After winning the ♦A, take your nine tricks, and go on to the next hand.

## Hand 1.3

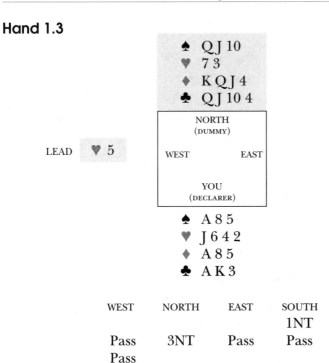

♠ Q J 10
♥ 7 3
♦ K Q J 4
♣ Q J 10 4

NORTH
(DUMMY)

LEAD   ♥ 5

WEST         EAST

YOU
(DECLARER)

♠ A 8 5
♥ J 6 4 2
♦ A 8 5
♣ A K 3

| WEST | NORTH | EAST | SOUTH |
|------|-------|------|-------|
|      |       |      | 1NT   |
| Pass | 3NT   | Pass | Pass  |
| Pass |       |      |       |

West leads the ♥5 against your 3NT contract. What are you think-ing about while the opponents are taking their heart tricks?

## Solution 1.3

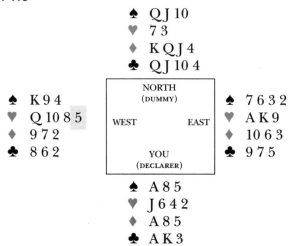

```
              ♠ Q J 10
              ♥ 7 3
              ♦ K Q J 4
              ♣ Q J 10 4

                   NORTH
                   (DUMMY)
♠ K 9 4                             ♠ 7 6 3 2
♥ Q 10 8 5   WEST        EAST       ♥ A K 9
♦ 9 7 2                             ♦ 10 6 3
♣ 8 6 2                             ♣ 9 7 5
                    YOU
                 (DECLARER)

              ♠ A 8 5
              ♥ J 6 4 2
              ♦ A 8 5
              ♣ A K 3
```

I hope you aren't worrying about whether or not you're in the right contract while the opponents are taking their tricks. Focus on your plan for taking nine tricks. If the opponents can take the first five heart tricks . . . on to the next hand. You want to concentrate on those situations in which you have a chance. On the actual hand, the opponents can take only four heart tricks before giving you the lead. The contract is there for the taking, if you've been careful.

Count your sure tricks; there's one in spades, four in diamonds, and four in clubs. As the opponents take their four heart tricks, you have to follow suit from your hand, but you'll have to discard two cards from the dummy on the third and fourth round of hearts. You've been counting on four tricks from both diamonds and clubs, so you can't discard either the low diamond or the low club from dummy. Otherwise, you'll no longer have your sure tricks! Instead, be prepared to discard dummy's ♠J and ♣10, leaving the singleton ♠Q in dummy. You need only one trick from the spade suit, and you have that with the ♠A in your hand.

As long as you focus on taking the nine tricks you need, finding the right discards from the dummy is straightforward. If you lose your concentration, you might let one of those little cards go from the dummy. Then, it would be too late to recover.

## Hand 1.4

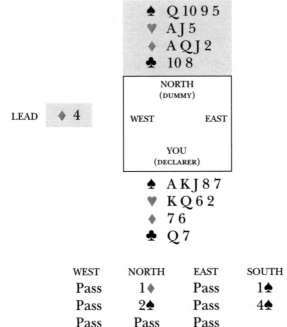

♠ Q 10 9 5
♥ A J 5
♦ A Q J 2
♣ 10 8

NORTH
(DUMMY)

LEAD ♦ 4

WEST          EAST

YOU
(DECLARER)

♠ A K J 8 7
♥ K Q 6 2
♦ 7 6
♣ Q 7

| WEST | NORTH | EAST | SOUTH |
|------|-------|------|-------|
| Pass | 1♦ | Pass | 1♠ |
| Pass | 2♠ | Pass | 4♠ |
| Pass | Pass | Pass | |

You reach a contract of 4♠, and West leads the ♦4. Do you visualize any problem in making your contract? Does it matter which diamond you play from dummy on the first trick? What do you plan to do once you win a trick?

## Solution 1.4

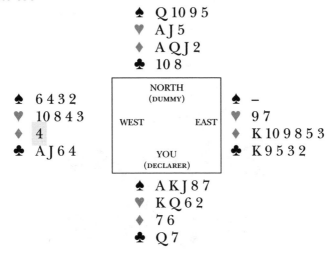

North (Dummy)
- ♠ Q 10 9 5
- ♥ A J 5
- ♦ A Q J 2
- ♣ 10 8

West
- ♠ 6 4 3 2
- ♥ 10 8 4 3
- ♦ 4
- ♣ A J 6 4

East
- ♠ —
- ♥ 9 7
- ♦ K 10 9 8 5 3
- ♣ K 9 5 3 2

You (Declarer)
- ♠ A K J 8 7
- ♥ K Q 6 2
- ♦ 7 6
- ♣ Q 7

The hand appears straightforward. You need to take ten tricks to fulfill your contract of 4♠. You can count five sure tricks in spades, four sure tricks in hearts, and the ♦A. That's enough for your contract.

When you have the number of tricks you need, it's tempting to start looking for something extra. You might consider playing dummy's ♦Q or ♦J on the first trick because, even if East has the ♦K, you still have your ten tricks. On the actual hand, however, this might lead to disaster. When East wins the ♦K, East could lead another diamond, and West will win the trick by trumping it. The defenders can now take two club tricks to defeat your "iron-clad" contract.

It would be unfortunate if this happened but also unnecessary. By counting your sure tricks, you know you have the tricks you need. All you have to do is take them. Don't put the contract at risk for the sake of an extra trick or two. Win the first trick with the ♦A, and then draw trump. You'll have to play spades four times before there are none left in the East-West hands. You can then take your four sure heart tricks, and you'll make the contract. Save your energy. Think about extra tricks for those hands which need them.

# Entries Are Everything

*"What we've got here is a failure to communicate."*

— DONN PEARCE,
*Cool Hand Luke,* screenplay 1967

I've always found the term "sure trick" to be a bit of a misnomer. There are many hands where there seem to be enough tricks at the start, but when it's all over, you end up with fewer tricks than you had at the beginning.

It all has to do with the last stage of the planning process, noting the order in which you have to play your cards. The order is connected to entries—the need to travel back and forth between your hand and the dummy. Entries play an important role in taking your sure tricks and in developing tricks. Before moving on to the various techniques for developing tricks, you need to become very familiar with entries.

## Entries

An entry from one hand to the other consists of two parts. First, you need a winner in the hand you're trying to reach. Equally important, you need a *link card* in the other hand which can be led to the winner. Take a look at each of the following suit combinations:

DUMMY
♠A 8 3

DECLARER
♠ 2

The ♠A is the winner which will provide an entry to the dummy. The ♠2 is the link card which can be played from declarer's hand to cross over to the dummy.

DUMMY
♥A K Q

DECLARER
♥ –

The importance of the link card can be seen in this layout. There are three winners in the dummy but no link card in declarer's hand. Dummy's heart winners are *stranded* unless there's an entry in another suit. When it comes to entries, the link card is as important as the winner.

DUMMY
♦4 3

DECLARER
♦A K 7

This suit provides you with two entries from the dummy to declarer's hand. Declarer has two winners, and dummy has two link cards. If there was only one diamond in the dummy, there would be only one entry to declarer's hand in this suit, even though declarer has two winners.

DUMMY
♣K Q J 3

DECLARER
♣ A

You have the top four cards in this suit. However, there's no entry to dummy in the club suit. You can use the ♣A as an entry to your hand, but the ♣K, ♣Q, and ♣J are stranded because there's no link card in declarer's hand. A suit like this is said to be *blocked.* You have four winners in the suit, but you can't take them without the help of an entry in another suit.

DUMMY
♠ 8 2

DECLARER
♠ A K Q J 10 9 3

Low cards have the potential to provide entries. The ♠8 is the winner in the dummy, and the ♠3 is the link card that will get you there.

DUMMY
♥ K 5 2

DECLARER
♥ A 8 6

From the point of view of sure tricks, this suit is not very interesting. There are two sure tricks and not much else. This suit is very valuable, however, when it comes to entries. It provides an entry to both hands. There will be many hands in which such suits play an important role, and the choice of which high card to play first could be crucial to the outcome of the hand.

DUMMY
♦ A Q 10 8

DECLARER
♦ K J 9 2

A suit like this can provide multiple entries to either hand. You could use it to give you four entries to the dummy: the ♦2 as the link card to the ♦8; the ♦9 as the link card to the ♦10; the ♦J as the link card to the ♦Q; and the ♦K as the link card to the ♦A. You could also use the suit to provide three entries to your hand: the ♦8 as the link card to the ♦9; the ♦10 as the link card to the ♦J; and the ♦Q as the link card to the ♦K.

In a suit contract, the trump suit is often a good place to look for entries between the two hands. You'll usually have high cards in both hands and may have to use them wisely during the play.

The trump suit can also provide an entry when one hand is void in a suit. Suppose spades are trump, and there are no hearts in the dummy. Declarer can lead a heart and trump it in the dummy to gain an entry to the dummy.

## Unevenly Divided Suits—Handle with Care

When you're taking sure tricks in a suit that's evenly divided between your hand and the dummy, there's no problem with entries.

You can take your three sure tricks in this suit in any order. For example, you could win the first trick with your ♣A, and then take two more tricks with dummy's ♣K and ♣Q. Or, you could win the first trick with dummy's ♣K, the second with your ♣A, and the third with dummy's ♣Q.

The order in which you take your tricks becomes much more important when a suit is unevenly divided between the two hands. Now, there's a *long side* and a *short side*.

In this suit, the dummy is the short side and declarer's hand is the long side. Suppose you win the first trick from the long side with your ♠A, playing the ♠3 from the dummy. You can win a second trick by playing your ♠5 over to dummy's ♠K, but now the ♠Q is stranded in your hand. You have no link card left in dummy in the spade suit. You'll need an entry in another suit, and if you don't have one, you'll never get to enjoy a trick with your ♠Q.

To avoid this problem, **play the high card from the short side first** when you're taking sure tricks in a suit that's unevenly divided. In the last example, start by winning a trick with the ♠K, high card from the short side. Now you have a link card, the ♠3, left in dummy to lead over to your ♠A and ♠Q. You can take your three sure tricks without the help of an entry in another suit.

Here's an example of this principle. The contract is 3NT, and the opening lead is the ♥K.

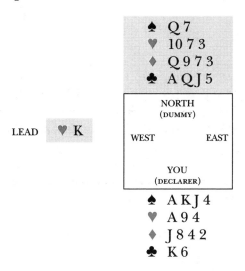

♠ Q 7
♥ 10 7 3
♦ Q 9 7 3
♣ A Q J 5

NORTH
(DUMMY)

LEAD ♥ K

WEST          EAST

YOU
(DECLARER)

♠ A K J 4
♥ A 9 4
♦ J 8 4 2
♣ K 6

Your target is nine tricks. Count your sure tricks; there are four in spades, one in hearts, and four in clubs. That's all you need for the contract, but note the order in which you have to take your tricks. When taking the four sure club tricks, start by playing the ♣K, high card from the short side. Your ♣6 is then the link card to travel over to dummy's ♣A, ♣Q, and ♣J. Play the spades in a similar fashion. Win the first trick with the ♠Q in dummy—the short side. The ♠7 can now be used to enter your hand for the remaining three winners in the spade suit.

# Blocked Suits

Suits that are blocked present entry problems.

## Totally Blocked Suits

Consider this example:

DUMMY
♥ Q J 7 3

DECLARER
♥ A K

There are four sure tricks in this suit but only if you can take them. After playing the ♥A and ♥K, there's no link card in the suit to cross over to dummy's remaining two winners. You'll need an entry in another suit to help you out.

To handle totally blocked suits, you'll often have to make good use of your entries in other suits. A good principle to keep in mind is to **keep an entry on the same side of the table as the long suit** in which you're trying to take tricks. This is best seen through an example.

Suppose you reach a contract of 1NT with the following hands, and the opening lead is the ♠J.

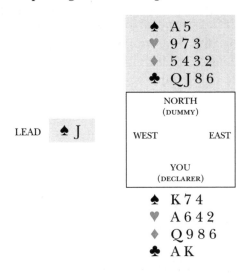

You have a choice of winning the first trick with the ♠A in dummy or the ♠K in your hand. Before you decide on the play in a particular suit, take a look at the complete hand. You need seven tricks in a contract of 1NT. There are two sure tricks in the spade suit, one in the heart suit, and four in the club suit. That's the seven tricks you need—provided you can take them all.

The problem on this hand is that the club suit is totally blocked. After winning the first two tricks in the club suit with your ♣A and ♣K, there's no link card left in the club suit to travel over to the dummy. You'll need an entry in another suit. The ♠A is the only possible entry to the dummy. You'll need to keep it with the long club suit in dummy. This tells you what to do on the first trick as you note the order in which you must play your cards.

Win the first trick with the ♠K in your hand. Next, play the ♣A and ♣K to *unblock* the suit. Now is the time to use your carefully preserved entry to the dummy. Play a low spade to dummy's ♠A, and then take your winners from the long side, the ♣Q and ♣J. Your ♥A is the seventh trick.

Be careful when you use guidelines such as "high card from the short side first." If you were to apply that principle in the spade suit on this hand, you'd win the first trick with dummy's ♠A. Playing the high card from the short side applies when you're planning to take sure tricks from an unevenly divided suit. Here, your focus is not on using the spade suit as a source of sure tricks—although it will provide two tricks. Your focus is on using the spade suit as a source of entries to help you take the club tricks to which you're entitled. Win the first trick with the ♠K; you're following the principle of keeping an entry on the same side of the table as your long suit—the club suit in this case.

## Partially Blocked Suits

Consider this suit:

DUMMY
♦K Q

DECLARER
♦A J 3 2

You can win the first two tricks with the ♦K and ♦Q in the dummy, but your ♦A and ♦J will be stranded in your hand unless there's an entry in another suit. If you need only three tricks from this suit, rather than four, you could win the first trick with dummy's ♦K, and then use the ♦Q as the link card. You could *overtake* dummy's ♦Q with your ♦A on the second round of the suit. That's a bit wasteful, but you'd now be in the right hand to take a third trick with the ♦J.

This suit is partially blocked. You can get an extra trick but only at the expense of playing two of your high cards on the same trick, thereby losing one of your sure tricks in the process.

Here's an example of handling entries to overcome a partially blocked suit in a trump contract. You've reached 4♠, and the opening lead is the ♦K.

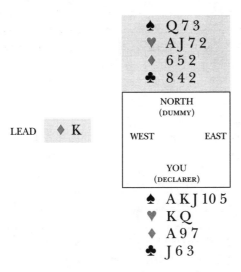

♠ Q 7 3
♥ A J 7 2
♦ 6 5 2
♣ 8 4 2

NORTH
(DUMMY)

LEAD   ♦ K

WEST                EAST

YOU
(DECLARER)

♠ A K J 10 5
♥ K Q
♦ A 9 7
♣ J 6 3

You need ten tricks, and on the surface, you appear to have them. There are five sure tricks in spades, four in hearts, and one in diamonds. The difficulty is that the heart suit is partially blocked. You can't take four tricks in the suit without an outside entry to the dummy.

In a trump contract, you're supposed to draw trump first when you have the tricks you need. This assumes you don't need the trump suit for anything else. On this hand, the only entry to the dummy outside of the heart suit is dummy's ♠Q. That's the card you'll have to use to help you get your heart tricks.

The order of play is very important on this hand. After winning the ♦A, you can start drawing trump by playing the ♠A and ♠K. Before playing a third round of trump, you must stop. You need to unblock the heart suit by playing your ♥K and ♥Q, while you still have an entry to the dummy. Once that's done, you can play a third round of trump, winning the trick with dummy's carefully preserved entry, the ♠Q. Now you're in the right place at the right time. If the defenders' five trump were originally divided with three in one hand and two in the other, there will be none left. You can safely take your two heart tricks and make the contract.

## Overtaking

Sometimes you can get around an entry problem by overtaking one of your high cards. Consider these suits.

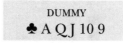

DUMMY
♣ A Q J 10 9

DECLARER
♣ K

There are five sure tricks in this suit, but with no low club in declarer's hand, it appears as though the suit is blocked. If you win the first trick with the ♣K, your remaining club winners will be stranded in the dummy. This inconvenience can be overcome by regarding the ♣K as the link card. Instead of winning the first round of clubs with the king, you could overtake the king with dummy's ace. Now you're in the right hand to continue taking your club tricks.

If you've heard the expression, "Don't play your ace on partner's king," now you know there are always exceptions!

DUMMY
♥ A Q

DECLARER
♥ K J 10 5

To take four tricks from this suit without using an entry in another suit, win the first trick with dummy's ♥A, lead the ♥Q, and overtake with the ♥K in your hand. You're in the right place to take the rest of your sure tricks.

Here's an example of overtaking in a full hand. The contract is
3NT, and the opening lead is the ♠2.

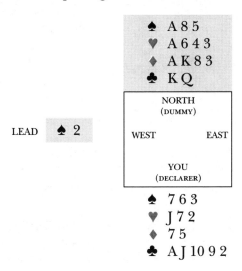

```
              ♠ A 8 5
              ♥ A 6 4 3
              ♦ A K 8 3
              ♣ K Q
         ┌──────────────────────┐
         │       NORTH          │
         │      (DUMMY)         │
LEAD ♠ 2 │  WEST          EAST  │
         │                      │
         │       YOU            │
         │    (DECLARER)        │
         └──────────────────────┘
              ♠ 7 6 3
              ♥ J 7 2
              ♦ 7 5
              ♣ A J 10 9 2
```

Count the sure tricks. There's a spade trick, a heart trick, two
diamond tricks, and five club tricks. You have the nine tricks you
need to make 3NT, but you'll have to be careful when you take them.
There's no entry to your hand outside the club suit, so you'll have to
take five club tricks using the club itself for transportation to your
hand.

After winning a trick with dummy's ♠A, lead the ♣K. Let the ♣K
win the trick, but when you lead the ♣Q, overtake with the ♣A so
that you'll be in the right hand. Now you can take three more club
tricks with the ♣J, ♣10, and ♣9. Together with your other sure tricks,
you make the contract.

Since overtaking uses up two of your high cards on the same trick,
you need to have enough high cards in the suit so that you can afford to overtake and still get the tricks you need. If you won't have
enough winners left after overtaking, you may have to look elsewhere
for your entries.

## Summary

When playing a hand, the order in which you take your tricks is important. The reason for focusing on the order is that you often need entries between the two hands. An entry consists of a winner in one hand together with a link card in the other hand with which to reach the winner. To help manage your entries effectively, keep the following principles in mind:

- Play the high card from the short side first when taking tricks in an unevenly divided suit.

- Keep an entry on the same side of the table as the long suit in which you're trying to take tricks.

- Use a high card as a link card, if necessary, by overtaking with a higher card on the other side of the table.

# Practice Hands

## Hand 2.1

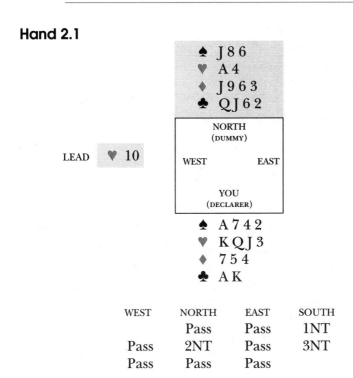

```
              ♠ J 8 6
              ♥ A 4
              ♦ J 9 6 3
              ♣ Q J 6 2
        ┌─────────────────────┐
        │       NORTH         │
        │      (DUMMY)        │
LEAD  ♥ 10│                     │
        │ WEST          EAST  │
        │                     │
        │       YOU           │
        │    (DECLARER)       │
        └─────────────────────┘
              ♠ A 7 4 2
              ♥ K Q J 3
              ♦ 7 5 4
              ♣ A K
```

| WEST | NORTH | EAST | SOUTH |
|------|-------|------|-------|
|      | Pass  | Pass | 1NT   |
| Pass | 2NT   | Pass | 3NT   |
| Pass | Pass  | Pass |       |

West leads the ♥10 against your contract of 3NT. Which card do you play from dummy on the first trick? Which suit do you plan to play after winning a trick?

## Solution 2.1

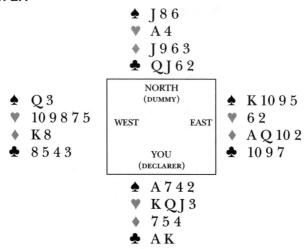

```
                    ♠ J 8 6
                    ♥ A 4
                    ♦ J 9 6 3
                    ♣ Q J 6 2
                ┌─────────────────┐
    ♠ Q 3       │     NORTH       │  ♠ K 10 9 5
    ♥ 10 9 8 7 5│   (DUMMY)       │  ♥ 6 2
    ♦ K 8       │ WEST      EAST  │  ♦ A Q 10 2
    ♣ 8 5 4 3   │                 │  ♣ 10 9 7
                │     YOU         │
                │  (DECLARER)     │
                └─────────────────┘
                    ♠ A 7 4 2
                    ♥ K Q J 3
                    ♦ 7 5 4
                    ♣ A K
```

If you were considering the heart suit all by itself, the best way to take four tricks in the suit would be to play the ♥A first—high card from the short side. Before deciding on how to play the heart suit, however, you must plan out the play for the entire hand.

You need nine tricks in your contract of 3NT. There's one sure trick in spades, four in hearts, and four in clubs. The tricks are there. All you have to do is take them—carefully. The club suit is blocked, so you'll need an entry to the dummy in another suit. The only sure entry is the ♥A. You can't afford to use that entry too early. You want to keep an entry with the long suit—clubs.

Note the order in which you must play your cards. Win the first trick in your hand with the ♥J—or the ♥K or ♥Q. Next, unblock the clubs by playing the ♣A and ♣K. Use your carefully preserved link card, the ♥3, to travel over to dummy's ♥A. Now you can play the ♣Q and ♣J. Finally, use the ♠A as an entry back to your hand to take your last two heart winners. You can graciously concede the rest to the defenders.

## Hand 2.2

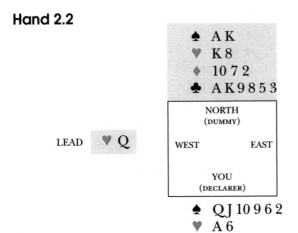

♠ A K
♥ K 8
♦ 10 7 2
♣ A K 9 8 5 3

NORTH
(DUMMY)

LEAD ♥ Q

WEST          EAST

YOU
(DECLARER)

♠ Q J 10 9 6 2
♥ A 6
♦ J 4 3
♣ 7 2

| WEST | NORTH | EAST | SOUTH |
|------|-------|------|-------|
|      |       | Pass | Pass  |
| Pass | 1♣    | Pass | 1♠    |
| Pass | 3♣    | Pass | 3♠    |
| Pass | 4♠    | Pass | Pass  |
| Pass | Pass  |      |       |

You reach a contract of 4♠, and West leads the ♥Q. Does it matter where you win the first trick? Why?

## Solution 2.2

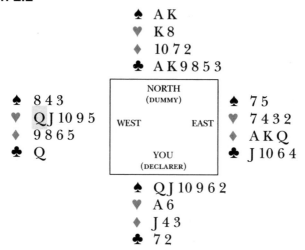

        ♠ A K
        ♥ K 8
        ♦ 10 7 2
        ♣ A K 9 8 5 3

NORTH (DUMMY)

WEST      EAST

YOU (DECLARER)

WEST:
♠ 8 4 3
♥ Q J 10 9 5
♦ 9 8 6 5
♣ Q

EAST:
♠ 7 5
♥ 7 4 3 2
♦ A K Q
♣ J 10 6 4

YOU:
♠ Q J 10 9 6 2
♥ A 6
♦ J 4 3
♣ 7 2

You have six sure spade tricks, two heart tricks, and two club tricks. The total of ten is exactly what you need to make your 4♠ contract. Be careful not to give the defenders an opportunity to trump one of your winners. You want to draw trump as soon as possible once you get the lead.

The only trouble here is the trump suit itself. After taking the ♣A and ♣K, you'll need to get over to your hand to draw the remaining trump. The best card for this is the ♥A. You want to keep that card with your long suit until you're ready to use it. That tells you to win the first trick with dummy's ♥K. Then play the ♠A and ♠K. Travel to your hand with the ♥A, and continue drawing trump until they're all gone from the defenders' hands. It's then safe to take your remaining winners, the ♣A and ♣K.

What might happen if you weren't concentrating on entries and won the first trick in your hand with the ♥A? You could play a spade to dummy's ♠A and ♠K but would have no quick way back to your hand to draw the last trump. If you try playing the ♣A and ♣K, West will trump the second club trick, and one of your sure tricks will have disappeared. If you lead a diamond, East can win three diamond tricks and lead a club or a heart. You'll be stuck back in the dummy. When you play your second high club, West will trump, and down you'll go. You're a little unlucky to go down because the clubs divide unfavorably. But you don't need to take that chance, if you handle your entries wisely.

## Hand 2.3

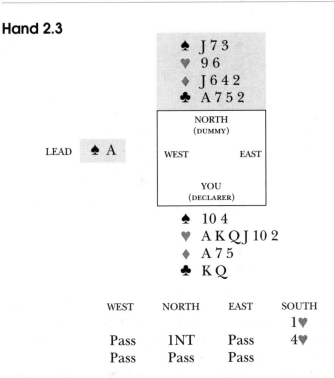

♠ J 7 3
♥ 9 6
♦ J 6 4 2
♣ A 7 5 2

NORTH
(DUMMY)

LEAD ♠ A

WEST          EAST

YOU
(DECLARER)

♠ 10 4
♥ A K Q J 10 2
♦ A 7 5
♣ K Q

| WEST | NORTH | EAST | SOUTH |
|------|-------|------|-------|
|      |       |      | 1♥    |
| Pass | 1NT   | Pass | 4♥    |
| Pass | Pass  | Pass |       |

You reach a contract of 4♥, and West starts off by leading the ♠A, followed by the ♠K and the ♠Q. How do you plan to make the contract? Can you afford to draw trump right away? If not, why not? Which card do you play on the third round of spades? Does it matter?

## Solution 2.3

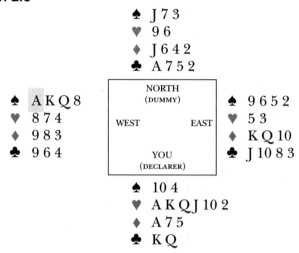

```
                      ♠ J 7 3
                      ♥ 9 6
                      ♦ J 6 4 2
                      ♣ A 7 5 2
                   ┌─────────────────┐
                   │     NORTH       │
  ♠ A K Q 8        │    (DUMMY)      │    ♠ 9 6 5 2
  ♥ 8 7 4          │                 │    ♥ 5 3
  ♦ 9 8 3          │ WEST      EAST  │    ♦ K Q 10
  ♣ 9 6 4          │                 │    ♣ J 10 8 3
                   │      YOU        │
                   │   (DECLARER)    │
                   └─────────────────┘
                      ♠ 10 4
                      ♥ A K Q J 10 2
                      ♦ A 7 5
                      ♣ K Q
```

You seem to have the ten tricks you need: six heart tricks, a diamond trick, and three club tricks. The only problem is the club suit. You can't take your three sure tricks without finding an entry to the dummy.

If you look hard enough, there it is—dummy's ♥9 will do the job. You must remember, however, that an entry consists of two parts: the winner and the link card to get to the winner. The only link card in your hand to dummy's ♥9 is your ♥2. If it's not around when you need it, you won't be able to get to dummy. When you trump the third round of spades, therefore, you must make sure to do so with one of your high hearts. Then you play the ♣K and ♣Q to unblock the suit. Use your carefully conserved ♥2 to travel over to dummy's ♥9 and play the ♣A. Only now can you draw the rest of the trump and make your contract.

This is another example of delaying drawing trump because you need to use the trump suit to provide a valuable entry to the other hand.

## Hand 2.4

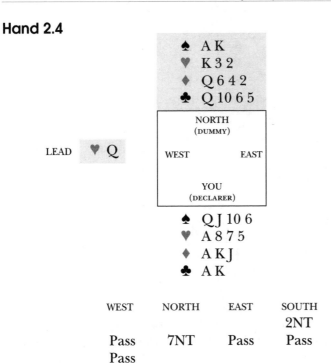

♠ A K
♥ K 3 2
♦ Q 6 4 2
♣ Q 10 6 5

NORTH
(DUMMY)

LEAD    ♥ Q

WEST            EAST

YOU
(DECLARER)

♠ Q J 10 6
♥ A 8 7 5
♦ A K J
♣ A K

| WEST | NORTH | EAST | SOUTH |
|------|-------|------|-------|
|      |       |      | 2NT   |
| Pass | 7NT   | Pass | Pass  |
| Pass |       |      |       |

Partner has taken you all the way to the seven level. You need all thirteen tricks. They're there, but you may have some trouble taking them all. Can you do it?

## Solution 2.4

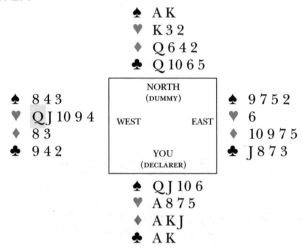

&spades; A K
&hearts; K 3 2
&diams; Q 6 4 2
&clubs; Q 10 6 5

NORTH
(DUMMY)

&spades; 8 4 3
&hearts; Q J 10 9 4
&diams; 8 3
&clubs; 9 4 2

WEST                EAST

&spades; 9 7 5 2
&hearts; 6
&diams; 10 9 7 5
&clubs; J 8 7 3

YOU
(DECLARER)

&spades; Q J 10 6
&hearts; A 8 7 5
&diams; A K J
&clubs; A K

You need all the tricks. There are four sure tricks in spades, two in hearts, four in diamonds, and three in clubs—but three of the suits are blocked. Only the heart suit presents no problem, but you have to choose where to win the first trick and play carefully thereafter. Try to visualize how the play will go. The order is very important. If you don't keep focused on your plan, you'll find yourself in the wrong place at the end of the hand, staring across the table at a winner you can no longer reach. Taking "sure" tricks can keep you busy.

Suppose you win the first trick in dummy with the &hearts;K—keeping the &hearts;A as an entry to the long spades. You must first unblock the diamonds and clubs. Take the high cards from the short side in those suits—the &diams;A, &diams;K, &diams;J, &clubs;A, and &clubs;K. Now that those suits are unblocked, cross back to dummy with the &spades;A to take &diams;Q and &clubs;Q—discarding the two low hearts from your hand. Finally, take the &spades;K to unblock that suit and cross back to your hand with the &hearts;A to take the last two tricks with the &spades;Q and &spades;J.

If you win the first trick with the &hearts;A—keeping the &hearts;K as an entry to the long clubs and diamonds—you must take the tricks in a different order. Unblock the spades by taking the &spades;A and &spades;K. Then cross back to your hand with a minor suit winner to take the &spades;Q and &spades;J—discarding a low heart and a low club from dummy. Finally, take the rest of the club and diamond winners in your hand, cross over to dummy with the &hearts;K, and take the last two tricks with dummy's &diams;Q and &clubs;Q.

# Promotion— Putting High Cards to Work

*"Really, if the lower orders don't set us a good example, what on earth is the use of them?"*

—OCSAR WILDE,
*The Importance of Being Earnest*
[1895]

On a warm afternoon in the park, I came upon two people playing checkers, one of the world's oldest board games. They were using some of the same ideas to win their games that bridge players use. A player would give up a piece in the hope of gaining more than was lost by the time the game was over.

As declarer, there will be many hands where your count of sure tricks falls short of those needed to make the contract. You have to start looking at ways to generate the extra tricks you need. *Promotion*, the first technique on your list of possibilities, is the most useful. When the conditions are right, it's a sure-fire way of developing additional winners.

## Promoting Winners

One of the most common ways to create tricks during the play is through *promotion*. This technique involves using your high cards to drive out the defenders' higher cards and to turn your side's lower-ranking cards into sure tricks. Consider this suit:

DUMMY

♠ K Q J

DECLARER

♠ 8 7 6

There are no sure tricks in the suit—tricks you can take without giving up the lead to the opponents—but there's great potential to develop tricks from this suit. Like the checker player, you have to give up something with the hope of getting something in return. In this suit, you have to give up one trick to the opponents by playing one of your high cards to drive out the defenders' ace. In return, your remaining two high spades have been promoted into sure tricks. That's a good trade.

DUMMY

♥ 7 4 3 2

DECLARER

♥ Q J 10 9

This suit also holds the promise of extra tricks, but you have to be more patient. The opponents have the ace and king. You have to lose two tricks to the defenders: one to drive out the ace and one to drive out the king. In the end, you've promoted two winners for your side.

DUMMY

♦ J 10 9 8

DECLARER

♦ 6 4 3 2

Patience is truly a virtue in this example. You'd have to lead this suit three times, driving out the opponents' ace, king, and queen. In return, you'd promote one of your cards as a winner. This may not seem worth the effort, but it could be the source of the one trick you need to make your contract.

DUMMY

♣ Q 10 4

DECLARER

♣ J 5 2

The high cards don't need to be in the same hand for promotion to work. You have the queen, jack, and ten between the two hands. That's enough to drive out the opponents' ace and king and still have a high card left that is now promoted into a winner.

DUMMY

♣ Q 6 4

DECLARER

♣ J 5 2

To promote winners, you need enough high cards between the two hands. This holding is similar to the previous example, but you don't have the ♣10. If you lead the ♣Q to drive out the opponents' ace and later lead the ♣J to drive out the opponents' king, the opponents' remaining high cards in the suit have been promoted.

## Note the Order

The technique of promotion can't be looked at in isolation. When it comes to the play of the entire hand, the order in which you play your cards can be important.

### Take Your Losses Early

Promotion is a sure-fire way of developing extra tricks because it doesn't depend on any particular distribution of the opponents' cards. Provided there are enough high cards, you can force out the opponents' higher cards and eventually create a winner.

There's one caution with promotion. You give up the lead to the opponents each time you drive out one of their high cards. This gives the opponents an opportunity to take their winners or to go about establishing additional winners for the defense. It's a race between the declarer and the defenders to see which side can establish and take their tricks first.

Whenever you give up the lead in order to promote tricks, it's with the expectation that you'll be able to regain the lead and take the established tricks. If you can't regain the lead, your promoted tricks won't do you much good. Generally, play the suit in which you're trying to promote tricks early on in the hand—while you still have enough strength in the other suits to prevent the defenders from winning the trick-taking race. As in any race, if you use up too many of your resources at the beginning, you may not have enough left at the end to reach the finish line.

The guideline for promotion is to **take your losses early**. Here's a straightforward example. The contract is 3NT, and the lead is the ♦Q.

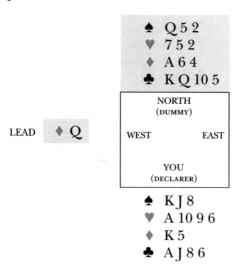

The race is on. The defense has led a diamond. There are two sure tricks in the suit, but if the defenders continue to lead diamonds at every opportunity, they will promote winners in the suit—perhaps enough to defeat your contract. In the meantime, you have work to do. Focus on the target: you need nine tricks. You have one sure trick in hearts, two in diamonds, and four in clubs. That's seven tricks, two short of your target. Going through the checklist of techniques to develop extra tricks, the spade suit offers the potential for promoting two winners by driving out the defenders' ace. That will give you the tricks you need.

Decide where the extra tricks are coming from, and note the order you should play your cards. Entries between the two hands don't seem to present any difficulties, but you're going to have to let the opponents gain the lead with their ♠A. Take your losses early. After winning the first trick with either the ♦A or ♦K, lead one of your high cards in spades right away, while you still have high cards in all the other suits. When the defenders take their ♠A, it won't matter which suit they lead. You can win the trick, and now that you have all the tricks you need, proceed to take your sure tricks. You win the race.

If you were to take all your winners in the other suits before going about promoting winners in the spade suit, you'd be establishing tricks for your opponents. Here's the complete hand:

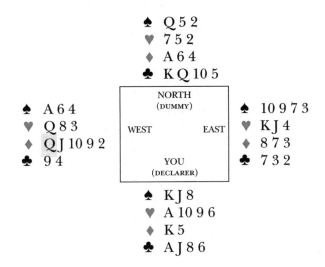

```
                    ♠ Q 5 2
                    ♥ 7 5 2
                    ♦ A 6 4
                    ♣ K Q 10 5
                  NORTH
                  (DUMMY)
  ♠ A 6 4                              ♠ 10 9 7 3
  ♥ Q 8 3        WEST        EAST      ♥ K J 4
  ♦ Q J 10 9 2                         ♦ 8 7 3
  ♣ 9 4                                ♣ 7 3 2
                  YOU
                  (DECLARER)
                    ♠ K J 8
                    ♥ A 10 9 6
                    ♦ K 5
                    ♣ A J 8 6
```

If you take your ♥A before promoting the two spade tricks, the defenders will have two heart tricks to take when they get the lead. If you take both the ♦A and ♦K as well, the defense will also be able to take three diamond tricks. It doesn't do any harm, on this hand, to take your four club tricks before promoting your spade winners, but neither does it do any harm to wait until you have all the tricks you need. When promoting winners, taking your losses early is a good guideline to follow.

Notice the teamwork among the suits. While the spades were being promoted, the other suits were providing protection, through their high cards, preventing the defenders from winning the promotion race. Without this protection, you wouldn't be able to enjoy the promoted winners in the spade suit.

Don't be afraid to give up the lead. Promotion is a common method of developing extra tricks. Very few hands contain all the tricks you need right away. What you want to do is control when you give up the lead. It's often to your advantage to give up the lead early on, before the opponents have had an opportunity to develop enough tricks to defeat the contract.

### First Things First

There are times when you'll need to promote winners in two suits in order to make the contract. In notrump, you should generally start with the suit containing the most combined cards. For example, suppose you're in 3NT on the following hand, and the opening lead is the ♠10.

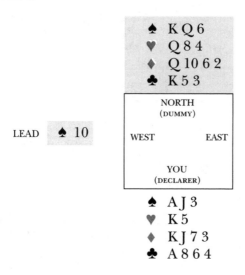

♠ K Q 6
♥ Q 8 4
♦ Q 10 6 2
♣ K 5 3

NORTH
(DUMMY)

LEAD    ♠ 10    WEST          EAST

YOU
(DECLARER)

♠ A J 3
♥ K 5
♦ K J 7 3
♣ A 8 6 4

There are five sure tricks: three in spades and two in clubs. You need four more to make the contract. You can develop one through promotion in the heart suit by driving out the ♥A, since you have both the ♥K and ♥Q between the two hands. You can also develop three tricks in the diamond suit through promotion by driving out the ♦A. That will provide you with the tricks you need. Does it matter which suit you start with?

Suppose you win the first spade trick and lead a heart, playing one of your high hearts to drive out the ace. The defenders may win the trick with their ♥A and decide that hearts isn't such a bad suit for them. Instead of continuing to lead spades, they may lead another heart, making you take your sure trick in that suit before you're ready. When you now try to establish the diamond suit, they may win the ♦A and be able to take enough tricks in the heart suit to defeat the contract.

There's no need to risk such an unfortunate outcome. Instead, start with the diamond suit. You don't mind if the opponents win the ♦A and lead another diamond. You've got three tricks in that suit. Once the ♦A has been driven out, you can now go after the one trick you need in hearts. It's too late for the opponents to prevent you from making the contract. As soon as you get that one extra trick from the heart suit, you'll have the nine tricks you need for the contract.

When you're playing in a trump contract, you'll frequently need to use promotion in the trump suit itself. If you're also going to have to promote tricks in another suit, it's usually best to start with the trump suit. This follows the general principle of drawing trump first. For example, suppose you're in a contract of 3♦ on the following hand, and the opening lead is the ♥K.

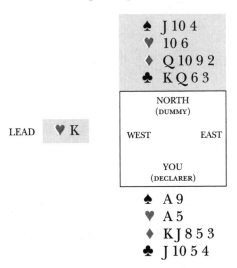

You need nine tricks to make your 3♦ contract, and have only two sure tricks, the ♠A and ♥A. You can promote four tricks in diamonds by driving out the ♦A, and three tricks in clubs by driving out the

♣A. Which suit do you start with after winning the first trick with your ♥A?

Lead the diamonds first. Once the ♦A is driven out and you regain the lead, you can draw the rest of the defenders' trump. Now it's safe to drive out the ♣A and establish the three tricks you need in the club suit. If you were to lead clubs first, the complete hand might be something like this:

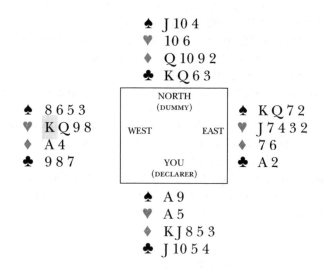

♠ J 10 4
♥ 10 6
♦ Q 10 9 2
♣ K Q 6 3

|  |  |  |
|--|--|--|
| ♠ 8 6 5 3 | NORTH (DUMMY) | ♠ K Q 7 2 |
| ♥ K Q 9 8 | WEST    EAST | ♥ J 7 4 3 2 |
| ♦ A 4 |  | ♦ 7 6 |
| ♣ 9 8 7 | YOU (DECLARER) | ♣ A 2 |

♠ A 9
♥ A 5
♦ K J 8 5 3
♣ J 10 5 4

East might decide to win a trick with the ♣A and lead another club. Your remaining clubs have been promoted into winners, but when you now lead a diamond, West can win the ♦A and lead another club. East will trump this, and you'll end up a trick short of making your contract. Playing the trump suit first reduces the possibility that a defender will be able to trump one of your winning tricks.

## Handling Unevenly Divided Suits

Promoting tricks in an unevenly divided suit brings up another consideration about the order in which you should play your cards. Entries can be a problem, both when developing the suit and when trying to reach the winners once they're developed. To see this, take a look at the following layout of the diamond and club suits in declarer's hand and the dummy.

DUMMY

♦ K J 10 3
♣ A

DECLARER

♦ Q 2
♣ 4 3 2

There is one sure trick, the ♣A, which provides an entry to dummy. There are no sure tricks in diamonds, but the potential is there to establish three extra winners through promotion by driving out the opponents' ♦A. Does it matter which of your high diamonds you play first?

Suppose you start the diamond suit by leading the ♦2 and playing dummy's ♦K. If the opponents win this first trick with the ♦A and lead a club, driving out your ♣A, you have a problem. You can take one diamond trick by leading the ♦3 back to your ♦Q, but the remaining two diamond winners in dummy—the ♦J and ♦10—are stranded. Your entry has disappeared before you're ready to use it.

The opponents may choose not to win the first trick with their ♦A. You still have a problem. If you lead the ♦3 back to your ♦Q, they may also let you win that trick too. That's not too bad, since you have two of the three diamond tricks you were hoping to promote, but you can't establish the third trick. You're in your hand and have no link card left in diamonds. You can use the ♣A to get to dummy so that you can lead another diamond and drive out the ♦A, but now your remaining diamond winner is stranded. Once again, you've had to use your sure entry, the ♣A, too soon.

Fall back on the same principle used when taking sure tricks in an unevenly divided suit: **play the high card from the short side first**. Start by playing the ♦Q, high card from the short side, and the opponents can do nothing to stop you from getting all three of your diamond tricks. If they win the first trick with the ♦A and lead a club, you win and take your three established winners in the dummy. If they don't win the first trick, you can use your ♦2 as a link card to continue leading the suit. If they don't win the second trick, you're now in dummy and can lead the suit again to establish your last diamond as a winner. You still have the ♣A as an entry to dummy to get to your last diamond trick.

You always need a way to get to your winners, and the buses don't run every day. The ♣A is your one sure ride on the above layout, and careful play is required to make sure you don't miss the boat. (Okay, no more transportation references after this.)

When you plan to promote winners in an unevenly divided suit, try to **keep an entry on the same side of the table as the long side of the suit**. Let's see how this works in a complete hand. The contract is 3NT, and the opening lead is the ♦Q.

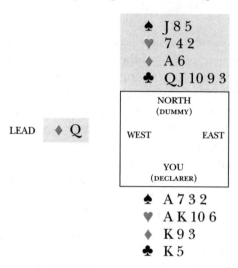

Focus on the target. Declarer needs to take nine tricks and has five sure tricks: one spade, two hearts, and two diamonds. Four more tricks need to be developed. The club suit offers an opportunity to generate all four of the required tricks by driving out the defenders' ♣A. Note the order. There are three considerations: the club suit should be played early, while you still have high cards in the other suits; the high card from the short side should be played when promoting the club tricks; an entry should be kept with the long side of the club suit which is being promoted. Let's see how all that translates into the correct order of play for this hand.

The first decision to be made is in a suit that isn't being promoted, the diamonds. Does it matter whether you win the first trick with the ace or the king? They're both winners. The suits work together as a team. The diamond suit will provide the sure entry once the clubs are established. Keep an entry with the long side. Keep the ♦A in the dummy with the long clubs, and take the first trick with the ♦K in your hand. Now go right to work on establishing the club winners you need. Play the ♣K, high card from the short side. If the defenders win this trick, you'll have no trouble taking your nine tricks as soon as you regain the lead. If the defenders let you have the first club trick, continue playing the suit by leading your link card, the ♣5, over to dummy's high clubs. Lead the suit until the defenders take their ♣A. Regardless of what suit the defenders lead next, you win the trick and can travel to dummy with the carefully preserved ♦A to take the rest of your established winners.

Playing the high card from the short side should be used in the right context. On this hand, for example, the diamonds were also unevenly divided, and yet playing the high card from the short side wasn't the correct play in that suit. The first trick had to be won with the ♦K on the long side in order to take nine tricks. Playing the high card from the short side applies when taking sure tricks or when promoting tricks in an unevenly divided suit. The play of a particular suit must always be made within the context of what's best for the entire hand. Good cooperation among all four suits is required to make the contract.

## Unblocking

Sometimes you need to consider overtaking one of your high cards to get around the problem of entries when promoting winners in a suit. Look at this example. You're in 3NT, and the opponents lead the ♥4.

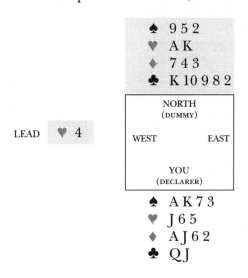

There are five sure tricks: two in spades, two in hearts, and one in diamonds. The four extra tricks you need to make 3NT can come from the club suit through promotion. You'll need to plan carefully the order in which you play your cards.

You have to win the first trick with one of dummy's high hearts. Now start by playing the ♣2 over to your ♣Q—or ♣J—playing the high card from the short side first. Suppose the opponents don't win the first round of clubs with their ace. Continue with your plan to promote winners in the club suit by leading the ♣J. This is where you must be careful. If you play a low club from the dummy on this trick, the defenders may be clever enough to let you win this trick also. All of a sudden, you're in trouble. Your only remaining entry to dummy is in the heart suit. Even if you use this entry to get over there and lead another club to drive out the ace, there's no way to get back to dummy. Your last two club winners will be stranded.

The solution is to overtake the last club from your hand with dummy's ♣K—putting two high clubs on the same trick. The advantage of this play is that the defenders are now helpless to prevent you from establishing and taking your winners in the club suit. If they win this trick with their ♣A, you still have the heart entry to the dummy. If they don't win this trick, you're in the right hand to keep leading clubs to drive out the ♣A, and you still have the high heart left in dummy as an entry.

## Creating an Entry

Promotion can serve more than the task of developing an extra winner. The promoted winner could be used as an entry to help out with another suit. Consider this hand. The contract is 1NT, and the opening lead is the ♣4.

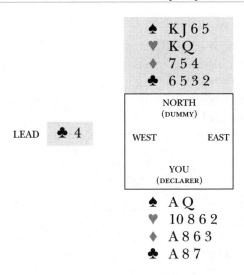

You'll need seven tricks to reach your target in 1NT. There are four sure tricks in spades, one in diamonds, and one in clubs. You can promote the extra trick you need in the heart suit, but before going about that, you should note the order of play for the complete hand.

There's a problem taking your four sure spade tricks. The suit is blocked, and you're going to need an entry to dummy. The heart suit will provide you with that entry at the same time as you promote your trick in the suit. After winning the first trick with the ♣A, be careful to take your ♠A and ♠Q next to unblock the suit. Now is the time to lead a heart. If the defenders take the first heart trick with the ace, you'll be able to use your promoted high heart as an entry to your two spade winners. If they don't take the ♥A right away, you'll win the first trick in the dummy and be able to take your remaining two spade tricks right away. Then you take the ♦A as your seventh trick. Timing is everything.

## Summary

When you need extra tricks to make your contract, one of the first items on your checklist of things to look for should be promotion—using your high cards to drive out the opponents' higher-ranking cards to promote your lower-ranking cards into winners.

| *Checklist* |
| --- |
| ✓ Promotion |
| Length |
| Finessing |
| Trumping Losers |
| Discarding Losers |

Provided you can afford to give up the lead to the opponents, promotion is a sure-fire method for developing extra tricks when you have sufficient high card strength in a suit. Keep the following guidelines in mind:

- Take your losses early by giving up the lead while you still have high cards in the other suits to use as entries and to protect against the defenders taking all their winners before you can take yours.

- If the suit to be promoted is unevenly divided between the two hands, play the high card from the short side first.

- Keep an entry on the same side of the table as the long side of the suit you're trying to promote.

# Practice Hands

## Hand 3.1

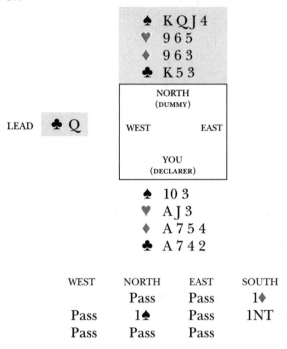

♠ K Q J 4
♥ 9 6 5
♦ 9 6 3
♣ K 5 3

NORTH
(DUMMY)

LEAD ♣ Q

WEST          EAST

YOU
(DECLARER)

♠ 10 3
♥ A J 3
♦ A 7 5 4
♣ A 7 4 2

| WEST | NORTH | EAST | SOUTH |
|------|-------|------|-------|
|      | Pass  | Pass | 1♦    |
| Pass | 1♠    | Pass | 1NT   |
| Pass | Pass  | Pass |       |

West leads the ♣Q against your contract of 1NT. How do you plan to make the contract? In which suits must you be careful of the order in which you play your cards?

## Solution 3.1

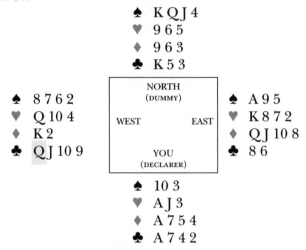

Seven tricks are needed to make the contract. There's one sure trick in hearts, one in diamonds, and two in clubs; a total of four tricks. The spade suit offers the potential to develop the three extra tricks required through promotion.

The spade suit is unevenly divided between the two hands, so you should plan to start the suit by playing the high card from the short side, the ♠10. You'll also need an entry to reach your spade winners once they're established. Let's see how this works.

You have a choice of winning the first club trick with the ♣K in the dummy, or with the ♣A in your hand. Since you want to leave an entry on the same side of the table as the length in the suit which you're trying to promote, win the first trick with the ♣A, leaving the ♣K in dummy. Before taking any of your other sure tricks, go to work on the spade suit. You're going to have to let the opponents win a trick, and the sooner the better. Play the ♠10, high card from the short side. If the defenders don't win this trick with the ♠A, lead the ♠3 over to one of dummy's high spades. Continue leading the suit until the ♠A is driven out. Whatever suit the defenders lead next, you can win the trick, and you still have the carefully preserved ♣K in the dummy as an entry to your spade winners. Now that your work is done, take your tricks and run.

**Hand 3.2**

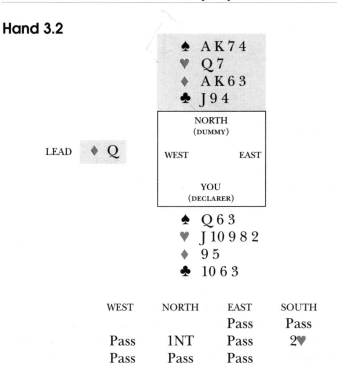

```
                    ♠ A K 7 4
                    ♥ Q 7
                    ♦ A K 6 3
                    ♣ J 9 4
                    NORTH
                    (DUMMY)
LEAD   ♦ Q      WEST          EAST

                    YOU
                    (DECLARER)
                    ♠ Q 6 3
                    ♥ J 10 9 8 2
                    ♦ 9 5
                    ♣ 10 6 3
```

| WEST | NORTH | EAST | SOUTH |
|------|-------|------|-------|
|      |       | Pass | Pass  |
| Pass | 1NT   | Pass | 2♥    |
| Pass | Pass  | Pass |       |

You've landed in a less than perfect trump fit, but it's still your job to make the contract. How do you plan to play your 2♥ contract after the opening lead of the ♦Q?

## Solution 3.2

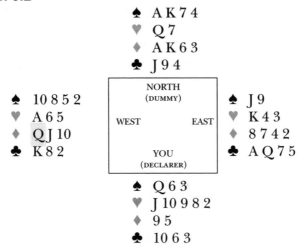

♠ AK74
♥ Q7
♦ AK63
♣ J94

NORTH
(DUMMY)

WEST          EAST

YOU
(DECLARER)

WEST
♠ 10852
♥ A65
♦ QJ10
♣ K82

EAST
♠ J9
♥ K43
♦ 8742
♣ AQ75

♠ Q63
♥ J10982
♦ 95
♣ 1063

You need to find eight tricks in your contract of 2♥. There are three sure tricks in spades and two in diamonds. You can develop the other three tricks in the trump suit by driving out the opponents' ♥A and ♥K.

After winning the first trick with one of dummy's high diamonds, start leading hearts right away. You do this for two reasons. First, you're going to have to give up two tricks in the suit, and you want to keep as many high cards as possible in the other suits to help regain the lead. Second, hearts is the trump suit, and it isn't safe to try to take your sure tricks in the other suits until trump have been drawn.

Start the heart suit by playing dummy's ♥Q, high card from the short side. If both opponents refuse to win this trick, you can lead another heart from the dummy. If one of the opponents wins the first heart trick, you'll lead another heart as soon as you regain the lead. Later on, you can use the ♠Q as an entry to your hand to play the third round of trump. Since the six missing hearts are divided with three in West's hand and three in East's hand, it will take only three rounds of the suit to draw all the trump. Now it's safe to take the rest of your sure tricks.

If you try to take your sure spade tricks before drawing trump, East will be able to play a low trump on the third round of the suit. One of your sure tricks will have disappeared, and you won't have enough tricks to make the contract.

## Hand 3.3

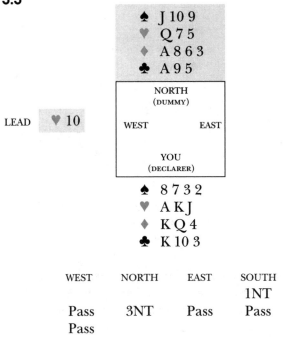

♠ J 10 9
♥ Q 7 5
♦ A 8 6 3
♣ A 9 5

NORTH
(DUMMY)

LEAD ♥ 10

WEST        EAST

YOU
(DECLARER)

♠ 8 7 3 2
♥ A K J
♦ K Q 4
♣ K 10 3

| WEST | NORTH | EAST | SOUTH |
|------|-------|------|-------|
|      |       |      | 1NT   |
| Pass | 3NT   | Pass | Pass  |
| Pass |       |      |       |

West leads the ♥10 against your contract of 3NT. Where's your ninth trick coming from?

## Solution 3.3

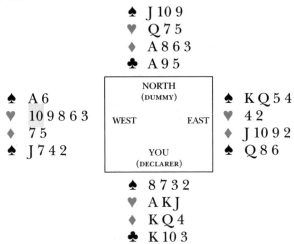

Nine tricks are required. There are three in hearts, three in diamonds, and two in clubs. One more trick must be found. As we'll discuss later, there's some possibility of getting another trick from the diamond suit, but there's a better place to look—spades. Even missing the top three cards, you have enough high cards to promote a trick—the lowly ♠8.

Because you have to give up the lead three times, start leading spades right away. After winning the first trick, lead a spade and drive out one of the high spades. Whichever suit is returned, win and lead a spade to drive out another high card. You have enough high cards left to win whatever suit is led next and play spades once more, driving out the defenders' last high card. You establish the extra trick you need— the ♠8 in your hand is the highest spade remaining. As long as the opponents haven't established enough winners, you win the race and make the contract. On the actual hand, West could promote two heart tricks—if the suit could be led three times and West could regain the lead. Unfortunately for the defenders—but fortunately for you—West doesn't have enough high cards to keep leading hearts and still end up with the lead when the defenders win their last spade trick.

Was it worth the effort of giving the opponents the lead three times so you could eventually enjoy one extra trick? The answer is definitely yes. It's the trick you needed to make the contract. A winner is a winner, even if it's only an eight.

## Hand 3.4

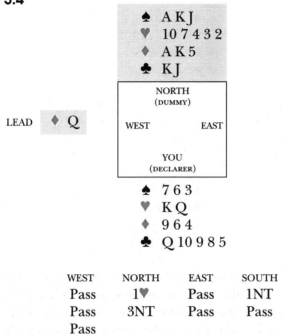

♠ A K J
♥ 10 7 4 3 2
♦ A K 5
♣ K J

NORTH
(DUMMY)

LEAD ♦ Q

WEST    EAST

YOU
(DECLARER)

♠ 7 6 3
♥ K Q
♦ 9 6 4
♣ Q 10 9 8 5

| WEST | NORTH | EAST | SOUTH |
|------|-------|------|-------|
| Pass | 1♥ | Pass | 1NT |
| Pass | 3NT | Pass | Pass |
| Pass | | | |

You've got only four sure tricks in your contract of 3NT. How will you get all the tricks you need after the opening lead of the ♦Q? Be sure to note the order in which you plan to play each suit.

## Solution 3.4

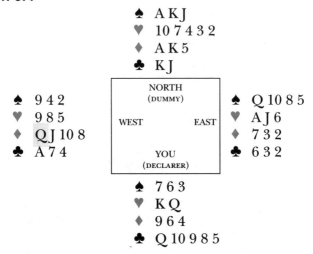

          ♠ A K J
          ♥ 10 7 4 3 2
          ♦ A K 5
          ♣ K J

                    NORTH
                    (DUMMY)
  ♠ 9 4 2                              ♠ Q 10 8 5
  ♥ 9 8 5      WEST          EAST      ♥ A J 6
  ♦ Q J 10 8                           ♦ 7 3 2
  ♣ A 7 4                              ♣ 6 3 2
                    YOU
                    (DECLARER)

          ♠ 7 6 3
          ♥ K Q
          ♦ 9 6 4
          ♣ Q 10 9 8 5

Count two sure tricks from the ♠A and ♠K and two more from the ♦A and ♦K. You need five more to meet your target. Since promotion is all you have on your checklist so far, that's what you have to use. You can promote a heart trick, by driving out the ♥A. You can also promote four club winners by forcing out the ♣A. In which order do you play the suits?

Play clubs first. They represent the main source of tricks, and you need an entry to reach them once they're established. The heart suit can provide the entry, but you don't want to use it too soon. Be careful to start clubs with the high card from the short side, the ♣K. If the opponents win the ♣A, you won't have any difficulty taking your tricks, but suppose the ♣K wins the trick. Continue clubs by leading the ♣J, but be careful to overtake with the ♣Q. If you don't, the opponents might let the ♣J win the trick. You'd be left in the wrong hand to continue leading clubs. By overtaking, it doesn't matter whether or not they take the ♣A. If they don't, you lead another club from your hand to drive it out.

Suppose West eventually wins the ♣A and leads another diamond. Win the trick in the dummy. You need to create an entry to the club winners in your hand. Now is the time to lead a heart. If the defenders take the ♥A, your remaining high heart is the entry you need—as well as being the ninth trick. If they don't take the ♥A, you win the trick in your hand and take the rest of your promoted club tricks. Then take the ♠A and ♠K to make the contract.

# Length—
# Putting Low Cards
# to Work

> *"A deck of cards was built like the purest of hier archies, with every card a master to those below it, a lackey to those above it. And there were the "masses"—long suits—which always asserted themselves in the end, triumphing over the kings and aces."*
>
> — ELY CULBERTSON,
> *Total Peace* [1943]

When you're looking for the extra tricks you need to make the contract, your initial focus is on the high cards, but don't overlook the low cards. They can often be your most important source of extra tricks. Turning those low cards into winners with the same power as an ace can become a pleasant pastime.

## Long Suits

A winner is any card that can take a trick; it could be the highest card in a suit, or the lowest. How many tricks would you expect to take with this suit playing in a notrump contract?

DUMMY
♦ 6 5 4

DECLARER
♦ A K Q J 3 2

You have the four highest cards in the suit and hold nine of the thirteen diamonds in your combined hands. That leaves the opponents with four diamonds between them. Even if one opponent holds all four of the missing diamonds, by the time you've played your ♦A, ♦K, ♦Q, and ♦J, the opponents will have no diamonds left. The two lowest cards in the suit, the ♦3 and ♦2, are now winners, since they're the only cards left in the suit. You'll end up taking six tricks from this suit. Your two low diamonds become winners due to the *length* in the suit.

This is the basic idea behind the second technique on the checklist for developing extra tricks—establishing winners through length. If you can keep leading a suit until the opponents have no cards left, your remaining cards in the suit have now become winners, whether they're high cards or low cards.

Let's make a small change to the above layout by replacing the ♦J with the ♦7.

DUMMY
♦ 6 5 4

DECLARER
♦ A K Q 7 3 2

Can you still count this as six sure tricks? No, although you'd certainly expect to get six tricks from this suit most of the time. It's possible, however, that one of the opponents holds all four of the missing diamonds, including the ♦J. After playing the ♦A, ♦K, and

♦Q, the next diamond trick would belong to the opponents. You have to be careful counting sure tricks when length is involved. You can count on only three sure tricks from the above suit. It will, however, be one of the first places to look when you need extra tricks to make the contract.

## Making the Length the Strength

Consider the following suit:

DUMMY
♣ 7 6 5 3

DECLARER
♣ A K 4 2

There are two sure tricks, the ♣A and the ♣K. At first glance, this may seem to be all that this suit has to offer. Those low cards are very low. The defenders have all of the other high cards in the suit, including the ♣Q, ♣J, and ♣10. Nonetheless, it's possible to establish an extra trick in this suit through length. Suppose the suit is distributed like this:

DUMMY
♣ 7 6 5 3

WEST              EAST
♣ Q 10        ♣ J 9 8

DECLARER
♣ A K 4 2

By taking two tricks with the ♣A and ♣K and then leading the suit a third time, declarer can develop an extra winner. The defenders would win the third trick with East's ♣J, but the defenders would now be out of clubs. The next time declarer gets the lead and plays the fourth round of clubs, declarer will win the trick because the only clubs left are the one in declarer's hand and the one in dummy.

**Developing tricks through length requires a favorable division of**

**the cards in the opponents' hands.** In the previous example, there's no guarantee that one opponent will have three of the missing clubs and the other will have two. The suit might be divided like this:

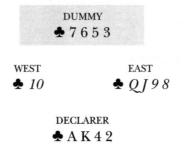

DUMMY
♣ 7 6 5 3

WEST          EAST
♣ 10          ♣ Q J 9 8

DECLARER
♣ A K 4 2

One opponent has four cards, and the other opponent has one. This is referred to as a 4–1 *break*. You can't build an extra trick if this is the distribution. Both opponents follow suit when you play the ♣A, but when you play the ♣K, West discards from another suit. Now East is left with two promoted winners. If you lead the suit again, East will win two club tricks.

If you're very unlucky, all five outstanding cards could be in one hand and none in the other: a 5–0 break. Here's what would happen when the distribution is very unfavorable:

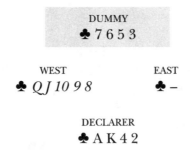

DUMMY
♣ 7 6 5 3

WEST          EAST
♣ Q J 10 9 8  ♣ –

DECLARER
♣ A K 4 2

When you play the ♣A, East will discard. You know immediately that West has all five clubs. If you continue to lead the suit, you'll promote three winners for the defenders and will get nothing in return. Maybe you could shift your attention to another suit if you're looking for extra tricks. At least you aren't playing for money.

## Expectations

How should you expect the outstanding cards to be divided between the opponents' hands? As you've seen, five cards could be divided 3–2, 4–1, or 5–0. As you might expect, it's unusual for all five cards to be in one defender's hand—although that might seem to be what happens every time you're trying to develop extra tricks! The following table shows the most likely division of the outstanding cards in a suit.

| *Number of Cards in the Defenders' Hands* | *Expected Division Between the Defenders* |
|:---:|:---:|
| 3 | 2 – 1 |
| 4 | 3 – 1 |
| 5 | 3 – 2 |
| 6 | 4 – 2 |
| 7 | 4 – 3 |
| 8 | 5 – 3 |

Suppose you have nine combined cards between your hand and the dummy. That leaves the defenders with four cards. The four missing cards could be divided 4–0, 3–1, or 2–2 between the defenders' hands. From the above table, you'd expect them to be divided 3–1 most of the time, rather than 4–0 or 2–2.

Instead of memorizing the above table, an easier way to remember its contents is to use the following guideline: **an even number of cards in the defenders' hands can be expected to divide slightly unevenly; an odd number of cards can be expected to divide as evenly as possible.** For example, six cards in the defender's hand will tend to be divided slightly unevenly, 4–2, rather than evenly, 3–3; seven cards will tend to be divided as evenly as possible, 4–3.

This expectation of how the defenders' cards divide is what you use when you don't have anything else to go on. Sometimes the auction will give you a better clue about the division of the cards in the opponents' hands, and you'll get more information as the play develops. Nonetheless, it's a useful starting point when you're looking for places to develop extra tricks.

## Opportunities for Extra Tricks

Suppose you have the following combination of cards between the combined hands. How many tricks might you expect to take from the heart suit?

DUMMY
♥ 8 6 3

DECLARER
♥ A K Q 5 2

You have eight combined cards, leaving five for the opponents. You'd expect the five cards in the defenders' hands—an odd number—to be divided as evenly as possible, 3–2. So, although you have only three sure tricks, you'd expect to take five tricks from this suit most of the time. The only way to find out how many tricks you're actually going to get is by playing the suit and watching the cards the opponents play. If both opponents follow suit when you take your first heart trick, so far so good. If they both play a heart on the second round, you're home free. The suit must have divided as you expected, 3–2. When you take your third trick with a high heart, the opponents' last heart will appear, and you can now take two more tricks with your low hearts.

If one of the opponents discards on the first round of the suit, you'll know it's not your day. The missing hearts are divided 5–0, and you won't get an extra trick from the suit. If both opponents follow suit on the first round but one of them discards on the second round of the suit, you'll have to compromise. The hearts have divided 4–1. You won't be able to take all five tricks in the suit, but you can still get four tricks. You'll have to give up one trick to the defender who holds the four hearts. After that, your remaining low heart will be a winner.

Let's take away the ♥Q, and replace it with a low heart.

DUMMY
♥ 8 6 3

DECLARER
♥ A K 7 5 2

You have two sure tricks in the suit, but you can still use the combined length in the suit as a source of extra tricks. You'd hope that the defenders' hearts are divided as you might expect, 3–2. If that's the case, you can take two sure tricks in the suit and give up one trick to the defenders. Your remaining two low hearts should now be winners.

Now let's replace the ♥K with a low heart.

DUMMY
♥ 8 6 3

DECLARER
♥ A 9 7 5 2

Only one sure trick. If the suit divides as you might expect, however, the hearts could provide you with three tricks. The complete layout might be something like this:

DUMMY
♥ 8 6 3

WEST                    EAST
♥ J 4                   ♥ K Q 10

DECLARER
♥ A 9 7 5 2

After taking your sure trick, you'd have to give up two tricks to the opponents. After that, the last two hearts in your hand would be winners.

Finally, let's remove the last high heart from declarer's hand:

DUMMY
♥ 8 6 3

DECLARER
♥ 9 7 5 4 2

Although this suit contains no high cards, it holds the potential for developing two tricks when the missing hearts are divided 3–2. You'll have to give up the lead three times, but it will be worth the effort when you need to find two extra tricks to make your contract. You won't do so well if the missing hearts are divided 4–1 or 5–0, but hopefully the full layout of the heart suit looks something like this:

DUMMY
♥ 8 6 3

WEST
♥ A J 10

EAST
♥ K Q

DECLARER
♥ 9 7 5 4 2

Developing tricks through length is similar to developing tricks through promotion. You have to be willing to give up tricks to the defenders with the expectation of getting something in return. Don't be afraid of letting the opponents win a trick or two during the play of the hand. As long as you can regain the lead before the opponents can take enough tricks to defeat the contract, you'll be able to develop the tricks you need. It's usually best to take your losses early, giving up tricks while you still have high cards left in other suits to regain the lead and take your established winners.

Here's an example in a complete hand. The contract is 1NT, and the opening lead is the ♦J.

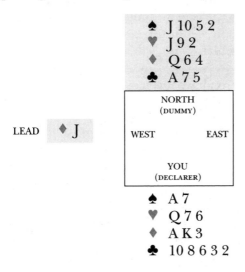

You need seven tricks to be successful in your 1NT contract. There are five sure tricks to start with: one spade, three diamonds, and one club. You need two more. Start at the top of your checklist of ways to develop extra tricks. There doesn't appear to be any suit in which you have enough high cards to promote winners. Move down the checklist, and look for opportunities to develop additional tricks through length. The club suit now comes into its own. There are eight combined cards, leaving the defenders with five. If the missing clubs divide as you might expect, 3–2, the club suit will provide both the extra tricks you need.

Win the first diamond trick, and go to work on the club suit right away. You want to take your losses early, while you still have high cards left in the other suits. Take your ♣A, and play a second round of clubs, giving up a trick to your opponents. You'll find out if you're going to be successful at this point. If both opponents follow suit on the second round of clubs, there's only one club left. The missing clubs were divided 3–2. Suppose the defenders lead another diamond. Win the trick, and lead a third round of clubs, giving up another trick in the suit. Now, the remaining two clubs in your hand have been established as winners. As soon as you regain the lead, you'll be able to take the rest of your winners and make the contract. Easy—once you know where to look for those extra tricks.

## Little Winners

Look to the long suits, in either dummy's hand or your hand, as a potential source of extra tricks. The longer the suit and the more combined cards you have in a suit, the better your chances for success. Here are some examples.

DUMMY
♠ K 6

DECLARER
♠ A 8 7 4 2

You have seven combined cards, leaving the defenders with six. Since there's an even number of missing cards, you'd expect them to be divided slightly unevenly—4–2 rather than 3–3. If they're divided as you might expect, you can develop one extra trick from this suit by taking your two winners and then giving up two tricks in the suit. Your remaining spade will be a winner. You might be lucky. If the defenders' cards happen to be divided 3–3, you'll end up with two extra winners. On the other hand, if the missing cards are divided 5–1 or 6–0, you won't get an extra trick from this suit.

DUMMY
♥ K 6 2

DECLARER
♥ A 8 7 4

Again you have seven combined cards, but you don't have as much length in your hand. This is not a good combination for developing an extra trick through length, especially if the six missing hearts are divided as you might expect, 4–2. Of course, if you're desperate to find an extra trick and this is the only potential source, you'll have to hope it's your lucky day and the suit is divided 3–3 in the opponents' hands.

DUMMY
♦ A K 7 6 4 2

DECLARER
♦ 8

You have the same seven cards as in the previous examples, but with the suit so unevenly divided between the two hands, there's lots of potential for extra tricks. In the best case, when the six missing diamonds are divided 3–3 in the defenders' hands, you can get five winners from this suit: two from your high cards and three from length. In the more likely case of a 4–2 division of the defenders' diamonds, you'll end up with four winners: your two high cards plus two tricks from length, after giving up two tricks to the opponents. This assumes you have enough entries to the dummy to keep playing the suit and to take your winners once they're established.

DUMMY

♣ A 9 7 6 5 4 2

DECLARER

♣ 8 3

There's one sure trick in this suit, but with nine cards in the combined hands and such length in the dummy, you could get five, or even six, winners from this suit. Such is the power of low cards. If the four missing clubs are divided slightly unevenly, 3–1, as you might expect, you'll have to lose two tricks in the suit but will end up with five winners—your ♣A plus four winners through length. On a good day, the missing clubs will divide 2–2, and this suit will provide you with six tricks. It's no wonder you give value to your long suits during the auction. Those low cards take on the power of aces and kings when you have a lot of them.

You'll encounter opportunities to develop tricks through length in almost every hand you play. The challenge is to recognize them and include them as part of your plan. Establishing tricks through length is useful in both notrump contracts and suit contracts. In a suit contract, the trump suit will be one of the longest combined suits between the two hands. You'll frequently need to rely on length when handling the trump suit itself.

Here's a typical example. You've reached a contract of 4♥ missing all the top cards in your trump suit. It's an excellent contract, nonetheless. All you have to do is look to the basic guidelines. The opening lead is the ♠J.

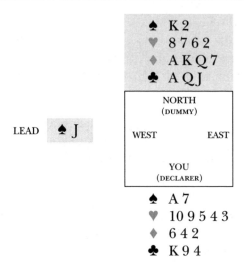

♠ K 2
♥ 8 7 6 2
♦ A K Q 7
♣ A Q J

NORTH
(DUMMY)

LEAD   ♠ J          WEST          EAST

YOU
(DECLARER)

♠ A 7
♥ 10 9 5 4 3
♦ 6 4 2
♣ K 9 4

You have eight sure tricks. You need two more to make your contract. Now that you know about length, the heart suit becomes your friend, rather than a source of concern. You have nine cards in the combined hands. If the four missing cards are all in one defender's hand, don't buy any lottery tickets today. Most likely, the missing hearts are divided 3–1, and you'll end up losing three heart tricks but nothing else. You'll have all the extra tricks you need.

All the basic principles guide you to leading hearts right away, after winning the first trick. It's part of the principle of drawing trump, to avoid letting the opponents trump one of your sure tricks. It falls under the guideline of taking your losses early. Win the first trick in either hand—you don't have any entry problems—and lead a heart. As long as both opponents follow suit, you're going to make the contract. The hearts can no longer be divided any worse than 3–1. All that's left is to find out if you're going to make an overtrick. You win a trick in whichever suit the defenders lead next and play another heart. If the missing hearts were originally divided 2–2, they'll come tumbling down together, and you have the rest of the tricks. If one defender started with three hearts, you'll graciously concede another heart trick to the defenders and claim your contract. Who needs aces and kings? Here's the complete hand:

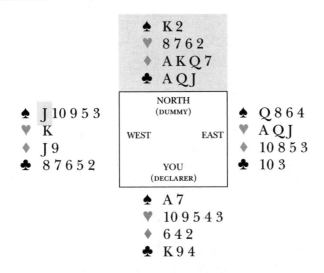

The defenders' hearts are divided 3–1, so you'll make exactly ten tricks in your 4♥ contract. Draw trump before trying to take your winners in the other suits, clubs and diamonds. If you were to play your ♦A, ♦K, and ♦Q first, for example, West would trump the third round of diamonds with the ♥K. One of your sure tricks would disappear, and East would still have three heart winners left with which to defeat the contract.

## Length and Entries

Suppose you decide to develop tricks through length when you make your plan. You still need to note the order in which you should play your cards. Entries are always an important consideration.

### Ducking

When you're trying to generate tricks through length in a suit that's unevenly divided between the two hands, be careful to avoid stranding your winners. Compare the layout of these two suits, both of which contain eight cards:

| 1) | DUMMY | 2) | DUMMY |
|----|-------|----|-------|
|    | ♥ A K 7 6 |    | ♥ A K 7 6 2 |

| DECLARER | DECLARER |
|----------|----------|
| ♥ 8 4 3 2 | ♥ 8 4 3 |

Assuming the five missing hearts are divided as expected, 3–2, declarer can establish one extra trick in the first layout by playing the ♥A, the ♥K, and then giving up a heart trick to the opponents. There will now be one heart left on each side of the table. The next time declarer gets the lead, whether in the dummy or in declarer's hand, the remaining heart can be led, and declarer will win the trick. Declarer doesn't need an entry to get to the established winner because the suit is evenly divided between the two hands.

In the second layout, the hearts are unevenly divided between the two hands. This provides an advantage. If the missing hearts divide 3–2, you'll end up with two extra tricks after playing three rounds of hearts. With the advantage, comes a challenge. If you play dummy's ♥A and ♥K and then lead the suit again, you'll establish the remaining two hearts in dummy as winners. There will be no hearts left in declarer's hand, however, and you'll need to find an entry to the dummy in another suit. If you don't have an entry to dummy, your two winners will be stranded.

Is there a way around this? In each layout, one trick had to be given to the opponents before the remaining cards were established through length. Declarer has a choice about when to give up that trick. Declarer could win the first two tricks with dummy's ♥A and ♥K and then give up a trick; declarer could win the first trick with one of dummy's high hearts and then give up a trick; or declarer could give up a trick right away by playing low hearts from both hands and then taking the ♥A and ♥K at the next opportunity.

In the first layout, when there are the same number of hearts in both hands, the order of playing the cards doesn't matter. In the second layout, where there's a long side and a short side, the order that the cards are played can make a big difference. Suppose this is the complete layout of the heart suit:

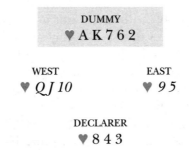

If you start by taking the first two tricks with dummy's ♥A and ♥K and then giving up a trick to West's outstanding ♥Q, the remaining cards in the suit look like this:

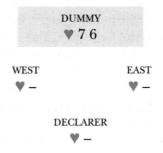

Dummy has two established heart winners, but they're stranded. Instead, suppose you give up a heart trick right away by playing a low heart from both your hand and the dummy. When West wins this trick, the remaining cards in the suit look like this:

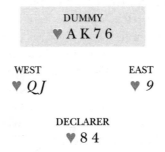

It no longer matters whether you regain the lead in your hand or in the dummy. You can't be stopped from taking the next four tricks in the heart suit. You don't need an entry to dummy in another suit because there is an entry within the suit itself. You have link cards left in your hand to travel over to dummy's winners.

Playing a low card from both hands when you could have won the trick is called *ducking*. In the above example, you ducked the first round of the suit, giving up a trick to the opponents. In the actual example, you could play the suit in a slightly different order. You could win the first trick with dummy's ♥A—or ♥K—and then duck a trick by playing low hearts from both hands. The remaining cards would look like this:

DUMMY
♥ A 7 6

WEST            EAST
♥ Q             ♥ –

DECLARER
♥ 8

You'll still get the four tricks to which you're entitled. You have left an entry in the suit on the long side, and you have a link card left in your hand with which to cross over to dummy.

Learning to duck at the right time is an important technique on many hands. It's another variation of the principles of taking your losses early and keeping an entry on the same side of the table as the long suit.

This next hand shows that it was no quack who suggested ducking as a way to make a contract. You're in 3NT, and the opening lead is the ♥4.

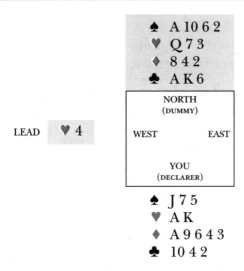

♠ A 10 6 2
♥ Q 7 3
♦ 8 4 2
♣ A K 6

NORTH
(DUMMY)

LEAD   ♥ 4

WEST            EAST

YOU
(DECLARER)

♠ J 7 5
♥ A K
♦ A 9 6 4 3
♣ 10 4 2

You start with seven sure tricks: one spade trick, three heart tricks, one diamond trick, and two club tricks. You'll need two more tricks to make the contract. The spade suit offers some possibility for an extra trick. If the missing spades divide exactly 3–3, for example, you'll be able to establish one extra trick in the suit. That's not how you'd expect the spades to divide; they're more likely to be divided 4–2. Besides, you need two extra tricks, not one. The diamond suit has good potential to establish the two tricks you need. If the five missing diamonds are divided 3–2, you'll be able to establish two additional tricks through length.

It may not appear that entries present much of a problem. You do have three entries to your hand. The opening lead, however, is going to remove one of those entries right away, before you're ready to use it. The order that the cards are played is important. After winning the first trick with one of the high hearts in your hand, suppose you start the diamond suit by playing the ♦A and then giving up a diamond trick. The defenders win this trick and lead another heart. You can win this in your hand and give up another diamond trick to establish the last two diamonds in your hand as winners. The operation was a success, but...you have no entries left to your hand. You're left holding on to the two diamond winners with no way to get to them.

Instead, after winning the first heart trick in your hand, it's time to put the duck to work. Play a low diamond from both hands, giving the opponents the first trick in the suit. Suppose they lead another heart, and you win the trick with the remaining high heart in your hand. It's not over yet. You must again play a low diamond from both hands—the second trick you've ducked to the opponents. Whichever suit they lead next, you can win in the dummy where you still have a diamond left as a link card to the carefully preserved ♦A in your hand. Now you're in the right place at the right time. Provided the missing diamonds divided 3–2, there are none left except those in your hand. Take your two low diamond winners and the rest of your tricks to make the contract.

## Another Look at Entries

Some suits appear identical, at first glance, and yet a closer look reveals that there's quite a difference. Compare these two suits:

| 1) DUMMY | 2) DUMMY |
|:---:|:---:|
| ♦ A K 7 6 4 | ♦ 7 6 4 3 2 |
| DECLARER | DECLARER |
| ♦ 8 3 2 | ♦ A K 8 |

Both suits have eight cards unevenly divided between the two hands in a 5–3 pattern—five on one side and three on the other. They're the same cards. The difference is that, in the first example, the high cards are both on the long side, and in the second example, the high cards are with the short side. Which holding would be preferable if you're trying to develop tricks from the suit through length?

Assuming that the five outstanding cards are divided 3–2 in the defenders' hands, you can establish two extra tricks in both cases by playing the suit three times, giving up one trick to the opponents. You'll need an entry to those established winners, however, and in this respect, the first layout is preferable. You can get around the entry problem in the first example by ducking the first or second round of the suit, keeping a high diamond in the dummy as an entry to your winners. That won't work in the second layout because there are no high diamonds on the side of the table that has the greatest length in the suit.

There are times when the suit being established can't provide the entries needed to reach the extra winners. You'll need to fall back on a familiar guideline: keep an entry on the same side of the table as the long suit. As an example, consider the following hand. The contract is 1NT, and the opening lead is the ♠Q.

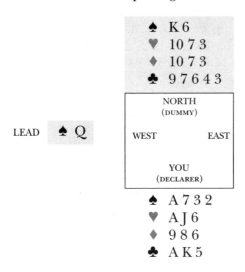

You need seven tricks, and you start with five: the ♠A and ♠K, the ♥A, and the ♣A and ♣K. Using your checklist, there's no place to promote extra winners. When it comes to length, however, the club suit is beckoning. Provided the defender's clubs are divided 3–2, you won't have a difficult time developing two extra tricks by playing the suit three times.

The challenge is to reach the club winners once they have been set up. Since there's no entry in the club suit itself, you'll need an entry in another suit. That's the clue that tells you how to handle the spade suit. You need to win the first trick in your hand. Then play the ♣A, the ♣K, and a third round of clubs. The opponents can no longer defeat you. They can take some diamond winners, but eventually they'll have to give you back the lead. Your carefully preserved ♠K is the entry you need to dummy's two club winners.

## Creating an Entry Through Length

When developing extra winners through length, the entry to the established winners can come from the suit itself or from another suit. There's another side to the coin. A winner established through length can itself become an entry. Remember, an entry doesn't have to be a high card. Consider this hand in a 3NT contract with the ♠5 opening lead.

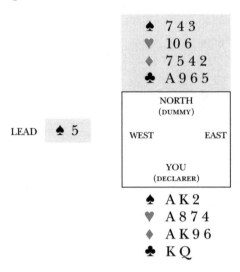

♠ 7 4 3
♥ 10 6
♦ 7 5 4 2
♣ A 9 6 5

NORTH
(DUMMY)

LEAD ♠ 5

WEST                    EAST

YOU
(DECLARER)

♠ A K 2
♥ A 8 7 4
♦ A K 9 6
♣ K Q

You need nine tricks and have two spade tricks, one heart trick, two diamonds tricks, and three club tricks. The diamond suit provides an opportunity to develop the extra trick you need, assuming the defenders' diamonds are divided 3–2. There aren't any problems within the diamond suit itself because the suit is evenly divided between the two hands, but there's a challenge to taking your three sure club tricks. The club suit is blocked. After taking two tricks with your ♣K and ♣Q, you'll need an entry to dummy to get to the ♣A. There are no other high cards in the dummy, so you'll have to look elsewhere.

You plan to develop an extra trick in diamonds by playing the suit three times. You will end up with a diamond in both hands which represents a winning trick. The final diamond trick may be able to provide the entry you need to the dummy. You have to be careful, however, in handling the diamond suit. You want to be left with a low diamond in your hand as the link card over to dummy's "high" diamond. The highest diamond in dummy is the ♦7 and the lowest diamond in your hand is the ♦6.

After winning the first trick with one of your high spades, play the ♦A and ♦K. If both opponents follow suit each time, the missing diamonds were originally divided as you hoped, 3–2. Now give up a diamond trick to the defenders by playing the ♦9 from your hand, making sure to keep the ♦6 as the last diamond in your hand and the ♦7 as the last diamond in the dummy. Whichever suit the opponents lead next, you win the trick and take your ♣K and ♣Q. Travel over to dummy, using the ♦7 as your entry, to take a trick with dummy's ♣A. You've got the nine tricks you need. Time for a pat on the back.

## Summary

When you need extra tricks to make your contract and can't find enough through promotion, the second thing to look for on your checklist should be length—using your long suits to develop low cards into winners.

| | Checklist |
|---|---|
| | Promotion |
| ✓ | Length |
| | Finessing |
| | Trumping Losers |
| | Discarding Losers |

Developing tricks through length doesn't always work. You often need a favorable division of the cards held by the defenders in the suit. Provided you can afford to give up the lead to the opponents, however, creating tricks through length is a good way to make the most of your low cards. Keep the following guidelines in mind:

- An even number of cards in the defenders' hands can be expected to divide slightly unevenly; an odd number of cards can be expected to divide as evenly as possible.

- Take your losses early by giving up the lead while you still have high cards in the other suits to use as entries and to protect against the defenders taking all their winners before you can take yours.

- Keep an entry on the same side of the table as the long side of the suit in which you're trying to develop tricks.

- If the suit is unevenly divided between the two hands, ducking may be a way of preserving an entry to the long side.

# Practice Hands

### Hand 4.1

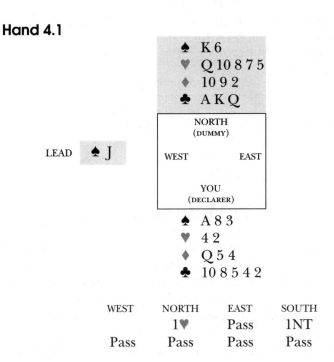

```
                    ♠ K 6
                    ♥ Q 10 8 7 5
                    ♦ 10 9 2
                    ♣ A K Q
              ┌─────────────────────┐
              │       NORTH         │
              │      (DUMMY)        │
LEAD   ♠ J    │  WEST        EAST   │
              │                     │
              │       YOU           │
              │    (DECLARER)       │
              └─────────────────────┘
                    ♠ A 8 3
                    ♥ 4 2
                    ♦ Q 5 4
                    ♣ 10 8 5 4 2
```

| WEST | NORTH | EAST | SOUTH |
|------|-------|------|-------|
|      | 1♥    | Pass | 1NT   |
| Pass | Pass  | Pass | Pass  |

West leads the ♠J against your contract of 1NT. How do you plan to make the contract? Why is the order in which you play your cards so important?

## Solution 4.1

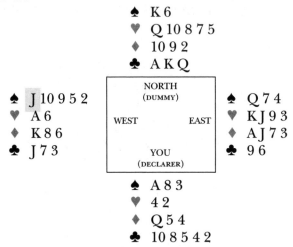

```
                    ♠ K 6
                    ♥ Q 10 8 7 5
                    ♦ 10 9 2
                    ♣ A K Q
                    ┌─────────────────┐
                    │     NORTH       │
♠ J 10 9 5 2        │    (DUMMY)      │    ♠ Q 7 4
♥ A 6               │                 │    ♥ K J 9 3
♦ K 8 6          WEST           EAST  │    ♦ A J 7 3
♣ J 7 3             │                 │    ♣ 9 6
                    │      YOU        │
                    │   (DECLARER)    │
                    └─────────────────┘
                    ♠ A 8 3
                    ♥ 4 2
                    ♦ Q 5 4
                    ♣ 10 8 5 4 2
```

Seven tricks are needed to make the contract. There are two sure tricks in spades and three in clubs; a total of five tricks. With nothing to promote, the club suit appears to offer the potential of providing the two extra tricks. If the five clubs in the defenders' hands are divided 3–2, as you might expect, you should be able to get five tricks from the club suit.

Note the order in which you must play your cards. There's no entry to the long clubs in your hand within the club suit itself. Your only outside entry is the ♠A. Since you want to keep an entry on the same side of the table as your long suit, you should win the first trick with dummy's ♠K, preserving your ace for later. Next, you can take the three club winners in the dummy, watching to see if all the missing clubs appear. When the clubs in the defenders' hands turn out to be divided 3–2, you cross to your hand using the ♠A as an entry and take the last two tricks you need with your ♣10 and ♣8. Seven tricks. On to the next hand!

## Hand 4.2

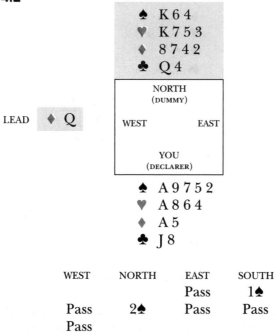

|  WEST  |  NORTH  |  EAST  |  SOUTH  |
|--------|---------|--------|---------|
|        |         | Pass   | 1♠      |
| Pass   | 2♠      | Pass   | Pass    |
| Pass   |         |        |         |

You're in a trump contract of 2♠. Where are your tricks going to come from after the opening lead of the ♦Q?

## Solution 4.2

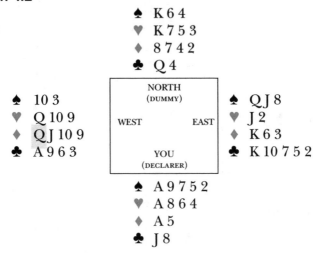

```
                    ♠ K 6 4
                    ♥ K 7 5 3
                    ♦ 8 7 4 2
                    ♣ Q 4
            ┌─────────────────────┐
♠ 10 3      │       NORTH         │      ♠ Q J 8
♥ Q 10 9    │      (DUMMY)        │      ♥ J 2
♦ Q J 10 9  │ WEST          EAST  │      ♦ K 6 3
♣ A 9 6 3   │                     │      ♣ K 10 7 5 2
            │       YOU           │
            │    (DECLARER)       │
            └─────────────────────┘
                    ♠ A 9 7 5 2
                    ♥ A 8 6 4
                    ♦ A 5
                    ♣ J 8
```

You need to find eight tricks in your contract of 2♠. There are two sure tricks in spades, two in hearts, and one in diamonds. You need to find three more. There's nothing to promote, so your extra tricks will need to come from your long suits. First, there's the trump suit, spades. You have eight spades in the combined hands. If the missing spades are divided 3–2, you'll get two tricks through length from the spade suit. The heart suit is the second place to look. Again, you have eight cards between your hand and the dummy. If the defenders' hearts are divided as you might expect, 3–2, you'll get one extra trick from this suit. That's all you need to make the contract.

After winning a trick with the ♦A, start by playing the spade suit. When this suit turns out to be divided 3–2, you can turn your attention to the heart suit. Play the ♥A and ♥K, and give up a heart trick to the opponents. Your one remaining heart in each hand is established as a winning trick. In total, you take four spade tricks, three heart tricks, and a diamond trick to make the contract.

**Hand 4.3**

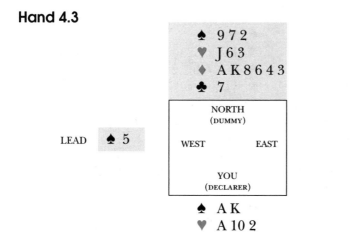

| ♠ | 9 7 2 |
| ♥ | J 6 3 |
| ♦ | A K 8 6 4 3 |
| ♣ | 7 |

NORTH
(DUMMY)

LEAD    ♠ 5

WEST              EAST

YOU
(DECLARER)

| ♠ | A K |
| ♥ | A 10 2 |
| ♦ | 7 5 2 |
| ♣ | A K 8 4 2 |

| WEST | NORTH | EAST | SOUTH |
|------|-------|------|-------|
|      |       |      | 1♣    |
| Pass | 1♦    | Pass | 2NT   |
| Pass | 3NT   | Pass | Pass  |
| Pass |       |      |       |

West leads the ♠5 against your contract of 3NT. How do you plan to handle the diamond suit?

## Solution 4.3

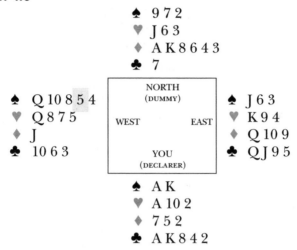

The target's nine tricks, and there are two in spades, one in hearts, two in diamonds, and two in clubs. You need two more. The obvious place to look for the extra tricks is diamonds. You have nine diamonds in the combined hands. If the four missing diamonds are divided 2–2, you can take all six diamond tricks. If the diamonds divide 3–1, you can still establish three extra tricks through length by giving up one trick.

At first glance, it might seem best to play the ♦A and ♦K after winning the first trick. If diamonds divide 2–2, you won't have to give up a trick and can continue to take your diamond winners. If diamonds divide 3–1, you can give up a trick, and the remaining diamonds in the dummy will be winners. Dummy, however, doesn't have any entries outside the diamond suit itself. You have no way to get back to your winners if you start by playing the ♦A and ♦K and find out diamonds are divided 3–1. Instead, duck the first round of diamonds by playing a low diamond from dummy. This gives up the chance of taking all six diamond tricks, but ensures that you can take five diamond tricks if the suit divides 3–1. Five diamond tricks is more than enough, and you want to keep an entry on the same side of the table as the long diamonds.

You could play the ♦A or ♦K on the first round, and then duck a diamond. That works on the actual hand. Proper technique, however, is to duck the first rounds. This leaves you with some chance of making the contract even if the diamonds divide 4–0.

## Hand 4.4

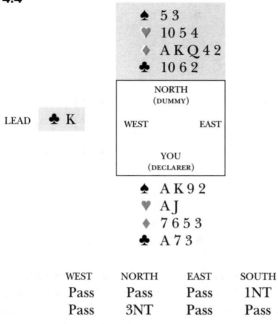

♠ 5 3
♥ 10 5 4
♦ A K Q 4 2
♣ 10 6 2

NORTH
(DUMMY)

LEAD ♣ K

WEST          EAST

YOU
(DECLARER)

♠ A K 9 2
♥ A J
♦ 7 6 5 3
♣ A 7 3

| WEST | NORTH | EAST | SOUTH |
|------|-------|------|-------|
| Pass | Pass | Pass | 1NT |
| Pass | 3NT | Pass | Pass |

You've got seven sure tricks in your contract of 3NT. Sometimes it's the easiest looking hand that can give rise to some interesting challenges.

## Solution 4.4

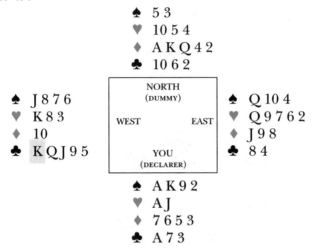

```
                    ♠ 5 3
                    ♥ 10 5 4
                    ♦ A K Q 4 2
                    ♣ 10 6 2
                       NORTH
                      (DUMMY)
  ♠ J 8 7 6                              ♠ Q 10 4
  ♥ K 8 3     WEST          EAST         ♥ Q 9 7 6 2
  ♦ 10                                   ♦ J 9 8
  ♣ K Q J 9 5          YOU               ♣ 8 4
                    (DECLARER)
                    ♠ A K 9 2
                    ♥ A J
                    ♦ 7 6 5 3
                    ♣ A 7 3
```

You start with seven sure tricks: two spades, one heart, three diamonds, and one club. Two more are needed to make 3NT. Going down the checklist, there don't appear to be any opportunities for promotion. When it comes to length, however, the diamond suit looks as though it can provide two extra tricks. You have nine diamonds, leaving the defenders with four. You'd expect the missing diamonds to divide slightly unevenly, 3–1. That shouldn't present a problem, since you hold the top three diamonds in the dummy. Only if all four diamonds are in one defenders' hand would you be unable to take all the diamond tricks.

As you can see, diamonds divide 3–1 on the actual hand, but you may still find a surprise when trying to take your tricks. After taking your ♦A, ♦K, and ♦Q, the defenders have no diamonds left, and the last two diamonds in dummy are established as tricks. You still have a diamond left in your hand, however. If it's not the ♦3, when you lead the fourth round of diamonds, you'll win the trick with the low diamond in your hand. Now there's no entry to get back to the last diamond in the dummy. Make sure the last diamond in your hand is lower than one of the diamonds in dummy. As you take the ♦A, ♦K, and ♦Q, carefully play the ♦5, ♦6, and ♦7 from your hand. Then take the fourth round of diamonds with dummy's ♦4, playing the ♦3 from your hand. You remain in dummy to take the last diamond trick with the ♦2. This is an unusual case of unblocking. Even those low cards can sometimes give you a problem.

♣ ◆ ♥ ♠ ♣ ◆ ♥ ♠ ♣ ◆ ♥ ♠   **5**   ♠ ◆ ♥ ♠ ♣ ◆ ♥ ♠ ♣ ◆ ♥ ♠

# *The Finesse— Putting Kings and Queens to Work*

> *"True Luck consists not in holding the best of the cards at the table:*
> *Luckiest he who knows just when to rise and go home."*
>
> —JOHN MILTON HAY,
> *Distichs, no. 15*

Aces are meant to take kings, or so the saying goes. That's wonderful for the ace but not satisfying for the king—the second-highest card in a suit, a card that could be expected to take a trick. It's time to see how to get the most out of your high cards when there are higher cards lurking in the defenders' hands.

In bridge, a *finesse* is an attempt to win a trick with a lower-ranking card by taking advantage of the favorable position of one or more higher-ranking cards held by the defenders. Let's see how it works.

---

## Putting the King to Work

In the following layout you're missing the ♠A, a higher ranking card than the ♠K. If either defender leads the ace, a low card can be played from both hands, and on the next trick, the king would be a winner. The defenders, however, can't be relied upon to be that co-operative. If you have to play the suit yourself, play your cards to get the most value from dummy's ♠K. In other words, you want to keep it from being captured by the ♠A.

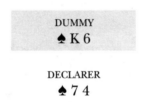

DUMMY
♠ K 6

DECLARER
♠ 7 4

To get a trick with dummy's ♠K, the basic idea is to order your play so that the defenders' ace is played on your low cards, not your king. Declarer can bring this about, but only if the ♠A is favorably located on declarer's left, *in front of* dummy. The type of layout of the spade suit that declarer has to hope for is something like this:

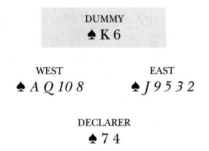

DUMMY
♠ K 6

WEST                EAST
♠ A Q 10 8     ♠ J 9 5 3 2

DECLARER
♠ 7 4

Leading a spade from the dummy won't work. If you lead the ♠K, West will win with the ♠A, and the defenders will have the remaining high spades; if you lead the ♠6, either defender can win the trick by playing a higher spade, and West will still have the ♠A to capture dummy's ♠K. So, the suit can't be played starting in the dummy. Let's try moving across the table and leading the first spade from declarer's hand, toward dummy's ♠K.

What a difference it makes when declarer changes the order of play and starts the suit by leading a low spade toward dummy! West has to choose a card to play to the trick before declarer has to choose the card to play from dummy. If West plays the ♠A, the ♠6 is played from dummy, and the ♠K has become a winner. If West plays a spade other than the ace, declarer can play the ♠K from dummy and win a trick right away because East doesn't have a higher spade.

This is the essence of the finesse. You need to order the play of the cards to **lead toward the card you hope will take a trick**. It's only a hope because you need the defenders' higher card to be favorably placed. The finesse wouldn't succeed if this were the layout of the suit:

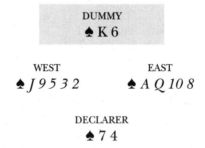

DUMMY
♠ K 6

WEST                    EAST
♠ J 9 5 3 2          ♠ A Q 10 8

DECLARER
♠ 7 4

If the ♠A is sitting in East's hand—*behind* the king, rather than in front of the king—you can't enjoy a trick with the king. When you lead toward dummy's ♠K, East will capture the king with the ace. After all, aces were meant to take kings—at least, some of the time. That's fine; the order of play gave declarer the best chance to take a trick with the king. This type of finesse has only a 50–50 chance of success—either the higher card is favorably placed, or it isn't. It's not a sure thing. Still, a 50% chance is better than nothing.

Here's a typical hand where the finesse can be put to good use. The contract is 2♣, and the opening lead is the ♠K.

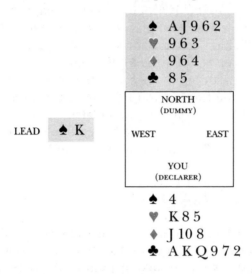

♠ A J 9 6 2
♥ 9 6 3
♦ 9 6 4
♣ 8 5

NORTH
(DUMMY)

LEAD  ♠ K   WEST          EAST

YOU
(DECLARER)

♠ 4
♥ K 8 5
♦ J 10 8
♣ A K Q 9 7 2

You need eight tricks for your contract. You have one sure trick with dummy's ♠A and can hope for six tricks from the club suit if the defenders' clubs are favorably divided, 3–2. That's still not enough. You need one more trick. There's nothing to promote, and other than the clubs, there are no low cards to develop through length. The only hope is to try to get a trick with your ♥K. To do that, you need to lead a heart from dummy toward your king.

There's no time like the present—especially since this is the last time you'll be in the dummy on this hand. Win the first trick with the ♠A, and lead a low heart. If the ♥A doesn't appear on your right, play the ♥K, and keep your fingers crossed. Here's the complete layout:

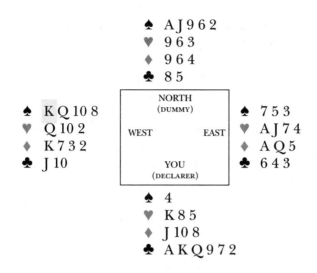

West doesn't have the ♥A, so your finesse is successful, and you make the contract. You needed two favorable things to happen on this hand. First, you needed a favorable division of the defenders' clubs, 3–2, so that you could get six tricks from your trump suit through length. Second, you needed a favorable placement of the ♥A so that you could get a trick out of your ♥K with a successful finesse.

It's not all luck, however. You also have to order your play of the cards correctly to take advantage of the situation. You have to recognize the potential in the heart suit early on and note that you want to lead a heart toward your king. It would be too late if you drew trump right away. Your only entry to dummy is the ♠A, and you're forced to use that on the very first trick. If you don't lead a heart right away, you may find yourself having to lead hearts from your hand later in the play, and you may end up with no winner in the suit. Entries go hand in hand with finesses. You need to be in the right place at the right time.

## Putting the Queen to Work

There are only five honor cards in each suit: the ace, king, queen, jack, and ten. During the play, both declarer and the defenders vie to capture each others' high cards, but surely each of these cards deserves its opportunity to take a trick. In these next examples, declarer wants to take a trick with the queen, even when the opponents have the king. How would you go about taking two tricks with this combination of cards?

DUMMY

♥ 3 2

DECLARER

♥ A Q

Taking the ace and then leading the queen won't work. The queen will be captured by whichever defender holds the ♥K. Instead, you'll have to fall back on the finesse—leading toward the card which you hope will win a trick. In this case, you're hoping to win a trick with your ♥Q, so you want to arrange to lead a low heart from the dummy. You're hoping the layout of the heart suit is something like this:

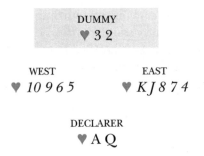

DUMMY

♥ 3 2

WEST           EAST

♥ 10 9 6 5      ♥ K J 8 7 4

DECLARER

♥ A Q

When you lead one of dummy's low cards, East's ♥K is trapped. If East plays the ♥K, you win the trick with the ♥A, and the ♥Q can win the next trick. If East plays a lower heart, you finesse the ♥Q. It wins the trick because West has no higher heart, and you get two tricks from this combination. Like the finesse against the ace, the finesse against the king is a 50–50 proposition. Your finesse wouldn't work if the layout were something like this:

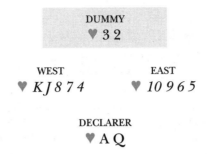

DUMMY
♥ 3 2

WEST          EAST
♥ KJ 8 7 4     ♥ 10 9 6 5

DECLARER
♥ A Q

Now, the ♥K is lying behind, or *over*, your ♥Q and is destined to capture the queen. There's no way you can play the suit to get around this unfortunate placement of the cards. Maybe next hand.

When the ace and queen are in the same hand, they work together to trap the king and provide you with two tricks without having to give up the lead to the defenders. Finesses, however, can come in various guises. Take a look at this combination:

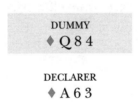

DUMMY
♦ Q 8 4

DECLARER
♦ A 6 3

Declarer again has both the ace and queen, but the high cards are divided between the two hands. This is not quite as strong a holding, since you can no longer take two tricks without giving the defenders a chance to take their king. Nonetheless, you can still win a trick with the ♦Q, in addition to your ♦A, provided the ♦K is favorably placed. You have to hope the ♦K is on your left, in front of dummy's ♦Q. The layout of the suit you're hoping for is something like this:

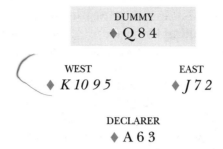

DUMMY
♦ Q 8 4

WEST              EAST
♦ K 10 9 5        ♦ J 7 2

DECLARER
♦ A 6 3

By leading a low diamond from your hand toward dummy's ♦Q, you make West play before dummy. If West plays the ♦K, you play a low diamond from dummy and later get a trick with dummy's ♦Q; if West plays a low diamond, you hop up with dummy's ♦Q, and it wins the trick. West can get a trick with the ♦K but can't prevent you from getting two tricks in the suit.

This holding has a disadvantage. You can't prevent West from taking a trick with the king. It has the advantage of providing its own entry. You can use the ♦A as the entry to your hand so that you can lead a low diamond toward dummy. Playing the ace first has another small advantage. You'd save yourself a trick if this were the actual layout of the diamond suit:

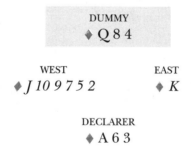

DUMMY
♦ Q 8 4

WEST              EAST
♦ J 10 9 7 5 2    ♦ K

DECLARER
♦ A 6 3

When you play the ♦A, East's singleton ♦K appears, saving you the trouble of leading toward dummy's queen. It's an unlikely holding, but you want to give yourself every chance of finding the cards favorably placed. It would be unfortunate, on this layout, if you were to start by leading a low diamond to dummy's ♦Q. Your finesse would lose, and when you later played your ♦A, you'd find out that you could have made two tricks after all.

Playing your ace first in these situations requires careful consideration. You can't always afford to do so. Suppose this is the combination of cards from which you're trying to get two tricks:

If you take your ♣A first, you'll leave the ♣Q all alone in dummy. When you next lead a low club, West can capture the ♣Q by playing the ♣K, restricting you to one trick in the suit. Instead, you should start the suit by leading a low club toward the dummy. You need the ♣7 in the dummy so that you can play it if West plays the ♣K.

Finesses come clothed in different guises. If West were to lead clubs first on the above layout—perhaps as the opening lead—it would be a finessing situation. You could hop up with dummy's ♣Q, hoping that East didn't have the king. This time, you'd get two tricks from the suit without giving West a trick with the ♣K. Unfortunate for West, but lucky for you.

Here's an opportunity to put your queens to work. The contract is 1NT, and the opening lead is the ♠J.

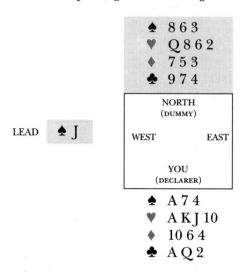

LEAD  ♠ J

You can count one sure trick in spades, four in hearts, and one in clubs. You need one more, and the only chance lies in the club suit. You'll need the ♣K to lie on your right so that you'll get two club tricks with the help of a successful finesse. To take the club finesse, you need an entry to the dummy, and the only one available is the ♥Q.

After winning a trick with your ♠A, you can take some heart tricks, but you must be sure to end up in dummy with the ♥Q. Now, you lead a low club from the dummy and finesse the ♣Q. If this wins, you'll have the seven tricks you need. If it doesn't...

On this hand, you have to make good use of your queens. The ♥Q is your entry to dummy. The ♣Q is the card you hope will be your seventh trick when you lead toward it.

## Putting the Jack to Work

Even a jack can play its part when the queen is outstanding. Consider this combination:

Two sure tricks can be taken with the ace and king. If you need an extra trick from the suit, you can try a finesse for the queen. Lead toward the jack, the card you hope will take a trick. This is how you're hoping the defenders' spades are positioned:

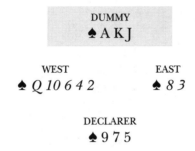

If the queen is favorably placed, in front of dummy's jack, your finesse will be successful, and you'll get three tricks from the suit. If East holds the queen, behind dummy's jack, you're out of luck. To take the finesse, you'll need an entry to your hand in this situation. Here's a layout with a built-in entry:

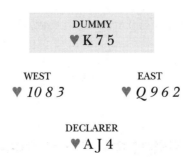

To take three tricks from this combination, you hope East holds the ♥Q. You can use the ♥K to cross over to dummy so that you can lead a low heart toward your hand. When East plays a low heart, you finesse your ♥J, winning the trick when West has no higher heart to play.

The following combination presents a different type of challenge when you're missing the queen:

DUMMY
♦ A 10 5

WEST          EAST
♦ ?           ♦ ?

DECLARER
♦ K J 6

You have a choice. If you think East has the ♦Q, you can play your ♦6 over to dummy's ♦A, and then lead a diamond from dummy toward your hand, intending to finesse the ♦J. That works if East has the ♦Q, as in this layout:

DUMMY
♦ A 10 5

WEST          EAST
♦ *9 7 3*      ♦ *Q 8 4 2*

DECLARER
♦ K J 6

It wouldn't be a success if West held the ♦Q, as would be the case if this were the layout:

DUMMY
♦ A 10 5

WEST          EAST
♦ *Q 8 4 2*    ♦ *9 7 3*

DECLARER
♦ K J 6

The presence of the ♦10 in dummy, however, gives you the opportunity to win three diamond tricks when West holds the ♦Q. You can win the first diamond trick with the ♦K in your hand and lead a diamond toward dummy, planning to trap West's ♦Q. If West plays the ♦Q, you capture with dummy's ♦A; if not, you finesse dummy's ♦10 and win the trick when East has no higher card.

Such a position is called a *two-way finesse* because you have a choice of which way to finesse. Which defender actually holds the ♦Q? Many times, it's a pure guess. Sometimes, however, you'll have a clue from the bidding or play. If West had bid during the auction, for example, you might suspect that West holds the missing high card.

Here's another layout in which you're missing the queen. The basic principle of the finesse still applies, but it may not be quite so obvious.

DUMMY
♣ A K 8 3

DECLARER
♣ J 4

You can expect to take two tricks from this suit with your ace and king, but what if you need three? You'll have to put the jack to work by leading toward it, hoping the full layout of the club suit is something like this:

DUMMY
♣ A K 8 3

WEST              EAST
♣ 10 7 6          ♣ Q 9 5 2

DECLARER
♣ J 4

You can't play dummy's ♣A or ♣K first because the ♣J would then be a singleton, easy prey to East's ♣Q. Instead, play dummy's ♣3 toward your ♣J. If East plays the queen, play your ♣4, and the remaining cards look like this:

DUMMY
**♣ A K 8**

WEST                              EAST
**♣ 10 7**                        **♣ 9 5 2**

DECLARER
**♣ J**

With the ♣Q gone, your ♣J is now a winner. After taking a trick with it, you'll need an entry to get back to dummy to take your ♣A and ♣K, but you'll end up with three tricks from the suit. If that's what you need, it will be worth the effort.

Let's see a finesse against the queen in action. On this hand you've reached a contract of 4 ♥, and the defenders have got off to a lead of the ♦K.

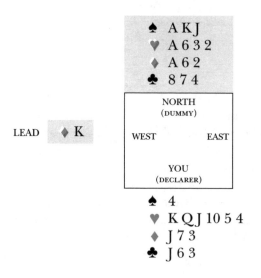

♠  A K J
♥  A 6 3 2
♦  A 6 2
♣  8 7 4

NORTH
(DUMMY)

LEAD   ♦ K       WEST            EAST

YOU
(DECLARER)

♠  4
♥  K Q J 10 5 4
♦  J 7 3
♣  J 6 3

You start with nine sure tricks: two spades, six hearts, and one diamond. You need one more to make the contract. There's no hope for an extra trick from the club suit, and your ♦J is also unlikely to provide a trick. The only chance appears to lie in the spade suit. You can get an extra trick by taking a finesse and hoping the ♠Q is on your left.

This takes some nerve. After winning the first trick with dummy's ♦A, draw the defenders' trump ending up in your hand. Lead a low spade, and when a low spade appears on your left, insert dummy's ♠J. This is the moment of truth. If the finesse works, you'll have ten tricks. If it loses, the opponents will probably take three club tricks and two diamond tricks, to go along with their ♠Q. You'll go down three tricks. Talk about all or nothing!

## Eight Ever, Nine Never

A missing queen raises an interesting issue when you also have some length in the suit. This is the situation:

DUMMY
♠ A K J 8 4

DECLARER
♠ 9 6 5 3 2

You lead one of the low spades from your hand and a low spade appears from your left-hand opponent. You could play dummy's ♠J, hoping the ♠Q lies on your left. With ten spades in the combined hands, however, a better choice would be to play dummy's ♠A or ♠K. The defenders have only three spades between them. As long as the missing spades are divided 2–1, you don't care which defender has the ♠Q; it will fall under your ace and king. Even if the player on your right were to discard on the first round of spades, you'd still be able to take all the spade tricks provided you have an entry back to your hand. With the knowledge that all three spades are on your left, you can cross back to your hand and lead another spade, finessing the ♠J on the second round.

So, length makes a difference, especially when you're missing the queen in a suit. The more cards you hold between the two hands, the more likely it is that the queen will "drop", or "fall", when you play your ace and king. Where do you draw the line? If you hold only six cards in the combined hands, leaving the opponents with seven, it's less likely that the queen will fall, and you should probably take a finesse rather than playing the ace and king.

The guideline used when you're missing the queen but hold the ace, king, and jack is **eight ever, nine never**. The "eight ever" means that, with eight or fewer combined cards, you should take the finesse. The "nine never" tells you to play the ace and king when you have nine or more combined cards—don't take the finesse. For example, compare these two holdings:

1) DUMMY
♥ K J 7 6

DECLARER
♥ A 4 3 2

2) DUMMY
♥ K J 7 6 5

DECLARER
♥ A 4 3 2

In the first layout, you have only eight combined cards. Suppose you take a trick with your ♥A and lead a low heart toward dummy. If the opponent on your left plays a low heart, the guideline suggests that you finesse for the missing ♥Q by playing dummy's ♥J—eight ever. In the second layout, you have nine combined hearts. After winning a trick with your ♥A and leading a low heart toward dummy, if the ♥Q hasn't appeared, the guideline suggests playing dummy's ♥K, hoping the ♥Q will fall—nine never.

Eight ever, nine never is a guideline, not a rule. Use it when you have nothing better to go on. As you have already seen, however, there are many hands where the best way to play a particular suit depends on your plan for the whole hand. We'll encounter some exceptions to the guideline later on, but for now see how you'd apply it on the following hand. You're in a contract of 3♠, and the opening lead is the ♣7.

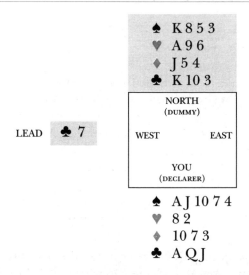

♠ K 8 5 3
♥ A 9 6
♦ J 5 4
♣ K 10 3

NORTH
(DUMMY)

LEAD   ♣ 7

WEST          EAST

YOU
(DECLARER)

♠ A J 10 7 4
♥ 8 2
♦ 10 7 3
♣ A Q J

There are two sure tricks in spades, one sure trick in hearts, and three in clubs. You'll need to take all five spade tricks to make the 3♠ contract. After winning the first club trick, start drawing trump. Play a spade to dummy's ♠K. Both opponents follow suit. When you lead a low spade from dummy toward your hand, the last low spade appears. Should you finesse the ♠J, hoping the ♠Q is on your right, or should you play the ♠A, hoping that the ♠Q will fall on your left?

With nothing else to guide you, play the ♠A. There are nine combined trump. The guideline suggests that playing the top two spades is better than taking the finesse. It's a close decision, and there are no guarantees. If it doesn't work, you can tell partner, "I was thinking of finessing, but you remember that book I was reading . . . ?"

## Summary

The third method of getting extra tricks on your checklist should be the finesse—trying to win a trick with a lower-ranking card by taking advantage of the favorable position of one or more higher-ranking cards held by the defenders.

| *Checklist* | |
|---|---|
| | Promotion |
| | Length |
| ✓ | Finessing |
| | Trumping Losers |
| | Discarding Losers |

Finesses don't always work. You need a favorable placement of the higher-ranking cards in the suit that are held by the defenders. Keep the following guidelines in mind:

- Lead toward the card you're hoping will win a trick.
- If you hold the ace, king, and jack, but are missing the queen, take the finesse when you hold eight or fewer cards in the combined hands. With nine or more combined cards, play the ace and king, hoping the queen will fall.

## Practice Hands

### Hand 5.1

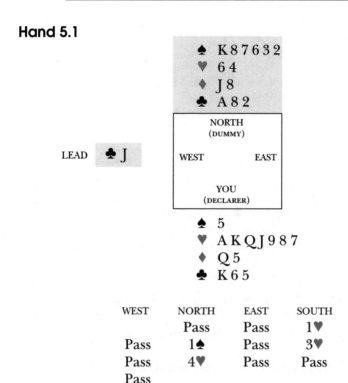

♠ K 8 7 6 3 2
♥ 6 4
♦ J 8
♣ A 8 2

NORTH
(DUMMY)

LEAD   ♣ J

WEST                    EAST

YOU
(DECLARER)

♠ 5
♥ A K Q J 9 8 7
♦ Q 5
♣ K 6 5

| WEST | NORTH | EAST | SOUTH |
|------|-------|------|-------|
|      | Pass  | Pass | 1♥    |
| Pass | 1♠    | Pass | 3♥    |
| Pass | 4♥    | Pass | Pass  |
| Pass |       |      |       |

West leads the ♣J against your contract of 4♥. How do you plan to make the contract? Does it matter in which hand you win the first trick?

## Solution 5.1

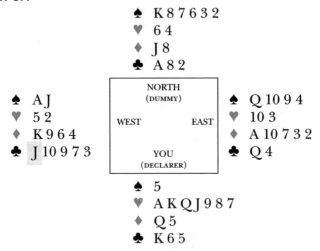

NORTH (DUMMY)
- ♠ K 8 7 6 3 2
- ♥ 6 4
- ♦ J 8
- ♣ A 8 2

WEST
- ♠ A J
- ♥ 5 2
- ♦ K 9 6 4
- ♣ J 10 9 7 3

EAST
- ♠ Q 10 9 4
- ♥ 10 3
- ♦ A 10 7 3 2
- ♣ Q 4

YOU (DECLARER)
- ♠ 5
- ♥ A K Q J 9 8 7
- ♦ Q 5
- ♣ K 6 5

Ten tricks are needed to make the contract. There are seven sure tricks in hearts and two in clubs; a total of nine tricks. You need one more. Using the checklist, there's nothing to promote, and it's doubtful you can do much with dummy's long spade suit because there aren't enough entries to the dummy. A finesse offers your best chance. If West holds the ♠A, you can establish a trick with dummy's ♠K.

Noting the order to play the cards. Be careful in both the spade suit and the club suit. In the spade suit, you want to be sure to lead from your hand toward the ♠K in dummy. Assuming your finesse is going to be successful, you'll also need an entry to dummy to reach the ♠K once it has been established as a winner. The only entry to dummy is the ♣A. That tells you where to win the first trick—with the ♣K in your hand. You can afford to draw the defenders' trump, and then it's time to lead a spade. West can take the ♠A, and the defenders can take two diamond tricks. Whatever they lead next, you'll get an opportunity to win a trick with dummy's carefully preserved ♣A and take a trick with dummy's established ♠K. That's your tenth trick.

## Hand 5.2

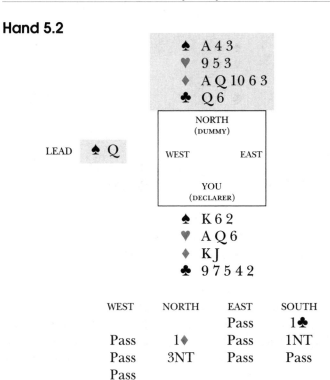

♠ A 4 3
♥ 9 5 3
♦ A Q 10 6 3
♣ Q 6

NORTH
(DUMMY)

LEAD   ♠ Q

WEST                    EAST

YOU
(DECLARER)

♠ K 6 2
♥ A Q 6
♦ K J
♣ 9 7 5 4 2

| WEST | NORTH | EAST | SOUTH |
|------|-------|------|-------|
|      |       | Pass | 1♣    |
| Pass | 1♦    | Pass | 1NT   |
| Pass | 3NT   | Pass | Pass  |
| Pass |       |      |       |

You're in a contract of 3NT, and the opening lead is the ♠Q. Why is the order important?

## Solution 5.2

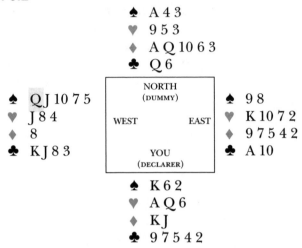

You need nine tricks in the 3NT contract. There are two sure tricks in spades, one in hearts, and five in diamonds. You need to find one more. You might consider using the club length to establish an extra trick. By the time you do that, however, the defenders will probably have established enough tricks of their own to defeat the contract. A better choice is available in the heart suit. You can plan to take a finesse of the ♥Q, hoping that the ♥K lies in the East hand. That's a 50–50 chance.

Order your play carefully. The diamond suit is blocked, and there's only one sure entry to the dummy outside of diamonds—the ♣A. You also need to get to dummy so that you can lead a heart toward your ♥Q. The ♣A will have to be used for that purpose as well. Win the first trick with the ♠K in your hand. Take the ♦K and ♦J to unblock the diamond suit. Cross over to dummy with the ♣A. While in the dummy, take the rest of the diamond winners, discarding low cards from your hand. Finally, lead a low heart from dummy, and when East plays a low heart, finesse the ♥Q. When this is successful, take your ♥A, congratulate yourself on your good play and good fortune, and go on to the next hand.

On this hand, you couldn't afford to focus only on the heart finesse. If you play dummy's ♣A too soon—planning to take the heart finesse—you won't be able to untangle your diamond winners. As always, you must look at the complete hand before deciding on the order in which to play each suit.

## Hand 5.3

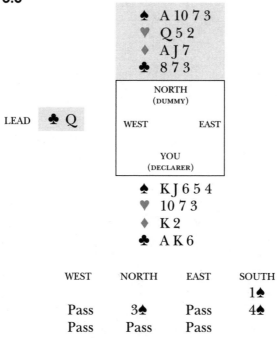

♠ A 10 7 3
♥ Q 5 2
♦ A J 7
♣ 8 7 3

|              | NORTH<br>(DUMMY) |              |
|--------------|:----------------:|--------------|
| WEST         |                  | EAST         |
|              | YOU<br>(DECLARER)|              |

LEAD   ♣ Q

♠ K J 6 5 4
♥ 10 7 3
♦ K 2
♣ A K 6

| WEST | NORTH | EAST | SOUTH |
|------|-------|------|-------|
|      |       |      | 1♠    |
| Pass | 3♠    | Pass | 4♠    |
| Pass | Pass  | Pass |       |

West leads the ♣Q against your contract of 4♠. How do you plan to play the trump suit? What's your best chance of making the contract?

## Solution 5.3

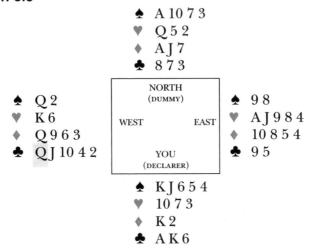

♠ A 10 7 3
♥ Q 5 2
♦ A J 7
♣ 8 7 3

NORTH
(DUMMY)

WEST          EAST

YOU
(DECLARER)

♠ Q 2
♥ K 6
♦ Q 9 6 3
♣ Q J 10 4 2

♠ 9 8
♥ A J 9 8 4
♦ 10 8 5 4
♣ 9 5

♠ K J 6 5 4
♥ 10 7 3
♦ K 2
♣ A K 6

Ten tricks are needed to make the contract. There are two sure tricks in spades, two in diamonds, and two in clubs. Four more tricks are needed. Three of the extra tricks can come from the spade suit. You have a choice of playing the ace and king, hoping the ♠Q will fall, or taking a finesse against the ♠Q. You actually have a two-way finesse for the missing ♠Q because you have both the jack and the ten. If you think East has the ♠Q, you could play dummy's ♠A, and then lead a low spade toward your hand, planning to finesse the ♠J if the queen doesn't appear. If you feel that West has the ♠Q, you could start by playing the ♠K, and then lead a low spade toward dummy, planning to finesse dummy's ♠10 if the queen doesn't appear. You have nine spades between the two hands, however, and the guideline "eight ever, nine never" suggests that you should simply play your ♠A and ♠K, hoping the ♠Q appears.

Assuming you can take five spade tricks, you still need to find one more trick. The only hope is the diamond suit. Dummy's ♦J offers you an opportunity. Plan to play the ♦K, and then lead the ♦2 toward dummy. If the ♦Q has not yet appeared, finesse dummy's ♦J, hoping West has the ♦Q. If the finesse is successful, you have ten tricks. With only five diamonds between the two hands, the finesse is a better chance than playing the ♦A and ♦K, hoping the queen will fall. The "eight ever, nine never" guideline suggests that, with eight or fewer cards in a suit that's missing the queen, the finesse is the recommended play.

## Hand 5.4

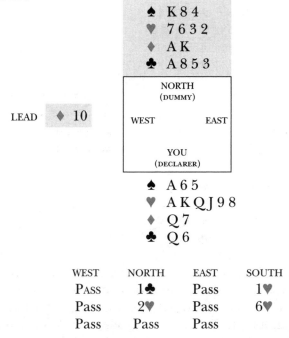

♠ K 8 4
♥ 7 6 3 2
♦ A K
♣ A 8 5 3

NORTH
(DUMMY)

LEAD   ♦ 10

WEST        EAST

YOU
(DECLARER)

♠ A 6 5
♥ A K Q J 9 8
♦ Q 7
♣ Q 6

| WEST | NORTH | EAST | SOUTH |
|------|-------|------|-------|
| PASS | 1♣ | Pass | 1♥ |
| Pass | 2♥ | Pass | 6♥ |
| Pass | Pass | Pass | |

Here's an opportunity to make a slam contract with the help of a queen. You're in a contract of 6♥, and the opening lead is the ♦10.

## Solution 5.4

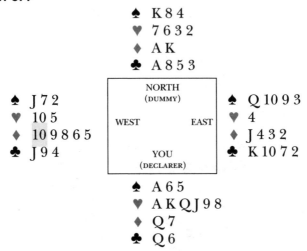

```
                    ♠ K 8 4
                    ♥ 7 6 3 2
                    ♦ A K
                    ♣ A 8 5 3
                  ┌──────────────┐
  ♠ J 7 2         │    NORTH     │      ♠ Q 10 9 3
  ♥ 10 5          │   (DUMMY)    │      ♥ 4
  ♦ 10 9 8 6 5    │ WEST    EAST │      ♦ J 4 3 2
  ♣ J 9 4         │              │      ♣ K 10 7 2
                  │     YOU      │
                  │  (DECLARER)  │
                  └──────────────┘
                    ♠ A 6 5
                    ♥ A K Q J 9 8
                    ♦ Q 7
                    ♣ Q 6
```

To make the small slam, you need twelve of the thirteen tricks. There are two spade tricks, six hearts, two diamonds, and one club— one trick short. There's nowhere to promote an extra trick, or to generate one from length. The finesse is your only hope. You need to get a trick with the ♣Q, and that requires the ♣K being favorably placed on your right.

It may not look like it, but entries to dummy could present a problem, if you aren't careful. You need to get there once to lead a club toward your ♣Q, and later to take a trick with dummy's ♣A. The defenders have already removed a diamond entry with the opening lead and may remove the other diamond entry when they win a trick with the ♣K. Since you're in dummy after winning the first trick, that's your opportunity to lead a low club. Suppose East wins the trick with the ♣K. Your finesse has been successful, but there's still work to do. Suppose East leads another diamond. Win this trick with dummy's remaining high diamond, and draw the defenders' trump. Once this is done, take a trick with your ♣Q. Now cross over to dummy with the ♠K, and take a trick with dummy's ♣A, discarding a low spade. The rest of the tricks are yours. Well done.

There are a couple of traps on this hand. You can't afford to play dummy's ♣A before leading a club toward the ♣Q. You also can't afford to draw trump before leading a club toward the ♣Q. There won't be enough entries to dummy if East wins the ♣K and leads a second diamond. Try it.

# More About Finesses

*"Play it again, Sam."*
—WOODY ALLEN,
*Take the Money and Run* [1969]

Finesses come in all shapes and sizes. Sometimes, you'll need to finesse for the same card more than once. At other times, you may have to finesse for more than one card.

## The Repeated Finesse

Many card combinations can be handled in more than one way. It all depends on your objective. Take a look at the following layout of the heart suit:

DUMMY
♥ 7 5 3

DECLARER
♥ K Q 6

If you need only one trick from this suit, you can get it through promotion. Play one of your high hearts to drive out the defenders' ace. Your remaining high heart is promoted into a winner. But suppose you have to take two tricks from these cards. You can't afford to sacrifice one of your honors to the ace; you need to take a trick with both the king and the queen. This sounds like a time to call on the finesse. Instead of leading toward the one card you hope will win a trick, however, you'll need to lead toward both cards with which you hope to take tricks.

You'll require a favorable placement of the defenders' higher-ranking card, the ♥A in this case. You'll need it to be on your right, in front of the king and queen, something like this:

DUMMY
♥ 7 5 3

WEST          EAST
♥ 10 9 4      ♥ A J 8 2

DECLARER
♥ K Q 6

The basic idea is that of the finesse. You lead a low heart from the dummy toward your hand, making your right-hand opponent, East, choose which heart to play before you have to decide. If East plays the ♥A, you play the ♥6, and you have established two winners with your king and queen. It becomes more interesting, however, if East doesn't take the ♥A right away, playing a low heart. You now play the ♥K—or ♥Q—which wins the trick because West has no higher heart to play. Your first finesse has been successful, and the following cards remain:

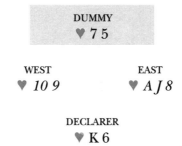

DUMMY
♥ 7 5

WEST                          EAST
♥ *10 9*                      ♥ *A J 8*

DECLARER
♥ K 6

Your work is not yet done. You must travel back over to dummy in another suit, and again lead a low heart toward your hand. This puts East back in the same dilemma. If East plays the ♥A, you play the ♥6, and your ♥K becomes a winner for later. If East plays a low heart, you play the ♥K which wins the trick. This type of play is referred to as a *repeated finesse*. You finesse more than once against the same card.

Since you're developing two tricks, rather than one, your development costs are higher. Unless East plays the ♥A on the first round of the suit, you'll need two entries to dummy: one to lead toward the ♥Q and one to lead toward the ♥K. You'll have to manage your entries carefully, and you may not always have the luxury of being able to repeat the finesse. That's why there are times you have to settle for a single trick from this suit, even though the ace is favorably located. Of course, if West holds the ♥A, all your work will be for naught. West will capture one of your high cards with the ace, limiting you to one trick in the suit.

Here's another combination that provides an opportunity for a repeated finesse:

DUMMY
♦ A Q J

DECLARER
♦ 7 6 4

You have one sure trick with the ♦A, and you could promote a second trick with your ♦Q and ♦J by driving out the ♦K in either defender's hand. To get three tricks from this suit, you'll need the ♦K favorably located, and you'll need two entries to your hand. Here's the type of layout you're hoping for:

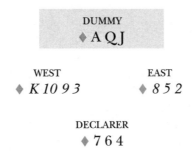

DUMMY
♦ A Q J

WEST         EAST
♦ K 10 9 3       ♦ 8 5 2

DECLARER
♦ 7 6 4

Lead a low diamond from your hand, and when West plays a low diamond, finesse dummy's ♦J. Your first finesse is successful because East doesn't have the ♦K. Cross back to your hand with an entry in another suit, and repeat the finesse by leading a low diamond toward dummy's ♦Q. West is powerless to stop you from taking three tricks in the suit.

Repeating finesses may require careful handling of your entries. Consider this hand. Your contract is 4♠, and the opening lead is the ♥J.

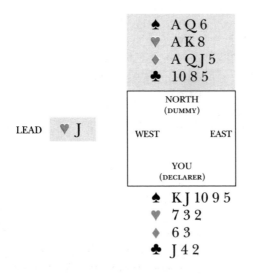

♠ A Q 6
♥ A K 8
♦ A Q J 5
♣ 10 8 5

NORTH
(DUMMY)

LEAD ♥ J

WEST       EAST

YOU
(DECLARER)

♠ K J 10 9 5
♥ 7 3 2
♦ 6 3
♣ J 4 2

There are five sure tricks in spades, two in hearts, and one in diamonds. Two more tricks are needed to make the contract. You can't get any extra tricks from the clubs or hearts, so you'll need to take three diamond tricks. That's possible, if the ♦K is favorably located on your left. You'll need to take two finesses, and there aren't many entries to your hand. You'll need to watch the order in which you play your cards.

After winning a trick with the ♥A, you can start drawing trump by playing dummy's ♠A. You continue by leading dummy's ♠Q but must overtake the queen with your ♠K. This gives you one of the entries you need to your hand. At this point, you can't afford to draw any more trump. You want to use the opportunity to lead one of your low diamonds toward dummy. When a low diamond appears on your left, play the ♦J, taking your first finesse. If this wins the trick, you're half way home. You can now afford to lead dummy's ♠6 back to your hand to draw the remaining trump. You're back in your hand for the second time and can lead your remaining low diamond toward dummy. Assuming another low diamond appears on your left, play dummy's ♦Q, repeating the finesse. Now you have enough tricks to make the contract. Here's the complete hand:

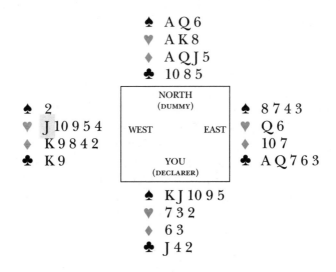

Notice the importance of overtaking dummy's ♠Q. If you let the ♠Q win the trick, you won't be able to get to your hand twice to repeat the diamond finesse. Sometimes, kings were meant to take queens—even your own. It's also important to delay drawing the rest of the trump. There are more important things to do. Once the first diamond finesse works, however, you can safely draw the remainder of East's trump before repeating the finesse. If you didn't do this, you might find East trumping one of your diamond winners after all that effort.

## Finessing Against More Than One Card

When I'm lecturing, I have the students wave one hand in the air to warm up for the topic of finessing against more than one card. You can do that now, if you're reading this book in a private place. Waving your hand is a way to remind yourself that there are only five honor cards in each suit: the ace, king, queen, jack, and ten. Consider this layout of the club suit:

There's one sure trick in the suit, the ♣A. There's no opportunity to promote winners in this suit because the opponents have both the ♣K and ♣Q. It does, however, have a vaguely familiar look. You'd like to win a second trick in the suit with the ♣J or ♣10, so perhaps you should be leading toward one of the cards you hope will win a trick. That's exactly what you should do. This is another form of the finesse. To see why you should start this suit by leading a low card from your hand toward the dummy, let's consider the four possible ways the missing king and queen could be located in the defenders' hands:

|   | *West* | *East* |
|---|--------|--------|
| 1 | ♣ K, ♣ Q | – |
| 2 | ♣ K | ♣ Q |
| 3 | ♣ Q | ♣ K |
| 4 | – | ♣ K, ♣ Q |

Let's consider the first case, when West holds both the king and queen. Does this mean, you could enjoy all three tricks? Not without a lot of help from West. By leading toward dummy, however, you'll always be able to get two tricks. Here's a typical layout:

DUMMY
♣ A J 10

WEST                    EAST
♣ K Q 7 2               ♣ 9 4 3

DECLARER
♣ 8 6 5

When you lead a low club from your hand, West must play a card before you choose the card from dummy. Suppose West chooses to play the ♣K, or ♣Q. This is referred to as *splitting your honors*. You capture West's honor with the ♣A, and now lead one of dummy's clubs to drive out West's remaining honor, promoting dummy's remaining club into a winner. You get two tricks from the suit.

Alternatively, when you lead a low club toward dummy, West may choose not to split the honors, playing a low club instead. You finesse the ♣J, or ♣10, and this wins the trick, since East doesn't have a higher club to play. You still have your ♣A as a second trick in the suit. You could come back to your hand and try leading another low club toward dummy, but West will likely play one of the honors this time to prevent you from taking all three tricks in the suit.

Let's see what happens in the second or third case, when each of the defenders holds one of the missing honors. The suit might look something like this:

DUMMY
♣ A J 10

WEST                    EAST
♣ K 7 2                 ♣ Q 9 4 3

DECLARER
♣ 8 6 5

When you lead a low club, it does West no good to play the ♣K. You can win the trick with the ♣A and use dummy's remaining clubs to promote a second trick in the suit by driving out East's ♣Q. Instead, suppose West plays a low club when you lead a club toward dummy. You finesse dummy's ♣J, or ♣10, and this finesse loses because East produces the ♣Q. It's not over yet, however. The remaining clubs now look like this:

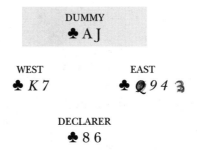

DUMMY
♣ A J

WEST                              EAST
♣ K 7                          ♣ Q 9 4 3

DECLARER
♣ 8 6

When you regain the lead, you can try leading another low club toward dummy. When West plays a low club, you try a second finesse by playing dummy's ♣J. This time, your finesse works because East no longer has a higher club. You end up with two tricks in the suit. Notice that it doesn't matter which defender has the ♣K and which defender has the ♣Q. When the missing honors are divided between the defenders' hands, your first finesse will lose, your second finesse will win.

Finally, what happens in the fourth case, when East holds both the ♣K and ♣Q?

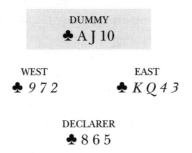

DUMMY
♣ A J 10

WEST                              EAST
♣ 9 7 2                        ♣ K Q 4 3

DECLARER
♣ 8 6 5

Unlucky! You try your first finesse by leading a low club to dummy's ♣10, and East wins the trick with the ♣Q. When you later get back to your hand and repeat the finesse, playing a low club to dummy's ♣J, East produces the ♣K. Both your finesses lose, and you end up with only the one trick you started with, the ♣A.

Although you get only one trick in this last layout, you get two tricks in the other three cases. That's pretty good odds. You win three out of four times—75%—by leading a low club toward dummy, planning to finesse the ♣10, and if this loses, repeating the finesse by leading low to dummy's ♣J. Let's see how you could profit from this technique on the following hand. You're in 1NT, and the opening lead is the ♥Q.

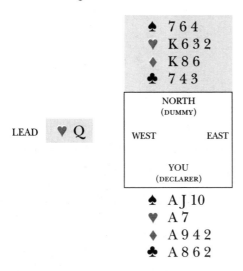

♠ 764
♥ K632
♦ K86
♣ 743

NORTH
(DUMMY)

LEAD ♥ Q

WEST            EAST

YOU
(DECLARER)

♠ A J 10
♥ A 7
♦ A 9 4 2
♣ A 8 6 2

You start with six top tricks: the ♠A, ♥A, ♥K, ♦A, ♦K, and ♣A. You need to find one more to make the 1NT contract. You go down your checklist, looking for ways to develop the extra trick you need. There's no suit that offers an opportunity for promotion, but there are two suits that offer some possibility for developing tricks through length. There are seven combined cards in both diamonds and clubs. If the defenders' cards are divided exactly 3–3 in either suit, you could establish an extra trick. This is not likely, however, since you expect six outstanding cards to divide slightly unevenly, 4–2.

A better opportunity for an extra trick is available in the spade suit. You can get two tricks from this suit if either the ♠K or the ♠Q are on your right. You'll need two entries to dummy, so you should win the first trick with dummy's ♥K. Lead a low spade toward your hand, finessing the ♠J, or ♠10. If your first finesse loses, you plan to get back to dummy with the ♦K and repeat the finesse. Here's the complete hand:

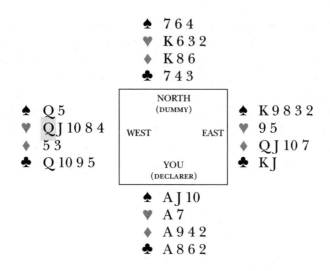

Your first finesse loses to West's ♠Q, but your second finesse is successful because East holds the ♠K. Neither the diamonds nor the clubs would have provided you with an extra trick. Playing the spade suit correctly, however, gave you a 75% chance of success. You'd have gone down in your contract only if West held both the ♠K and ♠Q.

## Leading Toward the Lower Card

There are many situations in which you need to take repeated finesses against two or more cards held by the defenders. The general principle to follow in such situations is to **start by leading toward the lower card you hope will win a trick**. For example, consider this combination:

Wave your hand to remind yourself that there are five honor cards. You have three of them, the ♠A, ♠Q, and ♠10; the defenders hold the other two, the ♠K and ♠J. You'd like to take as many tricks as possible from this combination, so you start by leading a low spade from your hand toward dummy. If West plays a low spade, which spade should you play from dummy, the ♠Q or the ♠10? The general principle suggests playing the ♠10 first, the lower card which you hope will win a trick. To see why, let's look at the possible placement of the missing honors in the defenders' hands:

|   | West | East |
|---|---|---|
| 1 | ♠ K, ♠ J | – |
| 2 | ♠ K | ♠ J |
| 3 | ♠ J | ♠ K |
| 4 | – | ♠ K, ♠ J |

In the first situation, you'd take all three tricks by playing the ♠10 on the first round of the suit. The complete layout would look something like this:

DUMMY
♠ A Q 10

WEST
♠ K J 4 2

EAST
♠ 9 8 5

DECLARER
♠ 7 6 3

When you lead a low spade and finesse dummy's ♠10, East can't win the trick. Now the remaining cards look like this:

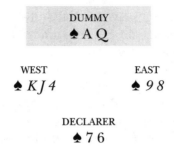

DUMMY
♠ A Q

WEST          EAST
♠ K J 4       ♠ 9 8

DECLARER
♠ 7 6

You can travel back to your hand and repeat the finesse, this time playing dummy's ♠Q. The defenders can't prevent you from taking three tricks.

Would it make a difference if you finesse the ♠Q the first time, rather than the ♠10? Yes. Your finesse would be successful, but the remaining spades would now look like this:

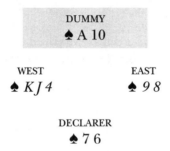

DUMMY
♠ A 10

WEST          EAST
♠ K J 4       ♠ 9 8

DECLARER
♠ 7 6

You could come back to your hand and try leading another spade toward dummy, but West could now split the honors, playing the ♠J. You could win dummy's ♠A, but that would be your last trick in the suit. You'd end up with two tricks, rather than three.

Let's look at the second situation, in which West holds the ♠K and East the ♠J:

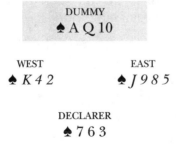

DUMMY
♠ A Q 10

WEST          EAST
♠ K 4 2       ♠ J 9 8 5

DECLARER
♠ 7 6 3

When you play a low spade to dummy's ♠10, your first finesse loses to East's ♠J. No problem. The remaining spades look like this:

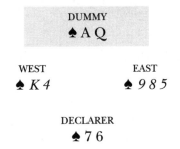

You get back to your hand and repeat the finesse. This time, you'll be successful. You'll end up with two tricks in the suit.

What happens in the third situation, where West holds the ♠J and East the ♠K?

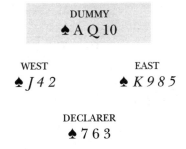

Instant success! When you play a low spade to dummy's ♠10, East has to win the trick with the ♠K. Now dummy's ♠A and ♠Q are both winners. You don't need any more finesses; you have two tricks from the suit.

Of course, you don't want to see what happens in the last case, when East holds both the ♠K and ♠J. Both your finesses lose, and you end up with the one trick you started with, the ♠A. Unlucky!

The point of all this is that, provided you have enough entries, playing to the lower card with which you hope to win a trick won't do any harm and is likely to do some good. Unless East has both the missing honors, you'll always get two tricks from the above combination, and you may get all three.

Here's a similar situation:

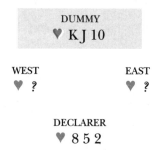

DUMMY
♥ K J 10

WEST          EAST
♥ ?           ♥ ?

DECLARER
♥ 8 5 2

When you lead a low heart toward dummy and West plays a low heart, which card do you play from dummy? You don't need to look at a table of all the possibilities. If you want the maximum number of tricks from the combination, start by playing dummy's ♥ 10, the lower card you hope will win a trick. You're hoping the layout looks something like this:

DUMMY
♥ K J 10

WEST          EAST
♥ Q 6 4       ♥ A 9 7 3

DECLARER
♥ 8 5 2

East will have to play the ♥ A to win the trick, and you can later repeat the finesse to get two tricks from the suit.

Let's try a hand that requires a similar approach. The contract is 4♠, and the opening lead is the ♥ 2.

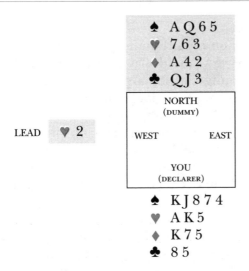

You start with nine sure tricks: five spades, two hearts, and two diamonds. To get a tenth trick, you'll need to make use of dummy's clubs. You're missing both the ♣A and ♣K, but if either of these cards is on your left, you'll be okay.

After winning the first heart trick, draw the defenders' trump, arranging to end up in your hand. Now lead a club toward dummy. If your left-hand opponent plays a low club, play dummy's ♣J, the lower card you hope will win a trick. If your right hand opponent wins this trick and leads a heart or a diamond, win the trick in your hand, and lead another club. You're hoping the complete hand looks something like this:

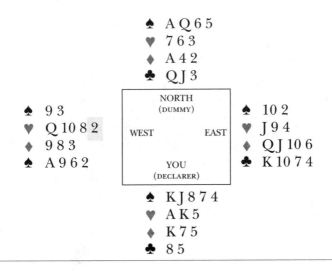

When you lead a low club toward dummy the first time, it does West no good to play the ♣A. You'd play dummy's ♣3 and could then use dummy's remaining club honors to drive out East's ♣K and promote a winner. If West plays a low club on the first round of the suit, you play dummy's ♣J and East wins the trick with the ♣K. When you regain the lead, you lead your last low club toward dummy. West is helpless. If West plays the ♣A, you play your low club from dummy and will later get your tenth trick with dummy's ♣Q. If West plays low a second time, dummy's queen will win the trick, and you again have ten tricks.

## Summary

When you're looking for extra tricks with the help of the finesse, you may need to arrange your entries so that you can repeat the finesse if necessary. When finessing against more than one card in the defenders' hands, use the following principle:

- Lead first toward the lower card which you hope will win a trick.

| | *Checklist* |
|---|---|
| | Promotion |
| | Length |
| ✓ | Finessing |
| | Trumping Losers |
| | Discarding Losers |

# Practice Hands

### Hand 6.1

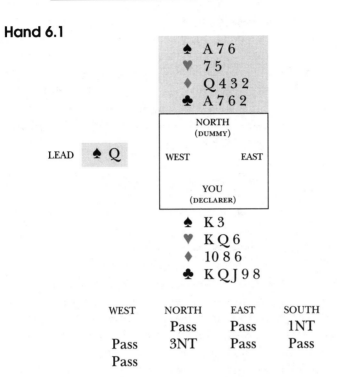

LEAD ♠ Q

NORTH
(DUMMY)
♠ A 7 6
♥ 7 5
♦ Q 4 3 2
♣ A 7 6 2

WEST          EAST

YOU
(DECLARER)
♠ K 3
♥ K Q 6
♦ 10 8 6
♣ K Q J 9 8

| WEST | NORTH | EAST | SOUTH |
|------|-------|------|-------|
|      | Pass  | Pass | 1NT   |
| Pass | 3NT   | Pass | Pass  |
| Pass |       |      |       |

West leads the ♠Q against your contract of 3NT. How do you plan to make the contract? Does it matter in which hand you win the first trick?

## Solution 6.1

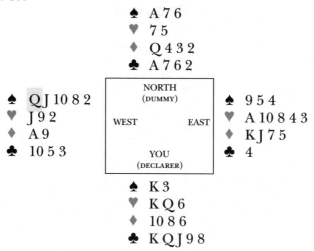

♠ A 7 6
♥ 7 5
♦ Q 4 3 2
♣ A 7 6 2

NORTH
(DUMMY)

WEST                    EAST

YOU
(DECLARER)

♠ Q J 10 8 2        ♠ 9 5 4
♥ J 9 2             ♥ A 10 8 4 3
♦ A 9               ♦ K J 7 5
♣ 10 5 3            ♣ 4

♠ K 3
♥ K Q 6
♦ 10 8 6
♣ K Q J 9 8

Nine tricks are required to make the contract. There are two tricks in spades and five in clubs; a total of seven tricks. You need two more. Using the checklist, the first possibility is to promote a trick in the heart suit, using one of your high cards to drive out the defenders' ♥A. But you'd still need one more trick. Moving down the checklist, the next possibility is length. There's some chance in diamonds. If the missing diamonds divide exactly 3–3, you could establish an extra trick. It's more likely that the defenders' six diamonds will divide 4–2. Also, by the time you establish an extra trick in diamonds, the defenders will likely have established enough tricks in the other suits to defeat the contract.

Going further down the checklist, you come to the finesse. The heart suit does provide the possibility for two tricks, if the ♥A is favorably placed on your right. You'll need to use a repeated finesse, so be careful about the order in which you play your cards. You need two entries to dummy so you can lead twice toward the high hearts in your hand. That tells you to win the first trick with the ♠A in the dummy. Then lead a heart toward your hand. Assuming East plays a low heart, play your ♥K, or ♥Q. You win the trick when West doesn't have the ♥A. You're halfway there. Cross back over to dummy with the ♣A, and lead another heart. East has no winning option. If East plays the ♥A, play your ♥6 and later take your remaining high heart as the ninth trick. If East plays low again, put up your remaining heart honor, and it wins the trick. Scamper home with nine tricks.

## Hand 6.2

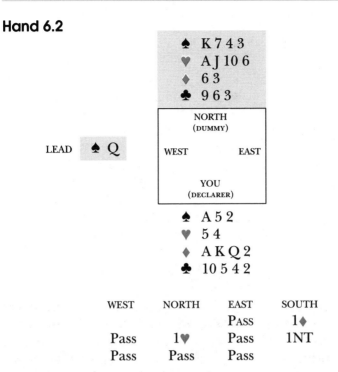

♠ K 7 4 3
♥ A J 10 6
♦ 6 3
♣ 9 6 3

NORTH
(DUMMY)

LEAD ♠ Q

WEST                     EAST

YOU
(DECLARER)

♠ A 5 2
♥ 5 4
♦ A K Q 2
♣ 10 5 4 2

| WEST | NORTH | EAST | SOUTH |
|------|-------|------|-------|
|      |       | PASS | 1♦ |
| Pass | 1♥ | Pass | 1NT |
| Pass | Pass | Pass | |

You're in a contract of 1NT, and the opening lead is the ♠Q. Where are your seven tricks going to come from?

## Solution 6.2

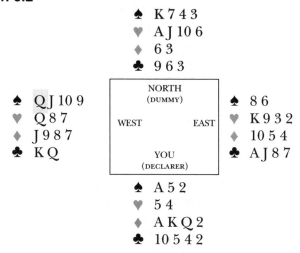

♠ K 7 4 3
♥ A J 10 6
♦ 6 3
♣ 9 6 3

NORTH
(DUMMY)

♠ Q J 10 9
♥ Q 8 7
♦ J 9 8 7
♣ K Q

WEST

EAST

♠ 8 6
♥ K 9 3 2
♦ 10 5 4
♣ A J 8 7

YOU
(DECLARER)

♠ A 5 2
♥ 5 4
♦ A K Q 2
♣ 10 5 4 2

You need seven tricks in your contract of 1NT. There are two sure tricks in spades, one in hearts, and three in diamonds. You need to find one more. You might consider using your spade length or club length to establish an extra trick. Either suit requires that the six cards held by the defenders divide exactly 3–3, an unlikely occurrence. A better chance is available in the heart suit. If West started with the ♥K, or the ♥Q, or with both heart honors, you can get an extra trick through a repeated finesse.

You want to start the heart suit by leading a low heart from your hand, so win your first spade trick with the ♠A. Lead a low heart, and when West produces a low heart, finesse dummy's ♥10, the lowest card you hope will win a trick. This loses to East's ♥K. Suppose East leads another spade. After winning with dummy's ♠K, cross back to your hand with a high diamond, and lead the last heart. When West plays a low heart, finesse dummy's ♥J, and keep your fingers crossed. On the actual layout, your second finesse is successful. Take dummy's ♥A and the rest of your diamond winners. That comes to seven tricks.

## Hand 6.3

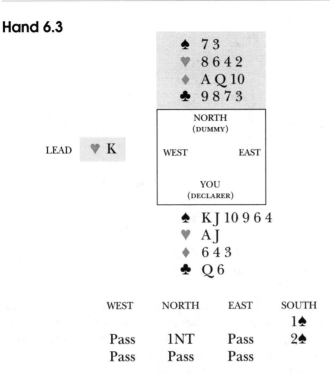

♠ 7 3
♥ 8 6 4 2
♦ A Q 10
♣ 9 8 7 3

NORTH
(DUMMY)

LEAD ♥ K    WEST          EAST

YOU
(DECLARER)

♠ K J 10 9 6 4
♥ A J
♦ 6 4 3
♣ Q 6

| WEST | NORTH | EAST | SOUTH |
|------|-------|------|-------|
|      |       |      | 1♠    |
| Pass | 1NT   | Pass | 2♠    |
| Pass | Pass  | Pass |       |

West leads the ♥K against your contract of 2♠. You have only two sure tricks to start with. You'll need to focus on getting the most from your spade and diamond suits. There are all sorts of finessing possibilities. What's your plan?

## Solution 6.3

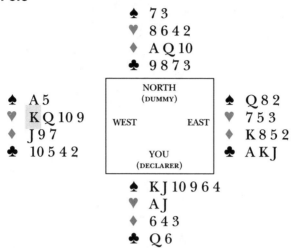

♠ 7 3
♥ 8 6 4 2
♦ A Q 10
♣ 9 8 7 3

NORTH
(DUMMY)

WEST                    EAST

YOU
(DECLARER)

♠ A 5
♥ K Q 10 9
♦ J 9 7
♣ 10 5 4 2

♠ Q 8 2
♥ 7 5 3
♦ K 8 5 2
♣ A K J

♠ K J 10 9 6 4
♥ A J
♦ 6 4 3
♣ Q 6

With only the ♥A and ♦A, you need six more tricks to make 2♠. The spade suit should provide most of them. You can develop two tricks through promotion: using the ♠K to drive out the ♠A, and the ♠J to drive out the ♠Q—promoting the ♠10 and ♠9 into winners. You expect two more tricks from the spade length. Once all the high spades are gone, the ♠6 and ♠4 should be winners. That's four tricks from the suit, but you may do better. By repeatedly leading spades from dummy toward your hand, you can finesse the ♠J and ♠10. If East holds the ♠Q, you get five tricks in the suit. That's still not enough. You need another trick from the diamonds. That's possible if West holds either the ♦K or ♦J, provided you handle the suit carefully.

With all these finesses to take, note the order you play your cards. After winning with the ♥A, you're in the wrong hand to try a spade finesse, but the right hand to lead a diamond. Lead a low diamond to dummy's ♦10, the card you'd like to win a trick. On the actual hand, this finesse loses to East's ♦K, but you now have two diamond winners. The defenders can take two club tricks and a heart trick, but you can then trump either suit. Cross to dummy with a diamond winner to lead a low spade, finessing the ♠9—the lowest card you hope will win a trick. West has to play the ♠A to win the trick. Whatever is led next, win the trick and return to dummy with the last high diamond. Lead dummy's last spade, and finesse the ♠J. When this wins, play the ♠K to draw the last trump—East's ♠Q. You end up with five spades, one heart, and two diamonds—just enough.

## Hand 6.4

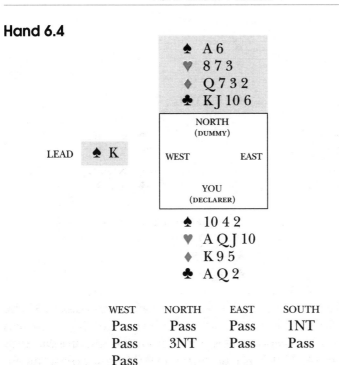

```
                    ♠ A 6
                    ♥ 8 7 3
                    ♦ Q 7 3 2
                    ♣ K J 10 6
              ┌─────────────────────┐
              │      NORTH          │
              │     (DUMMY)         │
              │                     │
   LEAD  ♠ K  │  WEST         EAST  │
              │                     │
              │       YOU           │
              │    (DECLARER)       │
              └─────────────────────┘
                    ♠ 10 4 2
                    ♥ A Q J 10
                    ♦ K 9 5
                    ♣ A Q 2
```

| WEST | NORTH | EAST | SOUTH |
|------|-------|------|-------|
| Pass | Pass | Pass | 1NT |
| Pass | 3NT | Pass | Pass |
| Pass | | | |

This hand provides an opportunity for a repeated finesse, but you'd better be careful with your entries. You're in a contract of 3NT, and the opening lead is the ♠K.

## Solution 6.4

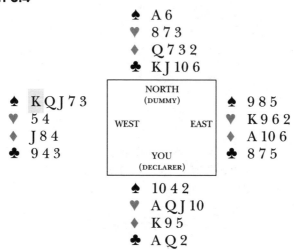

```
                    ♠ A 6
                    ♥ 8 7 3
                    ♦ Q 7 3 2
                    ♣ K J 10 6
                         NORTH
♠ K Q J 7 3              (DUMMY)           ♠ 9 8 5
♥ 5 4           WEST              EAST      ♥ K 9 6 2
♦ J 8 4                                     ♦ A 10 6
♣ 9 4 3                    YOU              ♣ 8 7 5
                        (DECLARER)
                    ♠ 10 4 2
                    ♥ A Q J 10
                    ♦ K 9 5
                    ♣ A Q 2
```

There's a sure trick in spades, one in hearts, and four in clubs, leaving you to find three more to make 3NT. You could promote two tricks in hearts, by driving out the ♥K, and one in diamonds, by driving out the ♦A. Unfortunately, you lose the race in the meantime. The defenders are about to drive out your only high card in spades. If you let them regain the lead with both the ♥K and ♦A, they can take more than enough tricks to defeat the contract. The only hope is to get four tricks from hearts without giving up the lead. You can do this using the finesse—provided the ♥K is favorably placed and there's enough entries to repeat the finesse. To get all four tricks, you may need to lead from dummy three times. The first entry is the ♠A. The other two have to come from clubs.

Order your play very carefully. After winning a trick with dummy's ♠A, use the entry to lead a low heart to the ♥10. When this first finesse works, you can breathe a sigh of relief, but there's lots left to be done. Play the ♣A, and then the ♣Q, overtaking with dummy's ♣K. You can afford this because dummy still has the ♣J and ♣10 to provide the tricks you need from that suit. You can't, however, continue to take your club winners. Use the entry to take another heart finesse by leading a low heart to your ♥J. When this wins, it's back to the club suit. Lead the carefully preserved ♣2 over to dummy's ♣10, and take the remaining club winner while you're in the dummy. Now lead dummy's last heart, and if the ♥K still hasn't appeared, finesse the ♥Q. Your ♥A is the ninth trick. Well done.

# 7

# Yet More Finesses

*"And thick and fast they came at last,*
*And more, and more, and more—*
*All hopping through the frothy waves,*
*And scrambling to the shore."*

—LEWIS CARROLL,
*The Walrus and the Carpenter*

The finesse is a powerful technique. On many hands, it seems as if the opportunities for finessing do indeed come thick and fast.

## Leading a High Card

Let's compare two suit combinations. On the surface they appear to be the same. See if you can spot the difference.

| 1) | DUMMY | 2) | DUMMY |
|----|-------|----|-------|
|    | ♥ A 5 3 |  | ♥ A 5 3 |

| DECLARER | DECLARER |
|----------|----------|
| ♥ Q 4 2 | ♥ Q J 10 |

Both combinations consist of six cards, evenly divided between the two hands. In both cases, dummy has the ♥A, and declarer has the ♥Q. The only difference is that declarer holds the ♥J and ♥10 in the second layout, in place of the ♥4 and ♥2. How much difference does that make?

In both combinations, the ♥A is a sure trick. In the first layout, there's a 50–50 chance for a second trick. If the ♥K is favorably located on declarer's right, you can make a second trick by leading toward your ♥Q.

For example, the complete layout of the suit might look like this:

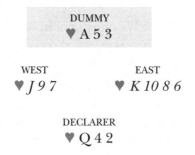

DUMMY
♥ A 5 3

WEST          EAST
♥ J 9 7       ♥ K 10 8 6

DECLARER
♥ Q 4 2

Declarer could play the ♥2 over to dummy's ♥A and then lead the ♥3 from dummy. If East plays the ♥K, declarer plays the ♥4 and later gets a trick with the ♥Q. If East plays a low heart on the second round, declarer can finesse the ♥Q, which wins the trick because West has no higher heart. It's a 50–50 proposition, because if West has the ♥K instead of East, your finesse will lose. In the most favorable situation, you get two tricks but have to give one up to the defenders.

It wouldn't be a good idea to lead the ♥Q originally. You'd end up with only one trick no matter which defender has the ♥K. If East holds the ♥K, as above, East simply wins the ♥Q with the ♥K, and dummy's ♥A is the only trick for declarer. If West holds the ♥K, the layout of the suit might look like this:

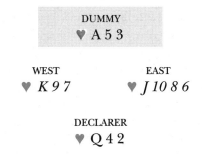

DUMMY
♥ A 5 3

WEST           EAST
♥ K 9 7       ♥ J 10 8 6

DECLARER
♥ Q 4 2

If declarer leads the ♥ Q, West can *cover* with the ♥ K, and declarer has to play dummy's ♥ A to win the trick. Both declarer's high cards go on the same trick, and the defenders have the remaining high cards in the suit.

This example emphasizes the basic principle of leading toward the card you hope will win a trick when you can't afford to lead the card itself.

Now let's turn our attention to the second example. The ♥ J and ♥ 10 make a big difference. First of all, you can always get two tricks from this combination no matter which defender holds the ♥ K. You can simply play the ♥ A and then use your remaining high hearts to drive out the ♥ K, promoting a second trick in the suit. You may, however, be able to do better than that. If the ♥ K is favorably placed, you can take three tricks from this combination without giving up the lead to the opponents. For example, suppose this is the complete layout of the suit:

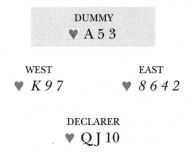

DUMMY
♥ A 5 3

WEST           EAST
♥ K 9 7       ♥ 8 6 4 2

DECLARER
♥ Q J 10

To take three tricks, you play the suit in almost the exact opposite fashion to the first example. First, you hope the ♥ K is on your left, rather than your right. Second, you lead the ♥ Q, instead of leading toward it. Look at the effect this has. When you lead the ♥ Q, West's

♥K is trapped. If West covers your ♥Q with the ♥K, you win the trick with dummy's ♥A, and your ♥J and ♥10 take the next two tricks. If West doesn't play the ♥K on your ♥Q, you play a low heart from dummy and win the trick because East doesn't have a higher heart. You can then repeat the finesse by leading the ♥J. West's ♥K is again trapped. If West covers the ♥J, dummy's ♥A wins, and the ♥10 is your third trick. If West doesn't cover, you finesse the ♥J, which wins the trick. Dummy's ♥A is the third trick.

Of course, if East started with the ♥K, your finesse would lose when you led the ♥Q and played a low heart from dummy. You'd be back to the two tricks you started with.

So, in the first example you lead toward the ♥Q to take a finesse, and in the second example you lead the ♥Q to take the finesse. This is quite a change in the order you play your cards, all due to the presence of that ♥J and ♥10. There will be many other situations in which you'll have a choice of leading toward a high card or leading the high card itself. How can you tell the difference?

The answer is to ask yourself, "Can I afford to have the defender cover my card with a higher card if I lead it?" If the answer is yes, lead the card. If the answer is no, lead toward the high card.

To see how this works, let's return to the examples. In the first example, if you lead the ♥Q, you can't afford to have the player on your left cover it with the ♥K. You'd have to win the trick with dummy's ♥A, and now you'd have no high cards left in the suit. This tells you to lead toward the ♥Q. In the second example, If you lead the ♥Q, you'll be happy if it's covered with the ♥K. You can win the ♥A, and your ♥J and ♥10 will have become winners.

You have to look at the combined cards you hold in the suit and ask yourself the question. Let's try other suit combinations.

DUMMY
♦ A J 2

DECLARER
♦ Q 10 6

You can afford to lead the ♦Q from your hand because you have both the ♦J and ♦10 between the two hands. You could lead the ♦10 rather than the ♦Q. It would have the same effect.

DUMMY

♣ 10 9 8

DECLARER

♣ A Q J 7 5

With this combination, lead the ♣10—or ♣9 or ♣8—from the dummy. You'd be happy to have it covered with the ♣K on your right. You'd win the ♣A and take all of the tricks. If the ♣10 isn't covered, play a low club from your hand, taking the finesse. If this works, lead another club from dummy and repeat the finesse.

DUMMY

♠ A K 6

DECLARER

♠ J 10 4

Lead the ♠J, hoping to trap the ♠Q on your left. If the ♠J is covered by the ♠Q, you're happy because you also have the ♠10. If you have enough entries, you could first play a high spade from dummy and the ♠4 from your hand. You could then cross to your hand and lead the ♠J, or ♠10, planning to finesse.

DUMMY

♥ J 9 3

DECLARER

♥ A Q 10 2

You can afford to lead a high card from dummy because you don't mind if it gets covered with the ♥K. Technically, the best card to lead from dummy is the ♥9. You take a finesse by playing the ♥2 from your hand. If this works, you can now lead the ♥J, repeating the finesse by playing the ♥10 from your hand if the ♥K has not appeared. Finally, lead dummy's ♥3, planning to finesse a third time by inserting the ♥Q if the ♥K still hasn't appeared. You'll get four heart tricks whenever the ♥K is on your right. If you lead the ♥J the first time and your finesse works, when you lead another heart from dummy, you'll have to win the second trick in your hand. Now you're in the wrong hand to repeat the heart finesse for a third time. Try it!

Here's a sample hand that requires knowing whether or not you can afford to lead a high card. You're in a contract of 4♠, and the opening lead is the ♣K.

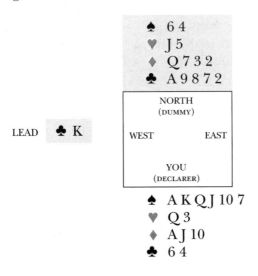

You can count six sure tricks in spades, plus your two minor suit aces. You need two extra tricks. You could promote an extra winner in diamonds by simply driving out the ♦K, but that's not good enough. Dummy has some length in clubs, but there is no way to reach dummy even if you could establish an extra club trick. The best bet is to try to take three tricks in the diamond suit. That's possible by way of repeated finesses if the ♦K is favorably placed on your right.

The difficulty on this hand is that there's only one entry to the dummy, the ♣A and it's about to be driven out very quickly. If you win a trick with the ♣A and lead a low diamond to your ♦10, or ♦J, the finesse might be successful, but there is no way to get back to dummy to repeat it. Instead, you can afford to lead dummy's ♦Q. You don't mind if it's covered with the ♦K. The advantage of leading the ♦Q is that, if it isn't covered, you can play the ♦10 from your hand. Assuming your finesse is successful, you're still in the dummy and can repeat the diamond finesse, playing a low diamond to your ♦J.

When your second finesse wins, it's time to draw trump. Once the trump are gone, it will be safe to take your ♦A. Here's the complete hand:

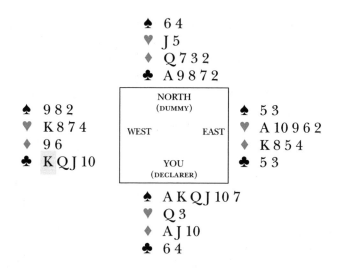

## Decisions, Decisions

In some suit combinations, it's difficult to decide whether or not you can afford to lead a high card and have it covered. It usually depends on how many tricks you need, how many entries you have, and whether or not you can afford to let the defenders win a trick. For example, look at this layout:

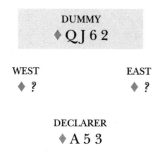

You have one sure trick, the ♦A. You can always promote a second trick by leading the ♦Q or ♦J, to drive out the defenders' ♦K. That's all right if you can afford to give up the lead to the opponents, but what if you need two tricks from the suit and can't afford to let them in? Perhaps they're in a position to take enough tricks to defeat your

contract if they get a trick with the ♦K before you get your two diamond tricks. If that's the case, your best play is to lead the ♦Q, or ♦J,
from the dummy, hoping the ♦K is with East on your right. You don't
mind if East covers your ♦Q with the ♦K. You'll win the trick with
your ♦A and have dummy's ♦J as your second trick in the suit, without giving up the lead.

Suppose you can afford to give up the lead to the opponents, but
you want to give yourself the best chance of taking three tricks from
this combination of cards. One possibility is that defenders' diamonds
could be divided exactly 3–3. You could take your ♦A and use one of
dummy's high diamonds to drive out the ♦K. That would promote
your remaining diamond honor as a winner, and you'd get your third
trick from length.

Relying on the six missing diamonds to be divided exactly 3–3
goes against the odds. The diamonds are more likely to divide 4–2
and could be 5–1 or 6–0. The best plan is to take your ♦A, and then
lead low diamonds twice toward dummy's ♦Q and ♦J. That will still
give you three tricks, no matter which defender has the ♦K, if the
diamonds divide 3–3. It will also give you three tricks any time West
has the ♦K, no matter how the diamonds divide. For example, suppose this is the full layout:

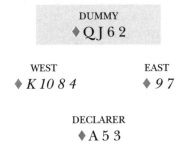

DUMMY
♦ Q J 6 2

WEST
♦ K 10 8 4

EAST
♦ 9 7

DECLARER
♦ A 5 3

If you lead the ♦Q, driving out West's ♦K, you'll get two tricks with
your ♦A and ♦J, but that's all. West will have a high diamond left
when the defenders' diamonds don't divide 3–3. Instead, if you start
by playing the ♦A and then leading a low diamond toward dummy,
West is helpless. If West rises with the ♦K, dummy's ♦Q and ♦J are
established as winners. If West plays a low diamond on the second
round of the suit, dummy's ♦J can be played to win the trick. Now
you come back to your hand and lead your remaining diamond to-

ward dummy. West is in the same dilemma. Sooner or later, you'll get a third trick with dummy's ♦Q.

The available entries to both hands may dictate the exact order in which you play the suit. If you don't have a second entry back to your hand outside of the diamond suit, you might start by playing a low diamond toward dummy. If West plays low, you win the trick with dummy's ♦J and can travel back to your hand with the ♦A to lead your last low diamond toward dummy's ♦Q.

So many possible variations. It all depends what you want to do. Try your luck with this combination:

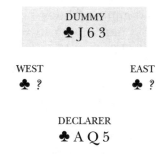

DUMMY
♣J 6 3

WEST          EAST
♣ ?           ♣ ?

DECLARER
♣A Q 5

There's one trick for sure and you can always promote a second trick by driving out the defenders' ♣K. If you need two tricks without letting the opponents get the lead, you can cross to dummy and lead a low club to your ♣Q, hoping East has the ♣K.

What if you're desperate to take three tricks from this combination? You might consider leading dummy's ♣J, but that's unlikely to work. If West has the ♣K, you were never going to get three tricks; and if East has the ♣K, East can cover the ♣J with the ♣K. That forces you to win the trick with the ♣A. You'll get a second trick with the ♣Q, but that's all. The defenders will have the rest of the high clubs. Is there any hope? If East has a singleton or doubleton ♣K, you can succeed by leading a low club from dummy toward your hand. This might be the full layout of the suit:

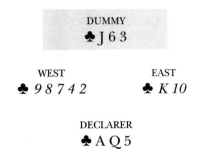

DUMMY
♣ J 6 3

WEST　　　　　　　　EAST
♣ 9 8 7 4 2　　　♣ K 10

DECLARER
♣ A Q 5

When you lead a low club from dummy and East plays the ♣10, you insert the ♣Q, and the finesse succeeds. When you play your ♣A, East's ♣K falls, and dummy's ♣J now becomes the third trick in the suit. It's amazing what happens when you start to visualize how the defenders cards might be placed favorably enough to let you to take the required tricks. Here's another card combination where the order in which you play your cards depends on how many tricks you need and perhaps how many entries you have:

DUMMY
♠ 7 5 4 2

WEST　　　　　　　　EAST
♠ ?　　　　　　　　♠ ?

DECLARER
♠ K Q 6 3

All three techniques we've discussed so far—promotion, length, and the finesse—are possibilities in this situation. If you need only one trick from the spade suit, you could lead one of your high cards, promoting the other into a trick. If you need two tricks, you could try a combination of promotion and length. You have eight cards, leaving the defenders with five. If the defenders' cards divide as you might expect, 3–2, you could lead the ♠K to drive out the ♠A, take a trick with your promoted ♠Q, and then give up a second trick to the defenders. You'd be left with a second winner in the suit.

You can never take all four tricks with this combination—you do have to let the defenders have the occasional trick, especially when they hold the ace of your suit—but you might need to take three of the four tricks. If that's the case, you'll have to try a combination of length and the finesse. You'll need the missing spades to be divided 3–2, and you'll have to find the ♠A located favorably on your right. Something like this:

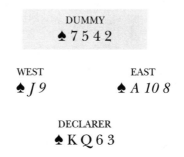

DUMMY

♠ 7 5 4 2

WEST        EAST

♠ *J 9*        ♠ *A 10 8*

DECLARER

♠ K Q 6 3

Start by leading a low spade from dummy. If East hops up with the ♠A, the rest is easy. You'll get one trick with your ♠K, one with the ♠Q, and a third trick when the defenders' spades divide 3–2. If East plays a low spade on the first round of the suit, you've got a little more work to do, but by now you can handle it. Win the trick by finessing your ♠Q, cross back to dummy with an entry in another suit, and lead another low spade toward your hand. It's all over for East. Whether East takes the ♠A on this trick, or lets you win the second trick with your ♠K, the defense gets only one trick, while you get three.

Of course, this last line of play assumes there are the entries to get over to dummy twice. If you don't, you may have to compromise on the way you play the suit. That's what makes the play of the hand so interesting. Each card has its role to play, and it's up to you to choose when it should play that role.

Here's a variation on the previous example:

DUMMY
♥Q 7 5 4

WEST          EAST
♥ ?           ♥ ?

DECLARER
♥K 6 3 2

You hold the same cards between the two hands, but now your high cards are on opposite sides of the table. That doesn't stop you from developing one trick through promotion. You could use either honor to drive out the ♥A. Also, you'll still be able to develop a second trick in the suit through length, if the defenders hearts divide 3–2. But what if you need three tricks? You can no longer try a repeated finesse by leading twice toward your high cards. One of the defenders must hold the ♥A.

This is a more complicated situation, and you're going to need both good luck and good judgment. First, the good luck. You're going to need to find the defender holding the ♥A with only two cards in the suit. The good judgment? You'll need to decide which defender holds the doubleton ♥A. For example, suppose you feel the player on your left holds the ♥A. You start by leading a low heart from your hand towards dummy's ♥Q. Assuming the player on your left plays a low heart and dummy's ♥Q wins the trick, the remaining cards now look like this:

DUMMY
♥7 5 4

WEST          EAST
♥ ?           ♥ ?

DECLARER
♥K 6 3

So far, so good. West must hold the ♥A. You now lead a low heart from dummy toward your hand and the ♥10 appears from East on your right. What do you do? Since you "know" the ♥A is in West's hand, there's not much point in playing your ♥K. Play a low heart from your hand, and hope the original distribution was something like this:

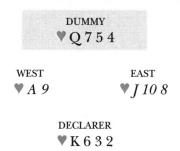

DUMMY
♥ Q 7 5 4

WEST                    EAST
♥ A 9                  ♥ J 10 8

DECLARER
♥ K 6 3 2

West's ♥A falls on your low heart on the second round of the suit. Your ♥K is now a second trick in the suit, and with the defenders' hearts dividing 3–2, you'll get a third trick from the suit. Lucky, but you needed to know how to tackle the situation. Incidentally, if your guessing shoes told you that East held the ♥A, you should start the suit by playing a low heart from dummy to your ♥K, then play a low heart from both hands on the second round. Playing a low heart from both hands on the second round of the suit is another form of the ducking play. The same concepts keep cropping up in different guises. In a later chapter, you'll encounter the duck in yet another form.

Time to try another hand. The contract is 3NT, and the opening lead is the ♥K. How do you plan to handle the spade suit?

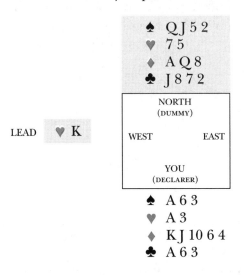

♠ QJ52
♥ 75
♦ AQ8
♣ J872

NORTH
(DUMMY)

LEAD  ♥ K

WEST        EAST

YOU
(DECLARER)

♠ A63
♥ A3
♦ KJ1064
♣ A63

Doesn't look too bad. You start with eight sure tricks: one spade, one heart, five diamonds, and one club. You have to find only one more. The spade suit appears to be the obvious choice. You can use one of dummy's spade honors to drive out the defender's ♠K, promoting a second trick in the suit. You might even be able to take three tricks in the suit by taking your ♠A and leading twice toward dummy's ♠Q and ♠J.

Before deciding the best way to play a particular suit, however, you must look at the entire hand. The opponents have led hearts and are about to drive out your ♥A. They have nine hearts between them. Even if their hearts divide as evenly as possible, 5–4, they'll be in a position to take four heart winners if you let them in with the ♠K. That will give them five tricks in total. You'll lose the race. The opponents will take the first five tricks. They may even take more if the hearts are divided 6–3, rather than 5–4.

You can't afford to play the spade suit in a manner that will allow the defenders to get the lead. What's the alternative? You can hope that the ♠K is favorably placed on your right and try the effect of leading the ♠Q from dummy. In this situation, you don't mind if it's covered. You'll be happy to escape with only two tricks from the spade suit. That's all you need. Here's the complete hand:

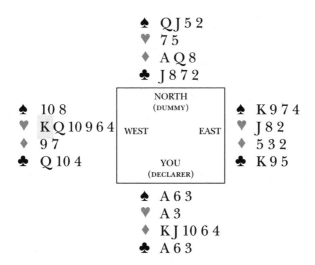

After winning a trick with the ♥A, cross to dummy using one of the high diamonds, and lead the ♠Q, or ♠J. If East plays a low spade, take the finesse. When this succeeds, scamper home with your nine tricks. If East covers your spade honor from dummy, win the ♠A, and again take your nine tricks. This wasn't the hand to give up a spade trick. If you let East win a trick with the ♠K, the defenders will take five heart tricks, and you'll be down two in your contract.

## Extra Care

There are times when it might be a good idea to take some of your high cards in a suit first, before taking a finesse.

If you need three tricks from this suit, you'd plan to lead a low diamond from dummy and finesse your ♦J, hoping East started with the ♦Q. That's fine, but if you have enough entries, it won't do any harm to play your ♦A or ♦K first, and then travel over to dummy and lead to a low diamond toward your hand. You'd get an unexpected bonus if this were the actual layout of the diamond suit:

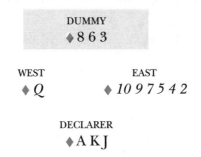

By playing the ♦A before going over to dummy, you'll find out that you don't need the finesse. Although this distribution is unlikely, there's no harm in taking a little extra care. It's like driving defensively.

Here are some other situations in which you might consider playing a high card first.

DUMMY

♣Q 8 6 3

DECLARER

♣A 7 5

You intend to lead a low club toward dummy, hoping the ♣K is on your left. It will usually do no harm to play the ♣A first, in case there's a singleton ♣K.

DUMMY

♠J 5 4 3

DECLARER

♠A K 6 2

You have two sure tricks and would like to get another by leading toward dummy's ♠J, hoping the ♠Q is on your left. You can't afford to lead the ♠J from dummy because you don't want to see it covered by the ♠Q. It's a good idea to start by playing the ♠A and ♠K.

If either defender has a singleton ♠Q, you can simply take three tricks in the suit. If either defender started with a doubleton ♠Q, you'll end up with all four tricks in the suit, since the defenders' spades must be divided 3–2. Only if the queen doesn't fall under the ace and king, would you need to lead toward the jack.

DUMMY

♥A K 7 3

DECLARER

♥J 10 9 8

Here you can afford to lead the ♥J, planning to take the finesse if a low heart appears on your left. As long as the ♥Q is on your left, you get four tricks from the suit. Taking the finesse is a better choice than playing the ♥A and ♥K because you have only eight cards in the combined hands—eight ever, nine never. It doesn't do any harm, however, to play one of dummy's high hearts first, in case your right-hand opponent started with a singleton ♥Q. If the queen doesn't appear, come back to your hand and lead the ♥J, trying to trap the ♥Q on your left.

DUMMY

♦A K J 10

DECLARER

♦4 3

This combination shows how difficult a choice it may be to decide whether or not to play a high card first. If you start by playing the ♦A to guard against a singleton ♦Q on your right, you can still come back to your hand and lead a diamond to dummy's ♦10 or

♦J, taking the finesse against the hoped-for queen on your left. Unfortunately, if your finesse is successful, you no longer have any low diamonds left in your hand with which to repeat the finesse. Unless the ♦Q now falls under your ♦K, you'll get only three tricks from this suit. The best play for four tricks is to immediately play a low diamond to dummy's ♦10. If the finesse works, cross back to your hand, and lead your remaining low diamond to dummy's ♦J, repeating the finesse. Your ♦A and ♦K will give you four tricks in the suit.

## Summary

While the basic principle of the finesse involves leading toward a card you hope will win a trick, there are times when you can afford to lead a high card, rather than lead toward it. When considering the possibility of a finesse, keep the following ideas in mind:

- Lead a high card only if you can afford to have the defenders cover it with a higher card.
- Decide how many tricks you need from a suit before deciding the best way to play the suit.
- Look for the safest way of playing the suit to get the number of tricks you need.

| | *Checklist* |
|---|---|
| | Promotion |
| | Length |
| ✓ | Finessing |
| | Trumping Losers |
| | Discarding Losers |

# Practice Hands

## Hand 7.1

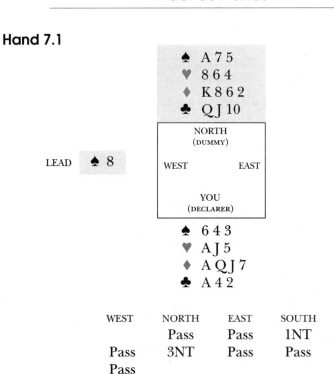

♠ A 7 5
♥ 8 6 4
♦ K 8 6 2
♣ Q J 10

NORTH
(DUMMY)

LEAD   ♠ 8

WEST          EAST

YOU
(DECLARER)

♠ 6 4 3
♥ A J 5
♦ A Q J 7
♣ A 4 2

| WEST | NORTH | EAST | SOUTH |
|------|-------|------|-------|
|      | Pass  | Pass | 1NT   |
| Pass | 3NT   | Pass | Pass  |
| Pass |       |      |       |

West leads the ♠8 against your contract of 3NT. How do you plan to make the contract?

## Solution 7.1

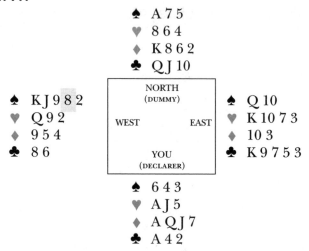

```
              ♠ A 7 5
              ♥ 8 6 4
              ♦ K 8 6 2
              ♣ Q J 10
                  NORTH
                 (DUMMY)
♠ K J 9 8 2                        ♠ Q 10
♥ Q 9 2     WEST          EAST     ♥ K 10 7 3
♦ 9 5 4                            ♦ 10 3
♣ 8 6                              ♣ K 9 7 5 3
                   YOU
                (DECLARER)
              ♠ 6 4 3
              ♥ A J 5
              ♦ A Q J 7
              ♣ A 4 2
```

You start with seven sure tricks: one spade, one heart, four diamonds, and a club. Two more tricks are required. By playing the ♣A and leading a second club, you could promote another winner in the club suit. But that's not enough to make the contract. You need to take three tricks from the club suit. To do that, you have to hope that the ♣K is favorably placed, on your right.

After winning a spade trick in dummy, lead the ♣Q. You certainly don't mind if it's covered—you can win with your ♣A and now have two more tricks in the suit. If East doesn't cover the ♣Q, take the finesse by playing a low club from your hand. When this works, continue by leading another club from dummy. Again, East's ♣K is trapped. Whether East plays the ♣K or a low club, you end up with three tricks in the suit—exactly what you required.

## Hand 7.2

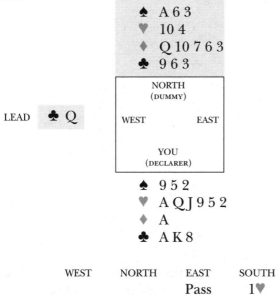

♠ A 6 3
♥ 10 4
♦ Q 10 7 6 3
♣ 9 6 3

NORTH
(DUMMY)

LEAD ♣ Q

WEST          EAST

YOU
(DECLARER)

♠ 9 5 2
♥ A Q J 9 5 2
♦ A
♣ A K 8

| WEST | NORTH | EAST | SOUTH |
|------|-------|------|-------|
|      |       | Pass | 1♥ |
| Pass | 1NT | Pass | 4♥ |
| Pass | Pass | Pass | |

You've reached 4♥, and West's opening lead is the ♣Q. Can you take ten tricks?

**Solution 7.2**

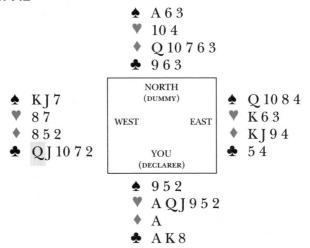

&spades; A 6 3
&hearts; 10 4
&diams; Q 10 7 6 3
&clubs; 9 6 3

NORTH
(DUMMY)

&spades; K J 7
&hearts; 8 7
&diams; 8 5 2
&clubs; Q J 10 7 2

WEST          EAST

&spades; Q 10 8 4
&hearts; K 6 3
&diams; K J 9 4
&clubs; 5 4

YOU
(DECLARER)

&spades; 9 5 2
&hearts; A Q J 9 5 2
&diams; A
&clubs; A K 8

You need ten tricks and start with five: one spade, one heart, one diamond, and two clubs. It looks as though all your extra tricks will have to come from the trump suit. You'll be able to take all six tricks in hearts provided East holds no more than three hearts, including the &hearts;K.

You'll need to be careful about entries. The only entry to dummy is the &spades;A, and you may need to repeat the heart finesse when East holds three hearts. After winning the club trick, play a spade over to dummy's &spades;A, and lead the &hearts;10. You don't mind if East covers this with the &hearts;K. You'll be able to take all six tricks in the heart suit. If East doesn't cover, play a low heart from your hand, taking the finesse. When this wins, you're still in dummy and can repeat the heart finesse. Lead the &hearts;4, and if East plays a low heart, finesse your &hearts;Q—or &hearts;J or &hearts;9. When your second finesse succeeds and West follows suit with a second heart, there's only one heart left. Lay down the &hearts;A, and East's &hearts;K will fall.

If you led dummy's &hearts;4, rather than the &hearts;10, you won't make the contract on the actual lie of the cards. You can take a successful finesse, but you can't reach dummy again to repeat the finesse. Lead a high card when you can afford to have it covered.

## Hand 7.3

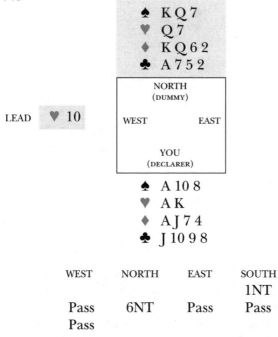

♠ K Q 7
♥ Q 7
♦ K Q 6 2
♣ A 7 5 2

NORTH
(DUMMY)

LEAD ♥ 10

WEST          EAST

YOU
(DECLARER)

♠ A 10 8
♥ A K
♦ A J 7 4
♣ J 10 9 8

| WEST | NORTH | EAST | SOUTH |
|------|-------|------|-------|
|      |       |      | 1NT   |
| Pass | 6NT   | Pass | Pass  |
| Pass |       |      |       |

West leads the ♥10 against your small slam contract. What are your plans for getting twelve tricks?

## Solution 7.3

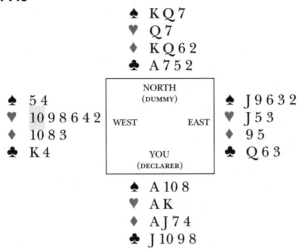

You have ten sure tricks: three spades, two hearts, four diamonds, and one club. You'll need to find two more. The club suit is the only potential source of extra tricks. You could take the ♣A and drive out the defenders' ♣K and ♣Q to promote one extra trick in the suit, but that's not good enough in your slam contract. You need to find a way to develop three tricks from the suit. That should be possible, with the help of a finesse, if West holds the ♣K, the ♣Q, or both club honors.

Win the first trick in your hand, and lead the ♣J—the ♣10, ♣9, or ♣8 would be equally effective. You don't mind if West covers your ♣J with a higher honor. You can capture the trick with dummy's ♣A and continue leading the suit to drive out the remaining high card held by the defenders. Suppose instead, West doesn't cover the ♣J. Play a low club from dummy and take the finesse. On the actual hand, this first finesse loses to East's ♣Q, but it's not over yet. You win the next trick in your hand and lead the ♣10, planning to repeat the finesse if a low club appears on your left—after all, one of your finesses should work. On the actual hand, West's ♣K appears, so you win the trick with dummy's ♣A. With the ♣K and ♣Q gone, your remaining clubs are winners, giving you the two extra tricks needed to make the contract.

## Hand 7.4

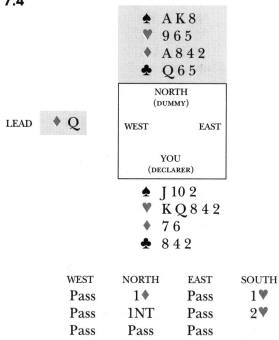

♠ A K 8
♥ 9 6 5
♦ A 8 4 2
♣ Q 6 5

NORTH
(DUMMY)

LEAD ♦ Q

WEST          EAST

YOU
(DECLARER)

♠ J 10 2
♥ K Q 8 4 2
♦ 7 6
♣ 8 4 2

| WEST | NORTH | EAST | SOUTH |
|------|-------|------|-------|
| Pass | 1♦ | Pass | 1♥ |
| Pass | 1NT | Pass | 2♥ |
| Pass | Pass | Pass | |

After the excitement of a slam on the previous hand, you stop in a quiet partscore on the next hand. How do you plan to take eight tricks in your 2♥ contract after the opening lead of the ♦Q?

## Solution 7.4

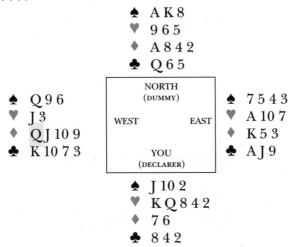

```
              ♠ A K 8
              ♥ 9 6 5
              ♦ A 8 4 2
              ♣ Q 6 5
                 NORTH
                 (DUMMY)
♠ Q 9 6                        ♠ 7 5 4 3
♥ J 3      WEST        EAST     ♥ A 10 7
♦ Q J 10 9                      ♦ K 5 3
♣ K 10 7 3    YOU              ♣ A J 9
           (DECLARER)
              ♠ J 10 2
              ♥ K Q 8 4 2
              ♦ 7 6
              ♣ 8 4 2
```

You have two sure tricks in spades and one in diamonds. You may be able to get one more trick from spades, if West holds the ♠Q. It looks like you'll need four tricks from the trump suit. That's possible only if the five hearts in the defenders' hands are divided 3–2 and the ♥A is favorably located. You can't afford to lead a high heart to promote a trick. Even if the hearts divide 3–2, the defenders would get two heart tricks.

Note the order you need to play your cards. After winning a trick with dummy's ♦A, you're in the right hand to start playing trump. Lead a low heart from dummy toward your hand. Assuming East plays a low heart, play the ♥Q or ♥K. When this wins, your chance of making the contract improves, since it looks as though East holds the ♥A. You need to return to dummy to repeat the finesse. You do this by playing the ♠2 over to one of dummy's high spades. Lead another heart toward your hand. East can't stop you from getting a trick with the other heart honor. When the defenders' trump divide 3–2, your troubles in that suit are over.

If East wins the second heart trick with the ♥A and continues to lead diamonds, trump the third round and draw East's last trump. You have one more thing to do. Lead your ♠J, or ♠10, and if West doesn't cover with the ♠Q, take the finesse. When this succeeds, you have your eight tricks. In spades, you can afford to lead a high card to trap West's ♠Q. In hearts, you can't afford to lead a heart honors. It depends on the combination of cards and how many tricks you need.

# Winners and Losers

*"Stake your counter as boldly every whit,*
*Venture as warily, use the same skill,*
*Do your best, whether winning or losing it,*
*If you chose to play!"*

— ROBERT BROWNING,
*The Statue and the Bust* [1855]

In a trump contract, one suit has significantly more power than the other three suits. The decisions surrounding the trump suit are like the receiving line at a state dinner; order is all important. The customary advice is to play the trump suit first, to get rid of the defenders' trump. Yet there are times when you can't afford to draw the trump right away, and in fact, there are hands in which you don't draw trump at all.

To help make a good decision about the order in which to play your cards, it's useful to switch your focus from winners to *losers*, those tricks which you may have to lose to your opponents.

## Losers

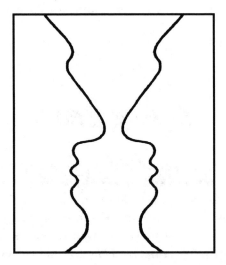

In the above illustration, you can see either the profiles of two people facing one another, or the outline of a Grecian vase. The lines don't change but your focus does. This is the same concept as counting winners and counting losers. The cards stay the same; your focus changes.

A winner is a trick that your side can take. A loser is a trick that the opponents can take—a winner for the opponents.

There are two types of winners: sure winners—those which you can take whenever you have the lead; and potential winners—those which you hope to develop through promotion, length, or the finesse. Similarly, there are types of losers: sure or *quick losers*—those tricks the defenders can take if they have the lead; and potential or *slow losers*—those tricks you'll eventually lose, if you don't do something about them. There is an advantage of focusing on losers in suit contracts. Due to the power of the trump suit, you can sometimes get rid of losers in ways that aren't available in a notrump contract.

## Counting Losers in a Suit

Let's take a look at the mechanics of counting losers. First, focus on one hand—the declarer's hand—and then look at the dummy for help. Suppose hearts are the trump suit, and this is the holding in the spade suit:

DUMMY

♠ 4

DECLARER

♠ A 8

There's one sure winner in this suit, the ♠A, but how many losers do you have? At first glance, you might feel that there are no losers. After you play the ♠A, you probably intend to lead the ♠8 and trump—or *ruff*—it in the dummy with one of your hearts. This line of thinking actually combines two steps into one. You recognize that the ♠8 is a potential loser, and you plan to get rid of it by trumping it in the dummy. You're making an assumption that there will still be a heart left in the dummy with which to ruff your loser when you get round to playing the ♠A and ♠8. While this is likely to be the case, there are those hands in which the trump seem to disappear before you're ready to use them.

Let's change the example:

DUMMY

♠ A 8

DECLARER

♠ 4

Now how many losers do you have? When counting losers, your principal focus is on only one hand. This is usually declarer's hand, since it's frequently the hand containing the most trump. You can consider the high cards on the other side of the table when determining whether or not you have any losers in the suit, but don't count the losers on the other side. Otherwise, you'll be double counting—and will end up with so many losers you'll give up on the hand!

In a trump contract, **don't count more losers in a suit than the number of cards held in declarer's hand.** You assume there will be some trump left in your hand to prevent the loss of any more tricks once you run out of the suit.

In the above layout, therefore, declarer has only one card in the spade suit, and dummy's ♠A will take care of that, so there are no losers in the suit.

Let's try examples of counting losers in a suit from declarer's perspective.

| | |
|---|---|
| DUMMY<br>♥ K 6 2 | Since dummy holds the ♥K to take care of your low heart, there are no losers in this suit. |
| DECLARER<br>♥ A Q 5 | |

| | |
|---|---|
| DUMMY<br>♦ A K | There are four low cards, and dummy's ♦A and ♦K will take care of two of them. That leaves you with two losers in the suit. Your losers are slow, since the defenders can't immediately take any tricks in the diamond suit. |
| DECLARER<br>♦ 8 6 5 3 | |

| | |
|---|---|
| DUMMY<br>♣ Q 8 5 2 | Although dummy has four clubs, declarer has only two. That counts as two losers, since dummy doesn't have enough help in the suit to prevent you from losing the first two club tricks. These are quick losers, since the opponents can win two club tricks if they get the lead. |
| DECLARER<br>♣ 6 3 | |

| | |
|---|---|
| DUMMY<br>♠ 7 4 | Count one quick loser in the suit, since you're missing the ♠A. |
| DECLARER<br>♠ K Q J | |

DUMMY

♥ A 8 5 3

DECLARER

♥ K Q 6 2

There are four cards in declarer's hand, and the ♥A, ♥K, and ♥Q will take care of three of them. That leaves you with one loser. Since you have eight combined cards in this suit, you won't have to lose a trick if the five hearts in the defenders' hands are divided 3–2. That's a hope, however, not a guarantee. The defenders' hearts could be divided 4–1 or 5–0. Many players simplify the count of losers by assuming that the opponents' cards will divide as expected, 3–2 in this case. That's okay, but once you're more familiar with the methods for eliminating losers, you can start to take into account an unfavorable division of the defenders' cards.

DUMMY

♦ 5 4 2

DECLARER

♦ A Q

There is one sure trick and you should count the ♦Q as a potential loser. You may be able to turn your loser into a winner with the help of a successful finesse, but that's leaping too far ahead. There's no guarantee that your finesse will succeed, and you may not even have an entry to the dummy which will let you take the finesse.

## Counting Losers in a Hand

To count all the losers in a hand, add up the losers in each suit. For example, suppose you're in a contract of 2♠ on the following hand:

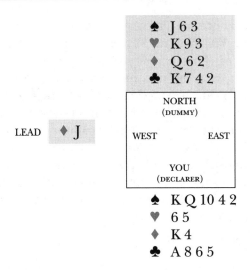

♠ J 6 3
♥ K 9 3
♦ Q 6 2
♣ K 7 4 2

NORTH
(DUMMY)

LEAD   ♦ J

WEST              EAST

YOU
(DECLARER)

♠ K Q 10 4 2
♥ 6 5
♦ K 4
♣ A 8 6 5

The spade suit is interesting. You have one loser for sure, the ♠A. If the defenders' spades divide as you might expect, 3–2, you won't have to lose any more tricks in that suit. Even if the spades divide 4–1, you won't have to lose a second trick in the suit because you hold the ♠10. If they divide 5–0, you'll have to lose two tricks—and may wish you were playing in a different contract. If you're an optimist, you count one loser initially, and then add to this total if the suit divides 5–0 during the play. If you're a pessimist, you assume you have two losers and breathe a sigh of relief when both opponents follow suit when you start drawing trump. We'll take the optimistic viewpoint and count one loser.

In the heart suit, you have two losers in your hand. You may be able to make use of dummy's ♥K during the play and reduce your losers by one, but that's only a 50–50 chance. Count two losers for now, and hope to eliminate one of them later on with the help of a successful finesse.

In diamonds, you have two cards in your hand, but the combination of the ♦K in your hand and the ♦Q in dummy leaves you with only one loser. Actually, it's not unusual for unexpected losers to crop up during the play of the hand. The opening lead of the ♦J could be a singleton, and the player on your right might win the first trick with the ♦A and lead another diamond which gets trumped on your left. All of sudden, one loser has turned into two. Nonetheless, that's a remote possibility. Assume a reasonable division of the outstanding cards. You'd count one loser, no more.

In clubs, you have four cards but hold the ♣A and ♣K between the two hands. That leaves you with two losers. Looking ahead, the five outstanding cards in the suit may divide 3–2, and you could turn one of your losers into a winner through length by playing the suit three times, giving up a trick to the defenders. That will be part of your plan for eliminating extra losers, but you should count two losers for now, since there's some work to be done even if the suit divides favorably.

In total, you have six losers: one spade loser, two heart losers, one diamond loser, and two club losers. To make your contract, you're going to have to eliminate at least one of your losers—but we'll get to that step later.

Some of your losers are quick. You really can't avoid letting the opponents take their ♠A, ♥A, and ♦A when they have the lead. Sometimes the defenders fail to take all the tricks to which they're entitled, but you don't want to count on that. It's especially difficult to avoid losing the ace of your trump suit when it's held by the opponents.

Other losers are slow. The second heart loser depends on the location of the ♥A. Even if it's unfavorably located on your right, the defenders may not be able to take both their heart tricks when they get the lead. On this hand, if you right-hand opponent has the lead, the defense can't take two quick tricks in hearts. Only if your left-hand opponent has the lead is there the danger that your ♥K could be trapped and the defenders could take two heart tricks. Your club losers are also slow. The defense can't take any tricks in that suit until your ♣A and ♣K are gone.

## Counting Losers and Having FUN

In the first chapter, we discussed the three things to keep in mind when you're declarer:

- **F**ocus on the target
- **U**se the checklist
- **N**ote the order

Let's see how looking at losers instead of winners affects this approach.

## Focus on the Target

The first step to having FUN during the play is to "Focus on the target." Playing in a notrump contract, you do this by determining the number of winners you need to make the contract and then counting the number of winners, or sure tricks, you hold. In a suit contract, you focus on the number of losers you can afford and the number of losers you have.

If the contract is 6♣, for example, the target is to lose no more than one trick. If you have two losers, that's one too many—hopefully, you can do something about it. If the contract is 4♥, you can afford to lose three tricks. If you have only two losers, it's not going to take long to play the hand.

Returning to our earlier hand:

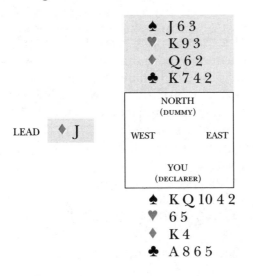

You're in a contract of 2♠, so you can afford five losers. There are six losers: one spade, two hearts, one diamond, and two clubs. Time to move on to the next step.

## Use the Checklist

The techniques available in notrump contracts—promotion, length, finessing—are equally available in suit contracts.

| *Checklist* | |
|:---:|:---|
| ✓ | Promotion |
| ✓ | Length |
| ✓ | Finessing |

In our sample hand, you'd be using the technique of promotion when playing trump suit itself. You'd drive out the ♠A and then draw the rest of the defenders' trump to make sure you end up with only one loser in the spade suit.

When looking for ways to eliminate the extra losers, you'd consider the length in the club suit. By taking your ♣A and ♣K and giving the defenders a trick in the suit, one of your losers will disappear if the defenders' clubs are divided 3–2. You'd also consider the finesse in the heart suit. You'd could try leading toward dummy's ♥K, hoping the ♥A is on your left. Your plan would be to try both possibilities. If either succeeded, you'd make the contract. If both succeeded, you'd make an overtrick. If nothing worked...

To this point, there's not much difference between focusing on losers and focusing on winners. If you were to look at this same hand from the point of view of winners, you'd start with two sure tricks in clubs. You'd expect to develop four winners in the spade suit through promotion and one winner in the diamond suit in the same fashion. That brings your total to seven. Your other winner would have to come from either a successful finesse in hearts—by leading toward dummy's ♥K—or through the length in the club suit.

The presence of the trump suit, however, gives you additional options when looking for ways to eliminate losers. That's what's going to go into those blank boxes on the chart. The two techniques we'll be discussing in the upcoming chapters are *trumping losers* and *discarding losers*. These aren't the only techniques available in a trump contract, but they're the ones that will highlight the importance of focusing on losers and the need for careful management of the trump suit.

## Note the Order

The importance of the order of play in a suit contract is the same as in a notrump contract. You'll need to watch your entries and choose which suit to play first. We've already touched on the consideration of drawing trump first in a suit contract when you can afford to do so. Managing the trump suit is an important aspect of playing in a suit contract.

On our sample hand, you should go to work on the trump suit first when you get the lead. Once trump are drawn, you could play the ♣A and ♣K to see how that suit divides. If the defenders' clubs are 3–2, give up a club trick to make the contract, perhaps trying the heart finesse for an overtrick later. If the clubs don't divide favorably, you can turn your attention to the heart finesse.

# Focusing on Losers

Focusing on losers can be important in both trump and notrump contracts. It may stop you from going down in flames—or up in smoke. Let's look at examples of both types of contract.

## Focusing on Losers in a Trump Contract

On this hand, the contract is 4♥, and the opening lead is the ♦Q:

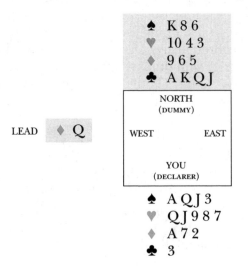

First, let's see what happens if you only focus on winners. You need ten tricks, and you have four sure tricks in spades, one in diamonds, and four in clubs. That's nine tricks. You can develop three more winners in the heart suit through promotion, by driving out the defenders' ♥A and ♥K. That would give you twelve winners in total. You might begin to suspect that there's something wrong with the total, since the defenders hold the ♥A and ♥K, but it certainly looks as though you have more than enough winners. Perhaps you'll finish with an overtrick.

Since you need to promote winners in the heart suit and it's generally a good idea to start by drawing the defenders' trump, you might lead a heart after winning a trick with the ♦A. Disaster! The defenders win the first heart trick with the ♥K and take two diamond tricks. They still have the ♥A, and your contract goes down one trick instead of making an overtrick. What went wrong?

You didn't focus on your losers. In a contract of 4♥, you can afford three losers. There's no losers in spades or clubs, but you have two losers in hearts and two in diamonds. That's one too many. If some of the losers were slow, you could perhaps worry about them later. Once your ♦A has been driven out, however, all your losers are quick. As you just saw, if the defenders get the lead, they can take two diamond tricks and two heart tricks.

The order in which the suits are played can make all the difference. The solution on this hand is to get rid of some of your losers before letting the defenders have the lead. You can't do much about the two heart losers, but after winning the first trick with the ♦A, you can play clubs before leading hearts. You take a trick with dummy's ♣A and then a second trick with dummy's ♣K on which you discard a low diamond from your hand. That leaves you with only one diamond loser in your hand. You can lead another high club from dummy and throw away the last diamond from your hand. Now you have no losers left in the diamond suit.

At this point, it's safe to lead a heart. The opponents can win a trick with a high heart, but if they try taking a diamond trick, you can trump in your hand. You drive out the other high heart, draw any remaining trump, and take the rest of the tricks. You lose only two tricks, the ♥A and ♥K. You're back to making an overtrick. What a difference counting losers makes.

## Focusing on Losers in a Notrump Contract

Although the focus in notrump contracts is on winners, it's sometimes important to consider losers. On this hand, your contract is
3NT, and the opening lead is the ♥K.

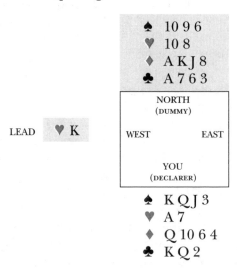

    ♠ 10 9 6
    ♥ 10 8
    ♦ A K J 8
    ♣ A 7 6 3

              NORTH
              (DUMMY)

LEAD  ♥ K    WEST        EAST

               YOU
             (DECLARER)

    ♠ K Q J 3
    ♥ A 7
    ♦ Q 10 6 4
    ♣ K Q 2

You need nine winners and start with eight sure tricks: one heart,
four diamonds, and three clubs. You can develop three more winners in the spade suit through promotion, giving you more than
enough tricks. But look what happens if you win the ♥A and lead a
spade. The defenders win a trick with the ♠A and proceed to take
four more tricks in the heart suit while you have to discard some of
your surplus winners.

Even in a notrump contract, you need to be aware of losers when
you have to give up the lead to the opponents. On this hand, if the
opponents had led a diamond or a club, you could win the trick and
lead a spade. You would end up with eleven sure tricks. Once they
lead a heart, driving out your ♥A, the picture changes. The defenders have nine hearts between them. Even if the hearts divide 5–4,
they'll have four tricks to take if they get the lead, since there's no
trump suit with which to stop them.

Once you realize that there will be too many losers if you try to
promote extra tricks in the spade suit, you can look at alternatives.
On this hand, the only other choice is the club suit. If the defend-

ers' clubs divide exactly 3–3, you'll get a fourth trick in the suit from length. It's not too likely that the clubs will be evenly divided—you'd expect them to be divided 4–2—but a slim chance is better than none. Besides, if you've taken the trouble to focus on losers as well as winners, you deserve a little luck. Here's the complete hand:

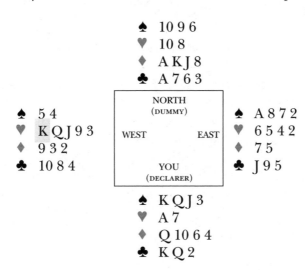

NORTH (DUMMY)
♠ 10 9 6
♥ 10 8
♦ A K J 8
♣ A 7 6 3

WEST
♠ 5 4
♥ K Q J 9 3
♦ 9 3 2
♣ 10 8 4

EAST
♠ A 8 7 2
♥ 6 5 4 2
♦ 7 5
♣ J 9 5

YOU (DECLARER)
♠ K Q J 3
♥ A 7
♦ Q 10 6 4
♣ K Q 2

## Summary

In a suit contract, you focus on losers—those tricks the defenders can take. Keep the following points in mind when counting losers:

- Don't count more losers in a suit than the number of cards held in your hand.
- Quick losers are those tricks the defenders can take immediately if they have the lead.
- Slow losers are those tricks you'll eventually lose, if you don't do something about them.

You still follow the FUN approach to playing the hand, but with the focus on losers, rather than winners.

- **F**ocus on the target.
  - How many losers can you afford?
  - How many losers do you have?
- **U**se the checklist if you need to eliminate losers.

| *Checklist* |
| --- |
| Promotion |
| Length |
| Finessing |
| ✓ Trumping Losers |
| Discarding Losers |

- **N**ote the order.
  - If you have the tricks you need in a suit contract, draw the trump first.
  - If you have too many quick losers, look for ways of getting rid of some of those losers before giving up the lead to the defenders.

## Practice Hands

### Hand 8.1

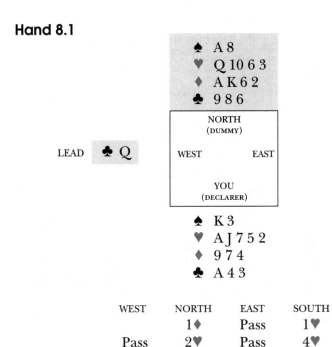

♠ A 8
♥ Q 10 6 3
♦ A K 6 2
♣ 9 8 6

NORTH
(DUMMY)

LEAD ♣ Q

WEST          EAST

YOU
(DECLARER)

♠ K 3
♥ A J 7 5 2
♦ 9 7 4
♣ A 4 3

| WEST | NORTH | EAST | SOUTH |
|------|-------|------|-------|
|      | 1♦    | Pass | 1♥    |
| Pass | 2♥    | Pass | 4♥    |
| Pass | Pass  | Pass |       |

West leads the ♣Q against your contract of 4♥. How many losers do you have? How do you plan to make the contract?

**Solution 8.1**

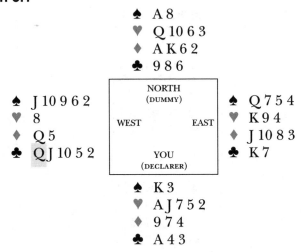

         ♠ A 8
         ♥ Q 10 6 3
         ♦ A K 6 2
         ♣ 9 8 6

                    NORTH
                    (DUMMY)
♠ J 10 9 6 2                          ♠ Q 7 5 4
♥ 8        WEST          EAST         ♥ K 9 4
♦ Q 5                                 ♦ J 10 8 3
♣ Q J 10 5 2         YOU             ♣ K 7
                    (DECLARER)

         ♠ K 3
         ♥ A J 7 5 2
         ♦ 9 7 4
         ♣ A 4 3

In a contract of 4♥, you can afford to lose three tricks. You have no losers in the spade suit. You have a potential loser in the heart suit because you're missing the ♥K. You have one loser in the diamond suit, since dummy has both the ♦A and ♦K. There are two club losers. That's a total of four losers, one more than you can afford.

There's nothing much you can do about the diamond and club losers. In the trump suit, you may be able to avoid a loser with the help of a finesse. After winning a trick with the ♣A, travel over to dummy using one of the high cards, and lead the ♥Q, or ♥10. If West covers with the ♥K, you win the ♥A, draw the rest of the trump, and take your other tricks. If West doesn't cover, play a low heart from your hand, taking the finesse. When this is successful, you can repeat the finesse, draw the trump, and take the rest of your tricks. You lose a diamond trick and two club tricks at the end of the hand.

It wouldn't have made much difference if you counted winners on this hand. You have two sure spade tricks, one sure heart trick, two diamond tricks, and a club trick. The four extra tricks you need can come from the heart suit with the help of a finesse. You'd play the hand exactly the same way.

## Hand 8.2

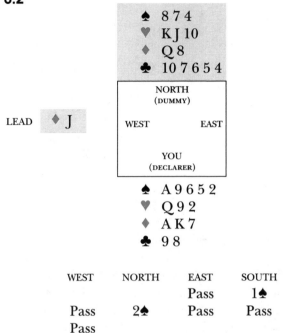

♠ 8 7 4
♥ K J 10
♦ Q 8
♣ 10 7 6 5 4

NORTH
(DUMMY)

LEAD ♦ J

WEST        EAST

YOU
(DECLARER)

♠ A 9 6 5 2
♥ Q 9 2
♦ A K 7
♣ 9 8

| WEST | NORTH | EAST | SOUTH |
|------|-------|------|-------|
|      |       | Pass | 1♠    |
| Pass | 2♠    | Pass | Pass  |
| Pass |       |      |       |

You're in a partscore contract of 2♠, and the ♦J is led. Count your losers. What do you need to happen in order to make the contract?

## Solution 8.2

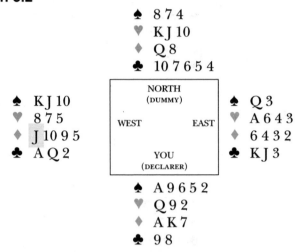

♠ 8 7 4
♥ K J 10
♦ Q 8
♣ 10 7 6 5 4

♠ K J 10
♥ 8 7 5
♦ J 10 9 5
♣ A Q 2

NORTH
(DUMMY)

WEST            EAST

YOU
(DECLARER)

♠ Q 3
♥ A 6 4 3
♦ 6 4 3 2
♣ K J 3

♠ A 9 6 5 2
♥ Q 9 2
♦ A K 7
♣ 9 8

You can afford five losers. It's uncertain exactly how many spade losers you have, but if the defenders' five spades divide 3–2, as you might expect, you'll have only two losers. If they divide 4–1, you'll have three losers. If they divide 5–0, you're lucky you aren't doubled. For now, take the reasonable view that you have two losers. You have a sure loser in hearts and two in clubs, but you have no losers in the diamond suit. You've got only five losers, provided the spades behave nicely.

Win the diamond with dummy's ♦Q, and lead a spade. Since you have to lose at least two tricks in spades, you could duck this trick completely. You'll be happy to see both defenders follow suit. That means the spades aren't divided 5–0. On the actual hand, you could also win the first spade trick with your ♠A and lead another spade. When the spades divide 3–2, your troubles are over. When you regain the lead, establish your two heart tricks by driving out the defenders' ♥A. Now you've got all the tricks you need. You'll lose two spade tricks, a heart trick, and two club tricks.

Counting winners would also work well on this hand. You need eight tricks and start with one spade trick and three diamond tricks. You can establish two more spade tricks through length, if the defenders' cards are divided 3–2, and you can promote two winners in the heart suit. All roads lead to Rome.

## Hand 8.3

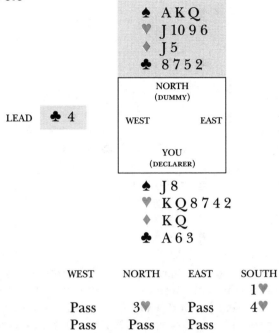

♠ A K Q
♥ J 10 9 6
♦ J 5
♣ 8 7 5 2

NORTH
(DUMMY)

LEAD  ♣ 4

WEST          EAST

YOU
(DECLARER)

♠ J 8
♥ K Q 8 7 4 2
♦ K Q
♣ A 6 3

| WEST | NORTH | EAST | SOUTH |
|------|-------|------|-------|
|      |       |      | 1♥    |
| Pass | 3♥    | Pass | 4♥    |
| Pass | Pass  | Pass |       |

West leads the ♣4 against your 4♥. How many losers do you have? Are you planning to draw trump as soon as you get the lead?

## Solution 8.3

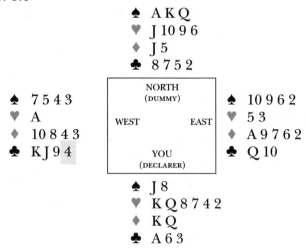

♠ A K Q
♥ J 10 9 6
♦ J 5
♣ 8 7 5 2

NORTH
(DUMMY)

WEST          EAST

YOU
(DECLARER)

♠ 7 5 4 3
♥ A
♦ 10 8 4 3
♣ K J 9 4

♠ 10 9 6 2
♥ 5 3
♦ A 9 7 6 2
♣ Q 10

♠ J 8
♥ K Q 8 7 4 2
♦ K Q
♣ A 6 3

In 4♥, you can afford to lose three tricks. You have no losers in spades, one in hearts, one in diamonds, and two in clubs. That's one too many. Since West has led a club, your ♣A is about to be driven out. That makes all your losers quick. If the defenders get the lead, they'll be able to take four tricks and defeat the contract.

All this tells you that you can't lead trump right away. You have to do something about one of the losers. There's nothing you can do about the heart and diamond losers, but you may be able to dispose of one of your club losers. After winning the ♣A, lead a spade over to dummy's winners. After taking two spade tricks, you can play dummy's third spade winner and discard one of your low clubs. That leaves you with only three losers. You can now lead a trump. The only tricks the defenders will take are the ♥A, the ♦A, and one club trick.

Counting winners might lead you astray on this hand. You start with three sure spade tricks and a club trick. Using promotion, you can develop five tricks from the heart suit and one trick from the diamond suit. That's the ten tricks you need. If you start going about drawing trump, however, you'll lose four tricks before you can win ten tricks. Counting losers steers you into playing your cards in the right order to make the contract.

## Hand 8.4

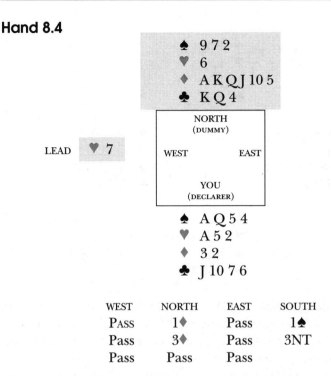

♠ 9 7 2
♥ 6
♦ A K Q J 10 5
♣ K Q 4

NORTH
(DUMMY)

LEAD ♥ 7

WEST     EAST

YOU
(DECLARER)

♠ A Q 5 4
♥ A 5 2
♦ 3 2
♣ J 10 7 6

| WEST | NORTH | EAST | SOUTH |
|------|-------|------|-------|
| PASS | 1♦ | Pass | 1♠ |
| Pass | 3♦ | Pass | 3NT |
| Pass | Pass | Pass | |

Although 5♦ might be a better contract, you find yourself in 3NT. There's an excellent source of tricks in dummy. How do you plan to get the nine tricks you need after the opening lead of the ♥7?

## Solution 8.4

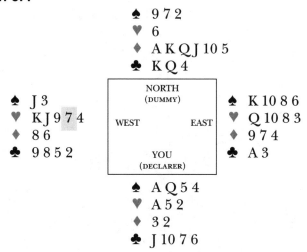

```
                   ♠ 9 7 2
                   ♥ 6
                   ♦ A K Q J 10 5
                   ♣ K Q 4
                        NORTH
 ♠ J 3                 (DUMMY)              ♠ K 10 8 6
 ♥ K J 9 7 4     WEST            EAST       ♥ Q 10 8 3
 ♦ 8 6                                      ♦ 9 7 4
 ♣ 9 8 5 2               YOU                ♣ A 3
                      (DECLARER)
                   ♠ A Q 5 4
                   ♥ A 5 2
                   ♦ 3 2
                   ♣ J 10 7 6
```

You need nine winners and start with eight. There are six sure diamond tricks, one spade, and one heart. Only one more needs to be developed. The club suit offers a sure-fire way of developing three extra tricks through promotion. That's more than you need.

If your planning stops there, you have ignored counting losers. The defenders have led hearts and will be able to drive out your ♥A. The defenders have nine hearts between them, so the best the hearts could be divided is 5–4. They'll get at least four heart tricks if you let them back in with the ♣A. Together with the club trick, that's enough to defeat your contract.

If the club suit can't be your source of extra tricks, what's the alternative? You have a 50–50 chance in the spade suit. If the ♠K is on your right, you can make the contract with the help of the finesse. If the ♠K is on your left, down you'll go. Still, that's better than giving yourself no chance at all. After winning a trick with the ♥A, you can take your six diamond winners, but then you have to lead a spade from dummy and finesse the ♠Q. This works on the actual hand—what else would you expect!

# *Trumping*
# *Losers*

*"Let spades be trumps! she said, and trumps they were."*

—ALEXANDER POPE [1712]

There are advantages to playing with a trump suit. Trump can be used to stop the defenders from taking their winners in a suit—you can ruff their tricks with a trump once you have no cards left in the suit. Trump can also be used to eliminate some of your losers and turn them into winners. At times it seems as if you're getting tricks from thin air.

## Tricks from Nowhere

Take a look at the following hand, and consider how many tricks you could take playing in a notrump contract.

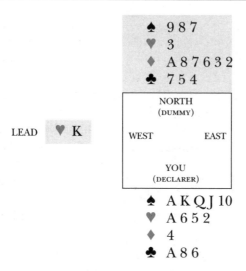

♠ 9 8 7
♥ 3
♦ A 8 7 6 3 2
♣ 7 5 4

NORTH
(DUMMY)

LEAD ♥ K

WEST          EAST

YOU
(DECLARER)

♠ A K Q J 10
♥ A 6 5 2
♦ 4
♣ A 8 6

There are five sure tricks in spades, one in hearts, one in diamonds, and one in clubs. That's a total of eight tricks, with no hope of taking any more. Even though there's some potential in the length of dummy's diamond suit, there are no entries to the dummy other than the ♦A. You can't establish winners in the diamond suit, and even if you could, you'd never be able to reach them. Playing in notrump, you can't afford to bid any higher than the two level.

Consider the same hand with spades as the trump suit. There are the same eight tricks on top, or looking at the hand from the viewpoint of losers, you have five losers—three hearts and two clubs. Yet amazingly enough, you can take eleven tricks with this hand after the opening lead of the ♥K.

Start by winning the ♥A. Dummy now has no hearts left. You can lead one of your low hearts—a loser—and ruff it with one of dummy's spades. You win this trick and have immediately gained one trick. You have turned a loser into a winner. You have won two tricks already and there are still five spade winners in your hand, together with the ♦A and ♣A. You're up to nine tricks.

Come back to your hand with the ♣A and lead another low heart, again trumping in dummy. A second extra trick. Four tricks already! You still have the ♦A plus the five spade winners in your hand. Now you have ten tricks.

You can take a trick with dummy's ♦A, lead a low diamond from dummy, and ruff it with one of your trump winners. This doesn't gain a trick because you already counted on winning a trick with each of the high spades in your hand. It does, however, give you an entry back to your hand. Lead your last low heart and ruff it with dummy's last spade. You've taken the first seven tricks and have four high spades left in your hand. You'll take eleven tricks, losing only the two club tricks to the defenders.

What a difference a trump suit makes! You could make an overtrick in a contract of 4♠ on the same hand with which you could take only eight tricks in a notrump contract. A trump suit won't always make that much difference, but it's easy to see how it can often be worth one or two extra tricks.

There are a number of important things to notice about this hand:

• You were able to get rid of your original heart losers by trumping—or ruffing—them in the dummy. *Trumping losers* is a new item to add to the checklist of techniques to use when there are more losers than you can afford.

• You gained a trick each time you trumped a loser in the dummy. You still had all the trump left in your hand that you were originally counting on to take tricks. In effect, by trumping three losers in dummy, you ended up winning eight trump tricks rather than five. On the other hand, you didn't gain a trick when you trumped a diamond to get back to your hand. You used up one of the tricks you already counted.

That's the general idea of trumping losers. You gain a trick by trumping in the hand with the fewer trump. This is usually the dummy. So, you should be looking for opportunities to trump losers in the dummy. Sometimes, both hands will have the same number of trump, but you'll still gain a trick by ruffing a loser in the dummy.

• The trump suit could be used for entries back and forth between the two hands. Dummy started with only one entry, the ♦A. Each time you trumped a loser in the dummy, you gained an entry. That wasn't particularly useful on this hand, but it's something to keep in mind. You did need to use the trump suit to get back to your hand so that you could trump your final heart loser. The trump suit is often your best source of entries to either side of the table.

• You can't have your cake and eat it too. You couldn't draw the defenders' trump right away if you wanted to ruff your heart losers in dummy. You started with eight spades, leaving the defenders with five. Even if the defenders' trump divided as you might expect, 3–2, you'd have to play the suit three times to draw them all. That would leave no spades in dummy with which to trump your heart losers.

• It wouldn't have been safe to be in a contract of 5♠ on this hand. Although you can take eleven tricks after the defenders lead the ♥K, it would be a different story if they led a trump originally. One of dummy's spades would disappear, and you'd be able to trump only two of your heart losers.

Not only must you be careful about drawing trump when you're planning to ruff losers, you must also watch out for the opponents. If they think that you're intending to trump losers in the dummy, they may lead the trump suit to try to prevent this from happening, if you give them the opportunity. That's a common defensive tactic.

• On this hand, you were able to safely ruff all your heart losers in the dummy. You held all the high trump, so there was no chance that one of the opponents could play a higher trump if they also had no hearts left. That's a potential danger when you're trying to trump losers and all the defenders' trump haven't yet been drawn. One of the defenders may be able to *overtrump*—play a higher trump—if they also have no cards left in the suit you're trying to ruff.

Let's take a more detailed look at some of these points associated with trumping losers.

## Opportunity Knocks

When you've counted your losers in a trump contract and you find more than you can afford, look for opportunities to trump losers. Because you usually trump losers in the dummy. **Look for a suit which has more cards in your hand than in the dummy.**

| DUMMY | This is an ideal holding for trumping a |
|---|---|
| ♥ 8 | loser. Dummy has a singleton and you hold |

the ace and a loser. You can take a trick with

| DECLARER | your ♥A, then lead the ♥6, and trump it in |
|---|---|
| ♥ A 6 | dummy. |

| DUMMY | This isn't the situation for trumping losers. |
|---|---|
| ♦ A 7 5 | First, you have no losers in your hand. |

Dummy's ♦A takes care of your ♦8. Second,

| DECLARER | dummy has more diamonds than declarer, |
|---|---|
| ♦ 8 | and that's not the pattern you want. Your |

point of view is important here. You can stop
the defenders from taking any diamond tricks because of your singleton ♦8. This doesn't, however, gain a trick.

| DUMMY | There are two losers in your hand, but |
|---|---|
| ♣ 8 6 3 | dummy has the same number of cards. This |

suit doesn't provide an opportunity to ruff

| DECLARER | losers. |
|---|---|
| ♣ A 7 5 | |

| DUMMY | This time, there are three losers in your |
|---|---|
| ♥ 9 | hand, and dummy has fewer cards in the suit |

than you do. There's work to do before you

| DECLARER | can actually trump one of your losers in the |
|---|---|
| ♥ J 4 3 | dummy. You'll have to give up one heart trick |

to the opponents. Now dummy will be void in
the suit, and you can trump your two remaining losers.

| DUMMY | There are four losers in your hand and |
|---|---|
| ♦ Q 4 | dummy has a doubleton. This is an opportu- |

nity to trump losers. You'd have to give up

| DECLARER | two diamond tricks to the defenders, then you |
|---|---|
| ♦ 10 9 7 5 | could lead one—or both—of your diamond |

losers and trump in dummy.

Here's a straightforward example of trumping losers in a complete hand. The contract is 2♥, and the opening lead is the ♣Q.

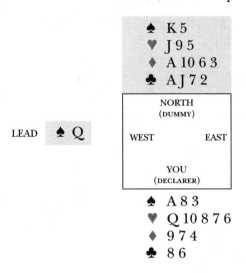

♠ K 5
♥ J 9 5
♦ A 10 6 3
♣ A J 7 2

NORTH
(DUMMY)

LEAD ♣ Q

WEST          EAST

YOU
(DECLARER)

♠ A 8 3
♥ Q 10 8 7 6
♦ 9 7 4
♣ 8 6

Count the losers: one in spades, two in hearts, two in diamonds, and one in clubs. That's six losers, one more than you can afford in your 2♥ contract. You have three spades, and dummy has two. That gives you an opportunity to trump a loser. Since you don't have many entries to your hand, be a little careful of the order in which you play your cards. Win the first trick with dummy's ♠K, and lead the ♠5 over to your ♠A. Now dummy has no spades left, and you're in the right hand to lead a third round of spades, trumping in dummy. That gets you down to five losers. Start drawing trump. You will lose only two heart tricks, two diamond tricks, and a club trick.

This next contract requires a little more work. You're in 4♠, and the opening lead is the ♦2.

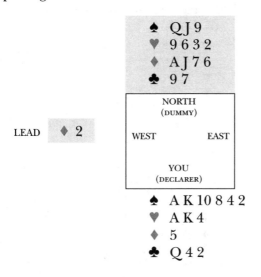

♠ Q J 9
♥ 9 6 3 2
♦ A J 7 6
♣ 9 7

NORTH
(DUMMY)

LEAD ♦ 2

WEST        EAST

YOU
(DECLARER)

♠ A K 10 8 4 2
♥ A K 4
♦ 5
♣ Q 4 2

You have one loser in hearts and three in clubs. You need to eliminate one of your losers. Since dummy has only two clubs and you have three, there's an opportunity to trump one of your club losers in the dummy. It will not gain a trick to trump dummy's diamonds in your hand. Focus on the club suit. You'll have to make dummy void in clubs. Win the first trick and lead a club, giving up a trick to the defenders. As soon as you regain the lead, lead another club, giving up a second trick in the suit to the defenders. Now dummy has no clubs remaining. When you regain the lead, lead your last club, and ruff it in the dummy. That takes care of your extra loser. You can draw any outstanding trump in the defenders' hands, and you'll eventually have to give them a heart trick at the end, but that's all.

A short suit in dummy is a prerequisite for trumping a loser, but sometimes you have to create the shortness yourself. On this next hand, you've reached 6♥ and have to find a way to make the contract after an opening lead of the ♣10.

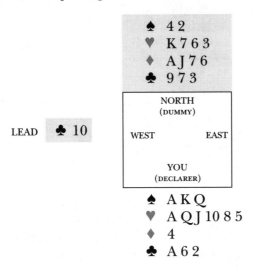

♠ 4 2
♥ K 7 6 3
♦ A J 7 6
♣ 9 7 3

NORTH
(DUMMY)

LEAD    ♣ 10    WEST            EAST

YOU
(DECLARER)

♠ A K Q
♥ A Q J 10 8 5
♦ 4
♣ A 6 2

There are no losers in any suit except clubs. Unfortunately, there are two losers in that suit, and that's one too many. With three clubs in both hands, it doesn't look like a suit in which you can trump a loser, but where there's a will…

After winning the first trick and drawing trump, you can play the three spade winners from your hand. On the third round of spades, discard a club from dummy. All of a sudden, dummy has one fewer clubs than you. Now you can give up a club trick to the opponents, and you'll be able to trump your last club in the dummy.

## Managing Dummy's Trump

It's generally a good idea to draw trump as soon as possible, but you need to weigh this against the need to **keep enough trump in dummy with which to ruff your losers**. Consider this hand. You've reached a partscore contract of 3♦, and the opening lead is the ♣K.

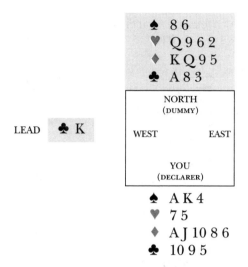

♠ 8 6
♥ Q 9 6 2
♦ K Q 9 5
♣ A 8 3

NORTH
(DUMMY)

LEAD ♣ K

WEST        EAST

YOU
(DECLARER)

♠ A K 4
♥ 7 5
♦ A J 10 8 6
♣ 10 9 5

There are five losers: one spade, two hearts, and two clubs. You can afford only four losers in your 3♦ contract, and your plan is to trump your spade loser in the dummy. Can you afford to draw trump first?

Yes and no. You need only one diamond left in dummy with which to trump your spade loser. You can certainly afford to play trump three times, and that will be sufficient if the defenders' diamonds are divided 2–2 or 3–1. If one defender has all four of the outstanding trump, however, you can't afford to draw them all. That would leave no diamond in dummy to take care of your spade loser.

The decision on whether or not to draw trump before ruffing your losers requires some foresight. On the above hand, after winning a trick with the ♣A, you could start leading trump. If both opponents follow suit, you'd continue until all the trump were drawn. You'd still have at least one diamond left in dummy. If one opponent fails to follow suit on the first round of diamonds, you'll know the diamonds are divided 4–0. You'll have to change tactics and ruff your spade loser in the dummy before drawing the rest of the trump.

Here's a hand which requires some careful thought. The contract
is 4♠, and the opening lead is the ♥10.

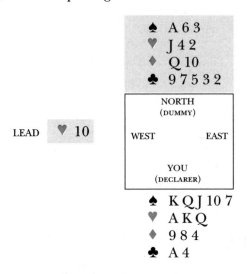

You have three diamond losers, and a club loser—one too many.
Dummy's doubleton in diamonds provides the opportunity to trump
one of your losers. You need only one spade in dummy to trump
your diamond loser, so it would appear that you can afford to draw
two rounds of trump before going about ruffing your loser. You'd
like to get rid of the defenders' low trump as soon as possible, so
they can't trump one of your heart winners. On this hand, however,
leading even one round of trump prevents you from making the
contract.

To trump your loser in the dummy, you're going to have to give
up the lead twice to the opponents. If they see that you're planning
to trump a losing diamond in dummy, they'll try to thwart your plans
by getting rid of dummy's spades. Suppose you win the first heart
trick and lead one round of spades before giving up a diamond trick
to the opponents. They can win the diamond trick and lead a second round of spades, leaving only one spade in the dummy. When
you give up the second diamond trick, they can lead another spade,
removing dummy's last trump. Now you're left with a losing diamond in your hand and nowhere to put it.

After winning the first heart trick, lead a diamond right away. That
way, you'll win the race. They can win the diamond and lead a trump,

but you win and lead a second diamond. They can lead a second round of trump, but you win and still have a trump in the dummy with which to ruff your last diamond loser. Now you can draw the rest of the trump and claim your contract.

When trumping a loser, you should **trump with the highest card you can afford**. That helps to avoid the possibility of a defender overtrumping—*overruffing*—and winning the trick. For example, suppose you've reached a contract of 4♥ on the following hand, and the defenders lead the ♦Q.

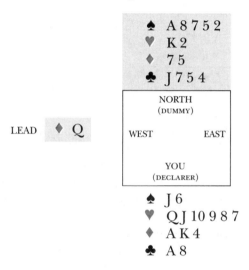

There is a spade loser, a heart loser, a diamond loser, and a club loser. You plan to get rid of your extra loser by trumping your low diamond in the dummy. You can't afford to draw trump first because you need a heart left in dummy to ruff your loser.

You take your ♦A and ♦K, and lead your ♦4, intending to ruff it in dummy. Since you have all the high cards in hearts except the ♥A, you can afford to trump this trick with dummy's ♥K, rather than the ♥2. This won't make much difference, unless the complete hand looks like this:

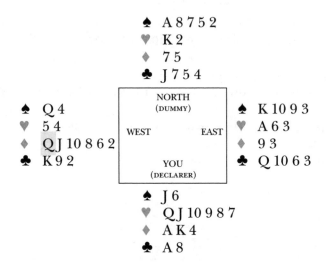

If you trump your ♦4 with dummy's ♥2, East can win the trick by overruffing with the ♥3. You still have to lose a spade trick, a club trick, and the ♥A, so you won't make the contract. If you trump your diamond loser with dummy's ♥K, no harm can befall you. You don't mind if East overtrumps with the ♥A; you had to lose that trick anyway. Of course, most of the time, East will simply follow suit with a diamond when you ruff your loser. But it doesn't hurt to be careful. Every now and then, caution will pay off.

## Managing the Entries

When playing a hand, note the order in which you need to play your cards. When trying to trump losers in the dummy, there's no exception. Entries are always a consideration. Take a look at this hand. The contract is 2♠, and the defense starts off with the ♥10.

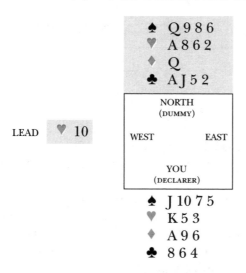

♠ Q 9 8 6
♥ A 8 6 2
♦ Q
♣ A J 5 2

NORTH
(DUMMY)

LEAD ♥ 10

WEST        EAST

YOU
(DECLARER)

♠ J 10 7 5
♥ K 5 3
♦ A 9 6
♣ 8 6 4

There are two spade losers, one heart loser, two diamond losers, and two club losers. That's two more than you can afford, so you plan to trump your two diamond losers in the dummy. You can't afford to draw trump before ruffing your losers because you need two trump left in the dummy.

You must also decide where you want to win the first trick—in your hand or in the dummy. To make that decision, you need to look ahead. After winning the first trick, you plan to play the ♦A and trump a diamond in dummy. You then need to get back to your hand so that you can lead your last diamond and trump it in dummy. The only entry back to your hand is the ♥K. That tells you that you should win the first trick with dummy's ♥A, preserving the ♥K until you're ready to use it.

On this next hand, you have to be even more thoughtful. You're in a game contract of 4♠, and the opening lead is the ♦K.

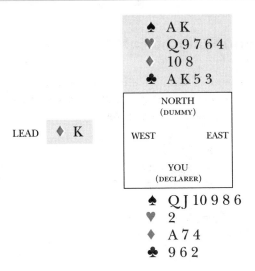

♠ A K
♥ Q 9 7 6 4
♦ 10 8
♣ A K 5 3

NORTH
(DUMMY)

LEAD   ♦ K

WEST              EAST

YOU
(DECLARER)

♠ Q J 10 9 8 6
♥ 2
♦ A 7 4
♣ 9 6 2

You can afford three losers, but you have a heart loser, two diamond losers, and a club loser. Dummy has only two diamonds, so you can plan to trump one of your diamond losers in the dummy. Seems simple enough. You know about leaving enough trump in dummy, so you win the first diamond trick and give up a diamond to the defenders. You're now ready to trump your loser, and there are still two trump left in dummy. Things are sailing along smoothly. But when the defenders see what you're planning to do, they take their diamond trick and lead a spade.

Suddenly, the sea has become a little rougher. You have to win this trick in dummy, and you have no immediate entry back to your hand. If you lead a heart, or take your two club winners and lead a club, the opponents win the trick and lead a second spade. Dummy's last trump disappears, and you still have a diamond loser left in your hand. What went wrong?

When the ♦K is led, you need to look ahead and visualize the entry problem. You then look for a way to overcome this challenge. Earlier in the book, we've seen one way to overcome entry problems, and that's our friend the "duck"—another way of saying "take your losses early." Instead of winning the first diamond trick and then losing the second, let's reverse the order. Duck the first diamond trick, playing a low diamond from both hands. The defense is now helpless. If they lead a trump, you win in the dummy, cross to your hand with the carefully preserved ♦A, and lead your last diamond. You ruff this with dummy's remaining trump, and your work's all done. Your only remaining losers are a heart and a diamond. Entries are everything.

## The Dreaded Crossruff

There are some hands on which trumping losers is so much fun that you never get around to drawing trump! Here's an example. The contract is 4♥, and the opening lead is the ♦K.

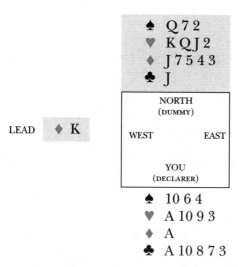

♠ Q 7 2
♥ K Q J 2
♦ J 7 5 4 3
♣ J

NORTH
(DUMMY)

LEAD ♦ K

WEST          EAST

YOU
(DECLARER)

♠ 10 6 4
♥ A 10 9 3
♦ A
♣ A 10 8 7 3

You have three spade losers in your hand and four club losers. You're going to have to get rid of four of them, and dummy's singleton diamond gives you a chance. You plan to trump all four of your club losers in the dummy. That means you can't draw any trump, since you need all four of dummy's trump.

After winning the first trick with the ♦A, you play the ♣A and then trump one of your club losers in the dummy. You now need an entry back to your hand so that you can trump another club loser. You can't afford to lead one of dummy's trump, but you can lead a diamond and trump it in your hand with a low heart. Now you lead another club and trump it in the dummy. To get back to your hand, you lead another diamond and trump in your hand. And so it goes. You ruff another club in dummy and ruff a diamond back to your hand. You ruff your last club in the dummy and come back to your hand by ruffing dummy's last diamond with your last heart.

You've never drawn a single trump, but you wind up with ten tricks: your two aces and eight trump tricks. All that's left are your three spade losers. Playing a hand in this manner is called a *crossruff* because you cross back and forth between the two hands through ruffing low cards. A danger of playing on a crossruff is that one of your opponents may be able to overruff one of your trump. On this hand, you take early ruffs with your low trump in both hands. Later on, you're ruffing with your high trump, so there's no danger of an overruff.

You won't get many hands like this, but it's fun when you do.

## Summary

When you count your losers in a trump contract and find you have more than you can afford, one technique to look for is the possibility of trumping losers.

| *Checklist* | |
|:---:|:---|
| | Promotion |
| | Length |
| | Finessing |
| ✓ | Trumping Losers |
| | Discarding Losers |

When looking to trump losers, keep the following guidelines in mind:

- Look for a suit that has fewer cards in the dummy than in your hand. You usually gain tricks by ruffing losers in the dummy, not in your hand.

- You may have to give up tricks to the opponents when preparing to ruff your losers in the dummy. Follow the general principle of taking your losses early.

- Keep enough trump in dummy with which to ruff your losers. You may have to delay drawing all of the defenders' trump.

- When trumping a loser, trump with the highest card you can afford, to avoid an overruff.

# Practice Hands

### Hand 9.1

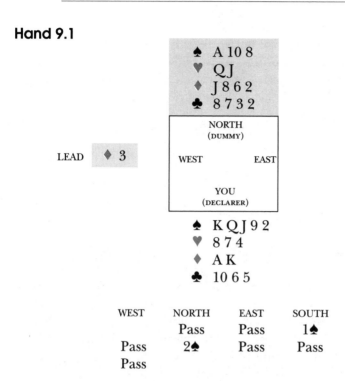

| ♠ | A 10 8 |
| ♥ | Q J |
| ♦ | J 8 6 2 |
| ♣ | 8 7 3 2 |

NORTH
(DUMMY)

LEAD ♦ 3

WEST          EAST

YOU
(DECLARER)

| ♠ | K Q J 9 2 |
| ♥ | 8 7 4 |
| ♦ | A K |
| ♣ | 10 6 5 |

| WEST | NORTH | EAST | SOUTH |
|------|-------|------|-------|
|      | Pass  | Pass | 1♠    |
| Pass | 2♠    | Pass | Pass  |
| Pass |       |      |       |

West leads the ♦3 against your contract of 2♠. How do you plan to make the contract? Should you start by drawing trump?

## Solution 9.1

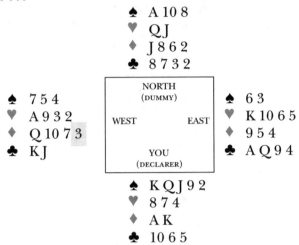

♠ A 10 8
♥ Q J
♦ J 8 6 2
♣ 8 7 3 2

NORTH (DUMMY)
WEST     EAST
YOU (DECLARER)

♠ 7 5 4
♥ A 9 3 2
♦ Q 10 7 3
♣ K J

♠ 6 3
♥ K 10 6 5
♦ 9 5 4
♣ A Q 9 4

♠ K Q J 9 2
♥ 8 7 4
♦ A K
♣ 10 6 5

You're in a trump contract, so you can focus on your losers. You can afford to lose five tricks in your partscore contract of 2♠. There are no losers in spades or diamonds, but there are three losers in hearts and three in clubs—one more than you can afford. When you go down the checklist looking for ways to eliminate extra losers, the heart suit offers the possibility of trumping a loser. There are fewer hearts in the dummy than in your hand. By giving up two heart tricks to the defenders, dummy will have none left, and you can ruff your last heart loser.

You can't afford to draw any trump. Even though you need to leave only one spade in the dummy with which to ruff your loser, you have to give up the lead twice to the opponents. If they see what you're up to, they might continue leading spades, removing dummy's trump. Instead, win the first diamond trick and immediately lead a heart, giving up a trick. If the defenders win this trick and lead a spade, win the trick in either hand and lead another heart. The defenders can lead a second round of spades, but you can win this in your hand and lead your last heart, trumping it with dummy's remaining spade. Come back to your hand, and draw the remaining trump. The only tricks you lose are two hearts and three clubs.

## Hand 9.2

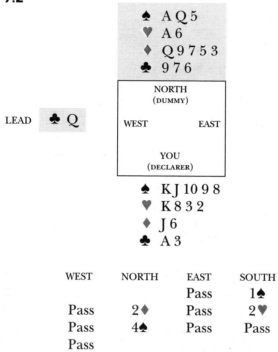

♠ A Q 5
♥ A 6
♦ Q 9 7 5 3
♣ 9 7 6

NORTH
(DUMMY)

LEAD ♣ Q

WEST        EAST

YOU
(DECLARER)

♠ K J 10 9 8
♥ K 8 3 2
♦ J 6
♣ A 3

| WEST | NORTH | EAST | SOUTH |
|------|-------|------|-------|
|      |       | Pass | 1♠    |
| Pass | 2♦    | Pass | 2♥    |
| Pass | 4♠    | Pass | Pass  |
| Pass |       |      |       |

You're in a contract of 4♠, and the opening lead is the ♣Q. How do you plan to get rid of your extra losers? Is there anything to be careful about?

## Solution 9.2

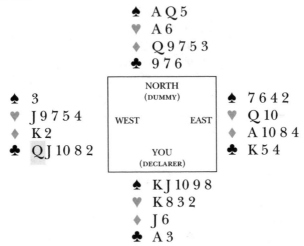

You can afford only three losers in your 4♠ contract. There are two in hearts, two in diamonds, and one in clubs. You'll have to eliminate two losers. The heart suit offers the best chance. You should be able to trump your two heart losers in the dummy.

You can't afford to draw any trump. You need two of dummy's trump for ruffing your losers, and you'll need the other trump as an entry back to your hand. Note the order in which you need to play the cards. After winning the first trick with your ♣A, play a low heart to dummy's ♥A, and play dummy's remaining heart back to your ♥K. Dummy has no hearts left, and you're in the right hand to lead one of your heart losers and trump it in the dummy.

You need to exercise some caution on this hand. You should trump your heart loser with dummy's ♠Q, or ♠A. You can afford to do this because you have all the other high spades in your hand. On the actual hand, if you ruff your heart loser with dummy's ♠5, East will overruff, and you won't make the contract. After trumping your first heart loser with one of dummy's high spades, come back to your hand by playing dummy's low spade to one of the winners in your hand. Lead the last heart, and trump with dummy's remaining high spade. Give the defenders their two diamond tricks and their club trick. The rest are yours.

## Hand 9.3

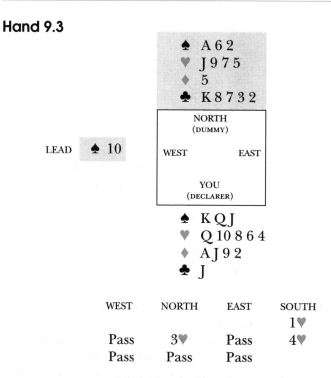

♠ A 6 2
♥ J 9 7 5
♦ 5
♣ K 8 7 3 2

NORTH
(DUMMY)

LEAD ♠ 10

WEST          EAST

YOU
(DECLARER)

♠ K Q J
♥ Q 10 8 6 4
♦ A J 9 2
♣ J

| WEST | NORTH | EAST | SOUTH |
|------|-------|------|-------|
|      |       |      | 1♥    |
| Pass | 3♥    | Pass | 4♥    |
| Pass | Pass  | Pass |       |

West leads the ♠10 against your contract of 4♥. Where should you win the first trick? Can you draw trump right away?

## Solution 9.3

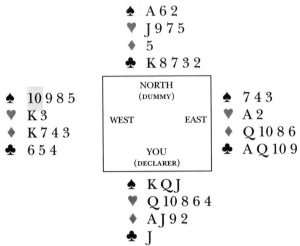

&spades; A 6 2
&hearts; J 9 7 5
&diams; 5
&clubs; K 8 7 3 2

**WEST**
&spades; 10 9 8 5
&hearts; K 3
&diams; K 7 4 3
&clubs; 6 5 4

NORTH (DUMMY)

**EAST**
&spades; 7 4 3
&hearts; A 2
&diams; Q 10 8 6
&clubs; A Q 10 9

YOU (DECLARER)

&spades; K Q J
&hearts; Q 10 8 6 4
&diams; A J 9 2
&clubs; J

There are two losers in the heart suit, three in the diamond suit, and one in the club suit. That's three more than you can afford. There's not much you can do about the losers in the heart and club suits, so you need to eliminate the three diamond losers from your hand. Fortunately, dummy's singleton diamond gives you the opportunity of trumping your losers.

You'll need three trump in the dummy to ruff all your losers, so you can't afford to draw trump too soon. You'll also need entries back to your hand so that you can keep leading diamonds. The spade suit provides you with two entries, but you'd better not use up one of the entries to your hand before you're ready.

Note the order in which you must play the cards. Win the first trick with dummy's &clubs;A, keeping your two spade entries for later. Play dummy's singleton diamond to your &diams;A, and lead a low diamond and ruff it in the dummy. Come back to your hand with one of your spade entries. Lead another low diamond, and trump it in the dummy. Cross back to your hand one more time with your second spade entry, and lead your last diamond. You trump this in dummy, and now it's safe to start leading trump. Two heart tricks and a club trick are all you lose.

## Hand 9.4

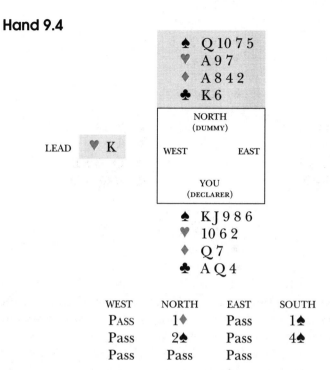

♠ Q 10 7 5
♥ A 9 7
♦ A 8 4 2
♣ K 6

NORTH
(DUMMY)

LEAD ♥ K

WEST                    EAST

YOU
(DECLARER)

♠ K J 9 8 6
♥ 10 6 2
♦ Q 7
♣ A Q 4

| WEST | NORTH | EAST | SOUTH |
|------|-------|------|-------|
| PASS | 1♦ | Pass | 1♠ |
| Pass | 2♠ | Pass | 4♠ |
| Pass | Pass | Pass | |

You're in a contract of 4♠, and the opening lead is the ♥K. You appear to have four losers. Is there anything you can do?

## Solution 9.4

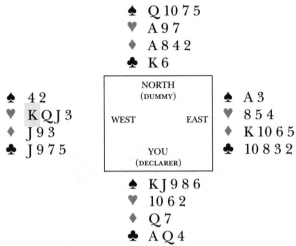

```
              ♠ Q 10 7 5
              ♥ A 9 7
              ♦ A 8 4 2
              ♣ K 6
                  NORTH
 ♠ 4 2            (DUMMY)         ♠ A 3
 ♥ K Q J 3                        ♥ 8 5 4
 ♦ J 9 3      WEST       EAST     ♦ K 10 6 5
 ♣ J 9 7 5                        ♣ 10 8 3 2
                   YOU
                 (DECLARER)
              ♠ K J 9 8 6
              ♥ 10 6 2
              ♦ Q 7
              ♣ A Q 4
```

You have one certain loser in the spade suit, and you're looking at two heart losers and a diamond loser. You'll need to find a way to reduce your number of losers by one. With the same number of hearts in both hands, there doesn't appear to be a way to trump one of your heart losers. But appearances can be deceiving. You have three club winners, and if you play them, you'll be able to discard one of dummy's hearts. That will leave dummy with fewer hearts than in your hand, and you'll be able to trump your second heart loser.

After winning the ♥A, you can't afford to lead trump right away. You have quick losers in spades and hearts. If you let the defenders win a trick with their ♠A, they can take their two heart winners and sit back and wait for their diamond trick. You need to do something about one of your heart losers right away. Win the first trick with dummy's ♥A, and play the ♣K—high card from the short side. Play dummy's link card, the ♣6, over to your ♣A, and play the ♣Q, throwing a heart from the dummy. Now it's safe to play trump. The defenders can take only one spade trick and one heart trick. You'll eventually ruff your last heart in the dummy. The defenders will get a diamond trick, but that's all.

# Discarding Losers

*"Remember, dummy and losers refer to the cards, not the players."*

You can't always turn losers into winners by trumping them. There are other choices when you count your losers and find that you have more than you can afford. The search is still on for unevenly divided suits. This time, however, look for more cards in the dummy than you have in your hand.

## Using Dummy's Extra Winners

Take a look at the following hand, and consider how many tricks you could take playing in a notrump contract.

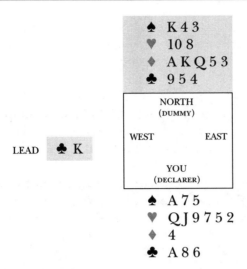

♠ K 4 3
♥ 10 8
♦ A K Q 5 3
♣ 9 5 4

NORTH
(DUMMY)

WEST            EAST

LEAD   ♣ K

YOU
(DECLARER)

♠ A 7 5
♥ Q J 9 7 5 2
♦ 4
♣ A 8 6

There are two sure tricks in spades, three in diamonds, and one in clubs, for a total of six. You could establish four more tricks in hearts through promotion, by driving out the defenders' ♥A and ♥K. You might also develop an extra trick from the diamond suit through length, if the defenders' seven diamonds are divided 4–3. Whatever you try, however, you're going to lose the race to the defenders. They're about to drive out your ♣A. Even if the defenders' clubs are divided 4–3, they'll have three tricks to take in the suit when they gain the lead. Since they also have two tricks in the heart suit, they'll be able to take at least five tricks before you can get any extra winners. You'd be lucky to end up with eight tricks in a notrump contract.

Consider the same hand with hearts as the trump suit. In a trump contract, you still have the same six winners, but your focus is on losers. There's one potential loser in spades, two certain losers in the trump suit, and two potential losers in clubs. Yet on this hand, you may be able to take ten or eleven tricks with hearts as the trump suit.

This all has to do with the power of the trump suit. For example, the defenders can't take more than two club tricks, even if one of them holds five or six clubs. After the third round of the suit, you have no clubs remaining in either hand. If they try to take another club trick, you can ruff with one of dummy's trump, or with one of the trump in your hand.

But you can do better than that on this hand. After winning the first trick with your ♣A, you could take three tricks with dummy's diamond winners and discard the two club losers from your hand. Now when the defenders get the lead, they can't take any club tricks. If they lead one of their established club winners, you can trump in your hand and win the trick.

On this hand, therefore, you can make a contract of 4♥, even though you could take only seven or eight tricks in a notrump contract. Playing in a trump suit is worth at least two extra tricks.

There are a few things to note about this hand:

- You were able to get rid of your original club losers by throwing them away on dummy's diamond winners. *Discarding losers* is another item to add to the checklist of techniques for eliminating extra losers.

- You gained a trick each time you discarded a loser on a winner in the dummy. That's the general idea of discarding losers. You look for opportunities to discard losers when you have extra winners in the dummy.

You don't gain a trick when you discard low cards from dummy on extra high cards in your hand. You don't count dummy's losers when totaling up your losers. In the last chapter, there was an example of discarding low cards by playing winners from your hand, but this had to do with creating shortness in the dummy so that you could trump losers from your hand. That's not quite the same thing.

- You had to discard some of your losers immediately, before letting the defenders gain the lead. That's because you had too many quick losers. The situation would be different if your losers were slow. Then you could afford to give up the lead to the defenders, since they couldn't immediately take enough tricks to defeat you.

For example, if the opening lead were a spade, rather than a club, there would be no hurry to discard losers. You could lead a trump, driving out one of the defenders' high cards in the suit. On winning the trick, they wouldn't be in a position to take any tricks in spades or clubs, since you still have winners in both suits.

- There was some danger in taking your diamond winners before drawing trump. If one of the defenders started with a singleton or doubleton diamond, they could ruff one of your winners, defeating the contract. When you're planning to discard losers, you'd prefer to draw trump first. It's only when you have too many quick losers and may have to let the opponents win a trick while drawing trump, that you delay drawing trump until you've disposed of enough losers.

It would actually be safer to discard only one of your club losers before going about drawing trump. You can afford to lose two heart tricks and one club trick. You'd later discard your spade loser on the last diamond winner in dummy.

- If the defenders' diamonds divide 4–3, you might be able to make an eleventh trick on this hand. After taking your three diamond winners, you could lead another diamond from dummy and trump it. You'd win the trick, and the defenders would have no diamonds left. Dummy's last diamond would be established as a winner. After drawing trump, you might be able to use this winner to discard your spade loser. Although you don't need to do this to make your contract on this hand, there are times when you'll need to manufacture an extra winner in the dummy so that you can discard one of your losers.

Let's discuss further some of the points related to discarding losers.

## Good Prospects

The opportunity to discard losers from your hand can come about only when there's a suit in which **dummy has more cards than are in your hand**. Dummy will also have to have some winners in the suit, or some cards that can be developed into winners. Consider each of the following suits.

DUMMY

♠ A K

DECLARER

♠ 3

This is an ideal suit to use for discarding a loser from your hand. Dummy has more cards in the suit than you do, and dummy has an extra winner. After taking a trick with the ♠A, you can use the ♠K to discard a loser.

| DUMMY | This is not a useful holding for discarding |
| ♥ 8 4 | losers, since you hold more cards in the suit |
| | than dummy. You can use the suit to discard |
| DECLARER | a card from the dummy, but that doesn't get |
| ♥ A K Q | rid of a loser from your hand. |

DUMMY
♥ 8 4

DECLARER
♥ A K Q

This is not a useful holding for discarding losers, since you hold more cards in the suit than dummy. You can use the suit to discard a card from the dummy, but that doesn't get rid of a loser from your hand.

DUMMY
♦ A 8 7 5

DECLARER
♦ 6

Dummy has more cards in the suit than you do, but with no extra winner in the dummy, you can't use the suit for discarding a loser from your hand. Dummy's ♦A is already accounted for, since you'd count no losers in this suit.

DUMMY
♣ A Q 4 2

DECLARER
♣ K 3

Dummy has an extra winner on which you could discard a loser. When playing this type of suit, you'd start with the high card from the short side, the ♣K. you can then travel over to dummy's ♣A using your link card, the ♣3. Finally, you'd discard a loser on dummy's ♣Q.

DUMMY
♠ K Q J

DECLARER
♠ 4

You have a loser in this suit and no immediate winners in the dummy. The suit, however, does offer some potential for discarding losers. Once the ♠A is driven out, you'll have two extra winners in the dummy on which you might be able to discard some losers.

Here's a typical hand in which you'd use the technique of discarding a loser. The contract is 2♦, and the opening lead is the ♣K.

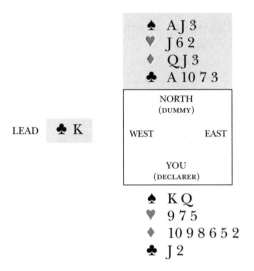

♠ A J 3
♥ J 6 2
♦ Q J 3
♣ A 10 7 3

NORTH
(DUMMY)

LEAD  ♣ K

WEST                    EAST

YOU
(DECLARER)

♠ K Q
♥ 9 7 5
♦ 10 9 8 6 5 2
♣ J 2

There are six losers: three hearts, two diamonds, and one club. You need to eliminate one of the losers. Since dummy has no short suit, you can't trump any of your losers. Instead, you look for an opportunity to discard one of your losers. Dummy has more spades than you and can provide the extra winner on which to discard a loser.

You'll have to dispose of your loser before playing trump, since all of your losers are quick once dummy's ♣A has been driven out. Win the first trick with dummy's ♣A, and play the ♠3 to your ♠K, or ♠Q. Now lead your remaining high spade and overtake with dummy's ♠A. That's the only way you can get to dummy without giving the defenders the lead. You're in the right hand to play dummy's ♠J and discard a loser from your hand. It doesn't matter whether you discard your club loser or one of your heart losers. They're all the same. Once you have your losers down to five, it's safe to start leading trump to drive out the defenders' high cards. They can take five tricks, but that's all.

## Quick and Slow

Before discarding losers, draw trump first if possible. If you can draw trump without giving up the lead to the opponents, it doesn't matter whether your losers are quick or slow. If you may have to give up the lead to the opponents while drawing trump, you can't afford to do so if you have too many quick losers.

On this hand, you're in a contract of 6♦, and the defense gets off to a lead of the ♠10.

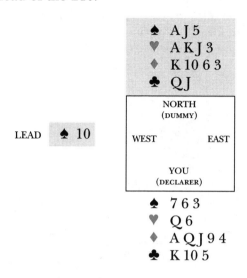

LEAD ♠ 10

NORTH
(DUMMY)

♠ A J 5
♥ A K J 3
♦ K 10 6 3
♣ Q J

WEST          EAST

YOU
(DECLARER)

♠ 7 6 3
♥ Q 6
♦ A Q J 9 4
♣ K 10 5

In a small slam contract, you can afford only one loser. On this hand you have three losers: two spades and one club. Not to worry. Dummy's extra heart winners look like a good spot on which to park your two spade losers. After winning the ♠A, all your losers are quick. The defenders can take three tricks, if you give them the lead. Should you dispose of your losers before drawing trump?

In this situation, there's no reason to delay drawing trump. You can draw the defenders' trump without giving up the lead. In fact, if you don't draw the trump before taking your heart winners, you won't be able to make the contract. The defenders have seven hearts between them. Even if they divide as evenly as possible, 4–3, one of the defenders will be out of hearts by the time you play your fourth winner in the suit. They'll play a trump on your winner, and you'll no longer have enough tricks to make the contract. If one of the defenders started with a singleton or doubleton trump, they'll ruff one of your winners even sooner.

After winning the ♠A, draw all four of the defenders' trump, playing as many rounds of diamonds as necessary. Then take your heart winners, starting with the ♥Q, high card from the short side. On dummy's third and fourth heart winners, discard your two remaining low spades. Now you can lead a club to promote your two winners in that suit. The defense can lead a spade after winning the ♣A, but it's too late. You can trump and take the rest of the tricks.

Contrast the previous hand with this one. The contract is 4♠, and the lead is the ♥J.

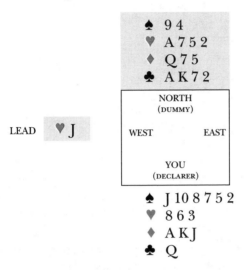

♠ 9 4
♥ A 7 5 2
♦ Q 7 5
♣ A K 7 2

NORTH
(DUMMY)

LEAD ♥ J

WEST          EAST

YOU
(DECLARER)

♠ J 10 8 7 5 2
♥ 8 6 3
♦ A K J
♣ Q

You're missing the top three spades and have two heart losers as well. After winning the first trick with dummy's ♥A, it's no time to draw trump. All your losers are quick, and the defenders will win the first spade trick. Instead, play a low club from dummy to your ♣Q. Travel back to dummy by playing your ♦J and overtaking with dummy's ♦Q. Play the ♣A and ♣K, discarding two hearts from your hand. Now it's safe to draw trump. Other than the three spade losers, the rest of the tricks are yours.

On many hands, you'll have both quick and slow losers. You'll have to judge carefully whether or not you can afford to draw trump. On the next hand, you're in a contract of 4♥, and the defense leads a club.

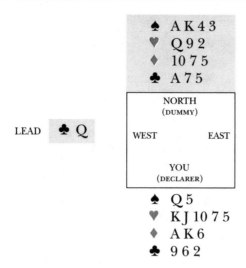

♠ A K 4 3
♥ Q 9 2
♦ 10 7 5
♣ A 7 5

NORTH
(DUMMY)

LEAD ♣ Q

WEST          EAST

YOU
(DECLARER)

♠ Q 5
♥ K J 10 7 5
♦ A K 6
♣ 9 6 2

You have a heart loser, a diamond loser, and two club losers. The spade suit provides an opportunity to discard one of your losers. After winning a trick with the ♣A, should you start drawing trump, or should you first discard one of your losers?

You have four losers and will have to let the opponents take the lead with their ♥A when you draw trump. Although you have too many losers, only three of them are quick—the heart loser and the two club losers. Your diamond loser is a slow loser. The opponents can't take a trick in that suit until your ♦A and ♦K are gone. Since you can discard any of your losers on the spade, you can plan to discard your diamond loser. There's no harm in playing the trump suit first, and it may be the only way to make the contract if all four hands look like this:

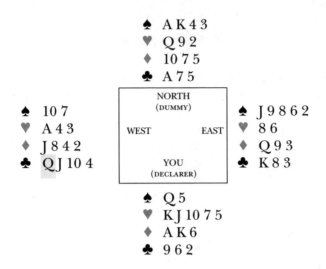

If you try to take three spade tricks before drawing trump, West will ruff the third round with the ♥3 after you've discarded one of your club losers. You'll still have to lose the ♥A, a diamond, and a club. That's one too many tricks.

Instead, win the ♣A and lead a trump, driving out West's ♥A. The defenders can take two club tricks, but whatever they lead next, you can win the trick and draw the rest of their trump. It's now safe to take your three spade winners, discarding the diamond loser from your hand. The remainder of the tricks are yours.

## Entries Again

When planning to discard losers, entries are always a consideration. Try this hand. The contract is 4♠, and the opening lead is the ♦K.

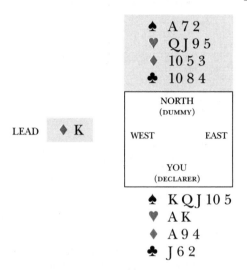

♠ A 7 2
♥ Q J 9 5
♦ 10 5 3
♣ 10 8 4

NORTH
(DUMMY)

LEAD ♦ K

WEST            EAST

YOU
(DECLARER)

♠ K Q J 10 5
♥ A K
♦ A 9 4
♣ J 6 2

The opening lead will drive out your ♦A and leave you with five quick losers. You plan to discard your two extra losers on dummy's ♥Q and ♥J, but there are some entry problems. The heart suit is blocked, and the only entry to dummy is the ♠A. You also need to draw trump before taking your last two heart winners. Even if the defenders' seven hearts divide 4–3, one defender will have no hearts left when you try to take your fourth heart trick.

Note the order in which you need to play your cards. Win the first diamond trick with the ♦A and draw two rounds of trump using two of the high cards in your hand, leaving the ♠A in the dummy. Unblock the heart suit by playing your ♥A and ♥K. Then cross over to dummy with the ♠A. If the defenders' trump divide 3–2, the last of their trump will be drawn when you take your ♠A. Now you're in the right place at the right time to take your two heart winners in the dummy and discard two of the losers from your hand. You'll end up taking five spade tricks, four heart tricks, and the ♦A, losing three tricks to the opponents at the end of the hand.

Here's another hand with an entry challenge. You're in a contract of 2♠, and the opening lead is the ♣Q.

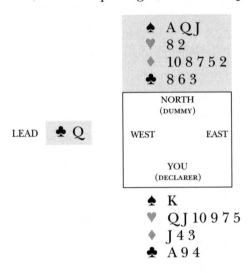

♠ A Q J
♥ 8 2
♦ 10 8 7 5 2
♣ 8 6 3

**NORTH**
(DUMMY)

LEAD ♣ Q

WEST          EAST

**YOU**
(DECLARER)

♠ K
♥ Q J 10 9 7 5
♦ J 4 3
♣ A 9 4

You can afford five losers but have seven: two heart losers, three diamond losers, and two club losers. They're all quick once your ♣A is gone. You need to get rid of two of your losers right away. There are extra winners in the spade suit, but you'll have to be careful in the way you play the spades, since your only entry to dummy lies in that suit.

Win the first trick with your ♣A, and lead the ♠K. To get around the entry problem, overtake your ♠K with dummy's ♠A. That puts you in the dummy, and you can take two spade tricks, discarding two of your losers. Now that you have the first four tricks, you can lead hearts and promote your other four tricks from that suit.

## Creating Winners for Losers

What do you do when you have too many losers, can't trump any in dummy, and have no winners on which to discard them? Time to start looking at ways of creating the extra winners that you need. Here's an example. You're in a contract of 3♦, and the opening lead is the ♥10.

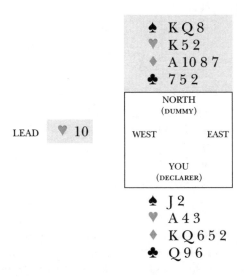

♠ K Q 8
♥ K 5 2
♦ A 10 8 7
♣ 7 5 2

NORTH
(DUMMY)

LEAD  ♥ 10

WEST          EAST

YOU
(DECLARER)

♠ J 2
♥ A 4 3
♦ K Q 6 5 2
♣ Q 9 6

You have a spade loser, a heart loser, and three club losers—one too many. There's no way to trump one of your losers in dummy, and there's no immediate winners on which you can discard a loser. But the spade can provide you with what you need. Once the ♠A has been driven out, dummy will have an extra winner on which to throw away one of your losers.

After winning the ♥A, draw the defenders' trump. Then drive out the defenders' ♠A, by playing the ♠J from your hand—high card from the short side. You promote two spade winners and can eventually discard your heart loser on the third round of spades. The only tricks the defenders take are a spade trick and three club tricks.

On the previous hand, you used promotion to develop the extra winner you needed. On this next hand, you'll need the help of a finesse. The contract is 4♠, and the defense gets off to a lead of the ♦Q.

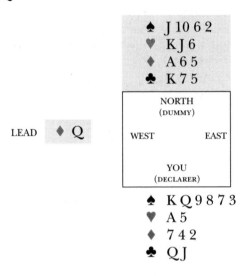

♠ J 10 6 2
♥ K J 6
♦ A 6 5
♣ K 7 5

NORTH
(DUMMY)

LEAD ♦ Q

WEST            EAST

YOU
(DECLARER)

♠ K Q 9 8 7 3
♥ A 5
♦ 7 4 2
♣ Q J

You have a spade loser, two diamond losers, and a club loser. You could use promotion to establish an extra winner in the club suit on which to discard a diamond loser, but the defense will win that race. They're about to drive out your ♦A, so all your losers are quick. If the defenders get the lead, they can take four tricks.

Since you have to do something about one of your diamond losers before giving up the lead, the only hope lies in the heart suit. After winning the ♦A, play a low heart to your ♥A, and lead the ♥5 back toward dummy. If a low heart appears on your left, finesse dummy's ♥J. This is a double or nothing play. If the finesse is successful, you can discard one of your diamond losers on dummy's ♥K and make the contract. If the finesse loses, you'll end up with five losers, rather than the four you started with.

In addition to promotion and finesses, you can always try establishing a long suit to give you the extra winners you need. On the following hand, you reach a contract of 4♥ and receive an opening lead of the ♣Q.

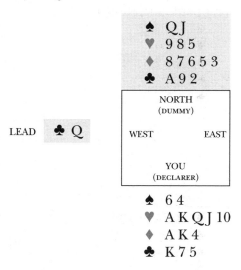

♠ QJ
♥ 985
♦ 87653
♣ A92

NORTH
(DUMMY)

LEAD    ♣ Q

WEST                EAST

YOU
(DECLARER)

♠ 64
♥ AKQJ10
♦ AK4
♣ K75

There are two spade losers, a diamond loser, and a club loser. You can't trump any of your losers in the dummy, and there are no winners on which to discard a loser. Dummy's five-card diamond suit, however, provides an opportunity for developing extra winners. The defenders have five diamonds between them, which hopefully will divide 3–2. One other thing to be careful about is the entries to dummy. The only entry you have is the ♣A. You'll need to keep that around until you're ready to use it.

Win the first trick with the ♣K in your hand. Draw the defenders' trump, and then play the ♦A, ♦K, and a third round of diamonds. If the defenders' diamonds divide 3–2, you'll be fine. In addition to the diamond trick, the defenders can take two spade tricks, but the rest of the tricks are yours. You can use dummy's ♣A as an entry to your established diamond winners. When you play one of your diamond winners, you discard the last club from your hand.

When developing tricks through length, the trump suit can sometimes come in handy. Instead of giving up tricks to the defenders, you may be able to establish the suit without losing a trick. Take a look at this hand. You've reached a contract of 7♠, so you can't afford to lose a trick, and the opening lead is the ♣K.

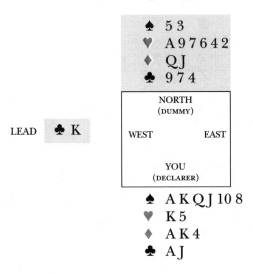

♠ 5 3
♥ A 9 7 6 4 2
♦ Q J
♣ 9 7 4

NORTH
(DUMMY)

LEAD   ♣ K

WEST          EAST

YOU
(DECLARER)

♠ A K Q J 10 8
♥ K 5
♦ A K 4
♣ A J

There's a club loser, and there's no way to trump it in the dummy. You also have no extra winner in the dummy on which to discard your loser. The long heart suit does offer some possibility. If the defenders' hearts are divided 3–2, you take your two winners in the suit and lead a third round, to drive out the defenders' remaining heart.

In a notrump contract, you'd have to give the third heart trick to the defenders. In a trump contract, there's another choice. You can trump the third round. This has the effect of getting rid of the last heart in the defenders' hands, without losing a trick to the defenders. Let's see how it works out when this is the complete hand:

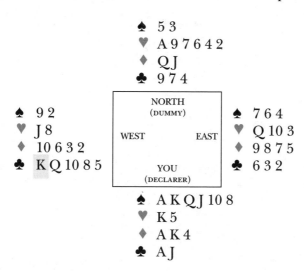

```
                    ♠  5 3
                    ♥  A 9 7 6 4 2
                    ♦  Q J
                    ♣  9 7 4
                         NORTH
   ♠  9 2             (DUMMY)        ♠  7 6 4
   ♥  J 8                            ♥  Q 10 3
   ♦  10 6 3 2    WEST      EAST     ♦  9 8 7 5
   ♣  K Q 10 8 5                     ♣  6 3 2
                         YOU
                      (DECLARER)
                    ♠  A K Q J 10 8
                    ♥  K 5
                    ♦  A K 4
                    ♣  A J
```

You win the first trick with the ♣A and play three of your high spades to remove the defenders' trump. Play the ♥K, high card from the short side and then the ♥5 over to dummy's ♥A. When both opponents follow suit, you can breathe a sigh of relief. Lead another heart from dummy, and when East's ♥Q appears, play a trump on the trick. You win this trick, and the defenders have no hearts left. Play your ♦4 over to dummy's ♦Q or ♦J, and lead one of your established hearts. On this trick, you discard the club loser from your hand. With no losers remaining, the rest of the tricks are yours.

Using the trump suit to help you establish a suit through length adds a whole new dimension to the play of the hand.

## Summary

In looking for ways to eliminate extra losers, one technique to keep in mind is discarding your losers on extra winners in the dummy.

| *Checklist* |
| --- |
| Promotion |
| Length |
| Finessing |
| Trumping Losers |
| ✓ Discarding Losers |

When planning to discard losers, keep the following guidelines in mind:

• Look for a suit that has more cards in the dummy than in your hand. You usually gain tricks by discarding losers from your hand, not from discarding dummy's low cards.

• You want to draw trump as early as possible, but if you have too many quick losers and will have to give up the lead while drawing trump, delay playing the trump suit until you've eliminated enough quick losers.

• If there aren't enough winners in dummy on which to discard your losers, look for opportunities to create extra winners in the dummy.

• When establishing winners through length, the trump suit can sometimes help you to avoid giving up tricks to the opponents.

# Practice Hands

**Hand 10.1**

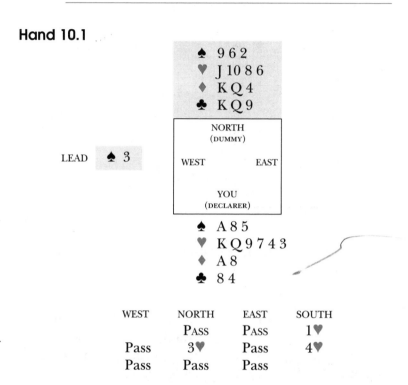

♠ 9 6 2
♥ J 10 8 6
♦ K Q 4
♣ K Q 9

| NORTH | |
| (DUMMY) | |

LEAD    ♠ 3

WEST         EAST

YOU
(DECLARER)

♠ A 8 5
♥ K Q 9 7 4 3
♦ A 8
♣ 8 4

| WEST | NORTH | EAST | SOUTH |
|------|-------|------|-------|
|  | PASS | PASS | 1♥ |
| Pass | 3♥ | Pass | 4♥ |
| Pass | Pass | Pass | |

West leads the ♠3 against your contract of 4♥. How do you plan to make the contract? Should you start by drawing trump?

## Solution 10.1

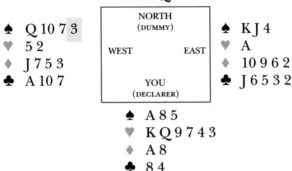

```
                    ♠  9 6 2
                    ♥  J 10 8 6
                    ♦  K Q 4
                    ♣  K Q 9
                         NORTH
  ♠  Q 10 7 3          (DUMMY)        ♠  K J 4
  ♥  5 2                              ♥  A
  ♦  J 7 5 3   WEST          EAST     ♦  10 9 6 2
  ♣  A 10 7                           ♣  J 6 5 3 2
                          YOU
                       (DECLARER)
                    ♠  A 8 5
                    ♥  K Q 9 7 4 3
                    ♦  A 8
                    ♣  8 4
```

Focus on the losers in your trump contract. You can afford to lose three tricks, but you have four losers: two spade losers, a heart loser, and a club loser. You can't trump any of your losers in the dummy, so look for places to discard your losers. There are opportunities in both diamonds and clubs, since there are more cards in dummy than in your hand in both suits. In diamonds, there is an extra winner in dummy. In clubs, you might be able to create an extra winner by leading twice toward the ♣K and ♣Q, hoping the ♣A is on your left.

You can't afford to give up a trick, however, before eliminating one of your losers. Once the defenders have driven out your ♠A, you'll have four quick losers. That tells you the order in which you need to play your cards. After winning a trick with the ♣A, take your three diamond tricks immediately. Start with the ♦A—high card from the short side—and play the ♦8 over to dummy's ♦K and ♦Q. On the third diamond trick, discard one of your spade losers. Now you can lead trump. The only tricks you lose are a spade trick, a heart trick, and a club trick.

It's important to discard a spade, not a club, on the third round of diamonds. Although you have a loser in the club suit, discarding one of your low clubs won't help—you'll still have a loser in the suit. Discarding a spade eliminates the appropriate loser.

## Hand 10.2

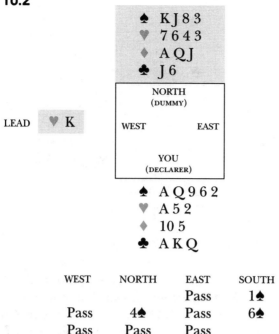

♠ K J 8 3
♥ 7 6 4 3
♦ A Q J
♣ J 6

NORTH
(DUMMY)

LEAD ♥ K

WEST          EAST

YOU
(DECLARER)

♠ A Q 9 6 2
♥ A 5 2
♦ 10 5
♣ A K Q

| WEST | NORTH | EAST | SOUTH |
|------|-------|------|-------|
|      |       | Pass | 1♠    |
| Pass | 4♠    | Pass | 6♠    |
| Pass | Pass  | Pass |       |

You're in a contract of 6♠, and the opening lead is the ♥K. What do you plan to do about your losers? Should you delay drawing trump?

## Solution 10.2

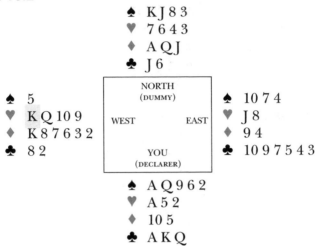

♠ K J 8 3
♥ 7 6 4 3
♦ A Q J
♣ J 6

NORTH
(DUMMY)

WEST          EAST

YOU
(DECLARER)

♠ 5
♥ K Q 10 9
♦ K 8 7 6 3 2
♣ 8 2

♠ 10 7 4
♥ J 8
♦ 9 4
♣ 10 9 7 5 4 3

♠ A Q 9 6 2
♥ A 5 2
♦ 10 5
♣ A K Q

You have three losers: two heart losers and a diamond loser. That's two more than you can afford. Going down the checklist, you can eliminate your diamond loser with the help of a successful finesse. That's a good start. Looking further ahead, if you repeat the finesse, you'll end up with an extra diamond winner in the dummy, on which you can discard one of your heart losers. That's the plan. You'll need a little luck, but you'll also have to be careful in the order in which you play your cards.

After winning a trick with the ♥A, you can afford to draw trump. You don't have to give up the lead to the opponents while drawing trump, so it's a good idea to do so. Now lead a low diamond from your hand toward dummy, and take your first diamond finesse. When this works, things are looking up. Travel back to your hand using one of your high clubs, and repeat the diamond finesse. Play dummy's ♦A, discarding one of your heart losers. All the defenders get is one heart trick, and you make your small slam contract.

Notice what would happen if you tried to get rid of your loser before drawing trump. Your two diamond finesses would be successful, but when you play your ♦A, planning to discard your loser, East would put a trump on the trick. There goes your contract!

## Hand 10.3

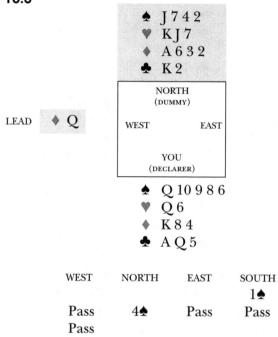

♠ J 7 4 2
♥ K J 7
♦ A 6 3 2
♣ K 2

NORTH
(DUMMY)

LEAD   ♦ Q

WEST        EAST

YOU
(DECLARER)

♠ Q 10 9 8 6
♥ Q 6
♦ K 8 4
♣ A Q 5

| WEST | NORTH | EAST | SOUTH |
|------|-------|------|-------|
|      |       |      | 1♠    |
| Pass | 4♠    | Pass | Pass  |
| Pass |       |      |       |

West leads the ♦Q against your contract of 4♠. Are your losers quick or slow? Can you afford to start drawing trump? Think through the hand carefully.

## Solution 10.3

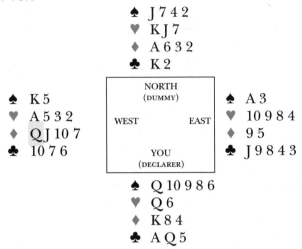

```
                     ♠ J 7 4 2
                     ♥ K J 7
                     ♦ A 6 3 2
                     ♣ K 2
                  ┌─────────────────┐
                  │     NORTH       │
♠ K 5             │    (DUMMY)      │       ♠ A 3
♥ A 5 3 2         │                 │       ♥ 10 9 8 4
♦ Q J 10 7        │ WEST      EAST  │       ♦ 9 5
♣ 10 7 6          │                 │       ♣ J 9 8 4 3
                  │      YOU        │
                  │   (DECLARER)    │
                  └─────────────────┘
                     ♠ Q 10 9 8 6
                     ♥ Q 6
                     ♦ K 8 4
                     ♣ A Q 5
```

There are two losers in spades, one in hearts, and one in dia-monds—one more than you can afford. There's nothing to be done with the heart and spade losers, so you need to eliminate a diamond loser from your hand. There are no immediate winners in dummy on which to discard a loser, but the heart suit provides the potential to promote an extra winner. Although you have four losers, only three are quick. If you let the defenders gain the lead in the trump suit, they can't take a diamond trick because you still have a dia-mond winner left. They can lead another diamond, however, to drive out your remaining high card. Now all your losers are quick, and you still haven't established an extra trick in hearts. You can't afford to start by drawing trump.

Instead, win the first diamond trick in your hand, and lead the ♥Q, promoting winners in the heart suit by starting with the high card from the short side. When the defenders take the ♥A, you have established an extra winner in the dummy. If they lead another dia-mond, win in dummy and take the heart winners, discarding the diamond loser from your hand. It's now safe to lead trump. You end up losing two trump tricks and the ♥A. You can afford that.

It doesn't make much difference where you win the first diamond trick, since you have an entry to dummy with the ♣K. Still, it doesn't hurt to win in your hand, following the general principle of keeping an entry on the same side of the table as the length in the suit you're establishing.

## Hand 10.4

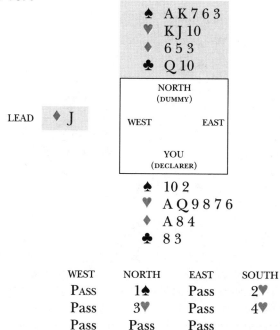

♠ A K 7 6 3
♥ K J 10
♦ 6 5 3
♣ Q 10

NORTH
(DUMMY)

LEAD   ♦ J

WEST         EAST

YOU
(DECLARER)

♠ 10 2
♥ A Q 9 8 7 6
♦ A 8 4
♣ 8 3

| WEST | NORTH | EAST | SOUTH |
|------|-------|------|-------|
| Pass | 1♠ | Pass | 2♥ |
| Pass | 3♥ | Pass | 4♥ |
| Pass | Pass | Pass | |

You're in a contract of 4♥, and the opening lead is the ♦J. You appear to have four losers. The only suit in which you have the possibility of establishing an extra winner is the spade suit. Can you make the contract if the defenders' spades divide 3–3? What if they divide 4–2? How do you plan to reach your extra winner once it's established? You'll need to plan the order of play very carefully on this hand.

## Solution 10.4

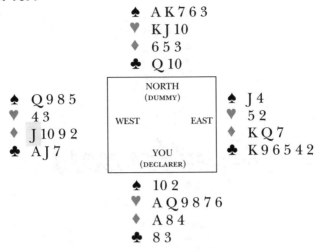

♠ A K 7 6 3
♥ K J 10
♦ 6 5 3
♣ Q 10

NORTH
(DUMMY)

♠ Q 9 8 5
♥ 4 3
♦ J 10 9 2
♣ A J 7

WEST                EAST

♠ J 4
♥ 5 2
♦ K Q 7
♣ K 9 6 5 4 2

YOU
(DECLARER)

♠ 10 2
♥ A Q 9 8 7 6
♦ A 8 4
♣ 8 3

You have four losers: two diamonds and two clubs. Going down the checklist, there's nothing you can do unless you can find a way to discard a loser on an extra winner in dummy. Since there are no extra winners in dummy, you need to create one. The only possibility is the length in spades. If the defenders' spades divide 3–3 or 4–2, you may be able to establish the suit. You have to be careful about entries on this hand. You need to use the trump suit to provide transportation to the dummy. You may need to get to the dummy more than once to establish the spade suit, and you need to get there once you've created the extra winner.

Note the order you need to play the cards. After winning a diamond trick, you can't afford to draw all the trump because you need the hearts for entries. Instead, take two spade tricks with dummy's ♠A and ♠K, and lead another spade. Trump this trick in your hand. If spades divide 3–3, your troubles are over. You can draw trump, ending in dummy, and take the two established spade winners, discarding two losers from your hand. You make an overtrick. On the actual hand, spades divide 4–2, and you have more work to do. Travel back to the dummy using one of the heart entries, then lead another spade and ruff it in your hand. After this trick, the defenders have no spades left. Play the ♥A and a low heart over to dummy. Trump are drawn, and you take your carefully established spade winner to discard a loser from your hand. There's a lot to do on this hand, but once you've made a plan, everything starts to fall into place.

# Togetherness

"A long pull, and a strong pull, and pull altogether."

— CHARLES DICKENS,
David Copperfield

All of the cards are part of a team, and you're the coach. The declarer makes a decision on when to play a particular card by focusing on the big picture. Let's see how all the techniques can be put together, both within a suit and within the whole hand.

## Combinations Within a Suit

Suppose you need tricks from this suit:

DUMMY
♥ 6 5 3

DECLARER
♥ K Q J 4 2

You have no sure tricks, but you can develop two tricks through promotion, by playing one of your high hearts to drive out the defenders' ♥A. In fact, you'd expect more than two tricks from this suit because of length. If the defender's hearts divide 3-2, you'll get four tricks from the suit: two through promotion and two through length. If the defenders' hearts are divided 4–1, you can still get three tricks from the suit. After driving out the defenders' ♥A, you can take two tricks with your promoted winners, and then lead another round of the suit, giving up a trick. Your remaining heart will be a winner.

You may actually be able to take four tricks from the suit, even if the defenders cards divide 4–1. For example, suppose this is the complete layout of the heart suit:

DUMMY
♥ 6 5 3

WEST                          EAST
♥ *10 9 8 7*                 ♥ *A*

DECLARER
♥ K Q J 4 2

If you start the suit by playing one of your high hearts to drive out East's ♥A and then taking tricks with your two promoted winners, you'll eventually lose a second trick to West's remaining heart. You can avoid this by incorporating the technique of the finesse into your play of the suit. Start by leading a low heart from the dummy toward your hand. East wins this first trick with the ♥A, and you don't have to waste any of your high hearts. You can use them to extract West's remaining hearts, and your last low heart is also a winner.

Using the finesse would also be a good idea if this were the layout:

DUMMY
♥ 6 5 3

WEST          EAST
♥ 7          ♥ A 10 9 8

DECLARER
♥ K Q J 4 2

When you lead a low heart from dummy, you'll get four tricks if East flies up with the ♥A on the first round of the suit. If East plays a low heart, you win the first trick with one of your high cards. You can then travel back to dummy and repeat the process. If East doesn't take the ♥A on the second round of hearts, travel back to dummy once more, and lead the last low heart from dummy. East is powerless to prevent you from winning four of the five heart tricks.

It won't always be practical to play the suit in this manner, since you need three entries to the dummy, but you can see how some combinations involve putting together the ideas of promotion, length, and the finesse. You can also bring the trump suit into consideration. Suppose spades are the trump suit, and you need to avoid losing a trick when you hold the following diamond suit:

DUMMY
♦ 6 5

DECLARER
♦ A Q 2

You'd start by crossing over to dummy and leading a low diamond toward your hand, finessing the ♦Q if a low diamond appears on your right. If your finesse is successful, you can take a trick with the ♦A, and lead your last diamond, trumping it in the dummy. You use a combination of the finesse and trumping a loser in the dummy to get the most out of this suit.

A lot of the fun in playing a hand comes from finding imaginative ways of combining the various techniques. In this next example, you're going to integrate promotion, the finesse, and ruffing a loser when handling a suit. You even get to take a finesse against an ace! Suppose spades are the trump suit—and you still have one left in dummy.

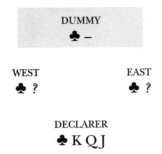

DUMMY

♣ —

WEST          EAST

♣ ?          ♣ ?

DECLARER

♣ K Q J

You can get two tricks through promotion by simply driving out the defenders' ♣A, but with the club void in dummy, you may not have to give up a trick in the process. Lead the ♣K, hoping the complete layout is something like this:

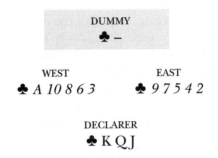

DUMMY

♣ —

WEST                    EAST

♣ A 10 8 6 3        ♣ 9 7 5 4 2

DECLARER

♣ K Q J

What can West do? If West covers your ♣K, you trump the trick in dummy—ruffing your loser—and your remaining two clubs are promoted into winners. If West doesn't cover the ♣K, you take a finesse by discarding a card from another suit. Since East can't win the trick, your finesse is successful, and you can repeat it by leading the ♣Q. This combination of techniques is called a *ruffing finesse*. It's a finesse because, if East holds the ♣A, your finesse will lose, although you'll still end up with two promoted winners.

Let's try a few more examples.

DUMMY

♠ A Q 7 5 2

DECLARER

♠ 8 4 3

You could hope to get four tricks from this suit with the help of a successful finesse and a friendly 3–2 division of the defenders' spades. Play a low spade to dummy's ♠Q. If this succeeds, play the ♠A, and give up a spade trick to the defenders. Dummy's last two spades will be winners, if the missing spades divide 3–2. Even if your finesse is not successful, you can still hope to establish extra tricks through length. Similarly, the finesse may work, but the spades may divide badly. If they're 5–0, you'll get only two tricks. If they're 4–1, you'll have to give up two tricks to establish one extra trick through length.

DUMMY
♥ A 7 4 3 2

DECLARER
♥ Q 6 5

Take a finesse by leading a low heart toward your ♥Q. If the ♥K is on your right, you'll get tricks with both your ♥A and ♥Q. Furthermore, if the defenders' hearts divide 3–2, you'll get four tricks, losing only one trick to the ♥K.

DUMMY
♦ Q 7 6 3

DECLARER
♦ K 10 5 2

Start by leading a low diamond toward dummy's ♦Q. If this is won on your right with the ♦A, too bad, but you'll still have promoted the ♦K into a trick. If the ♦Q wins the first trick, it looks like the ♦A is on your left. Lead a low diamond from dummy, and finesse the ♦10, hoping the ♦J is on your right. If your finesse works, driving out the ♦A on your left, you can take another trick with the ♦K, and your last diamond will be an established winner through length.

DUMMY
♣ 6 4 3

DECLARER
♣ Q J 5 2

Lead a low club from dummy toward your hand, playing the ♣Q or ♣J, if a low club appears on your right. If your first finesse loses to a high club on your right, get back to dummy, and try leading another low club toward your remaining honor. If either high club is on your right, you'll get one club winner in this manner. If the defenders' clubs divide 3–3, you can get a second trick through length. Even if they don't divide 3–3, you might have the opportunity of trumping your fourth club in the dummy, if you're playing in a suit contract.

The following hand shows how you can use a combination of techniques to land your contract. You're in 1NT, and the opening lead is the ♠Q.

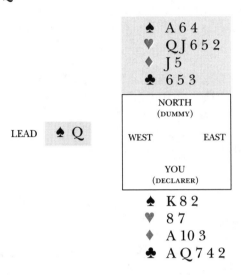

♠ A 6 4
♥ Q J 6 5 2
♦ J 5
♣ 6 5 3

NORTH
(DUMMY)

LEAD ♠ Q

WEST      EAST

YOU
(DECLARER)

♠ K 8 2
♥ 8 7
♦ A 10 3
♣ A Q 7 4 2

You start with four sure tricks: two spades, one diamond, and one club. Looking down the checklist of ways for getting the three extra tricks you need, you might first think about the heart suit. You could consider leading twice toward dummy's ♥Q and ♥J, hoping either of the higher hearts are on your left, and you might get some extra tricks through length. Looking ahead, however, even if you could establish extra tricks in hearts, it's unlikely you can ever reach them. As soon as the defenders win a heart trick, they'll probably drive out your remaining high spade, and you'll have no entry left to dummy.

Instead, the club suit offers some possibilities. You can get an extra trick with the help of a successful finesse against the ♣K on your right, and you can get two more tricks in the suit through length if the defenders' clubs divide 3–2. Since you also have lots of entries to your hand, that seems to be the route to go.

Note the order in which you have to play. Win the first trick in dummy with the ♠A, and play a low club to your ♣Q, taking the finesse. When this succeeds, play the ♣A and another club, giving up a trick to the defenders. As long as the clubs divide 3–2, you'll have all the tricks you need when you regain the lead.

## Entries Again

As might be expected, entries usually play an important role when you're combining various techniques. Look at this hand. You've reached a contract of 3NT and are faced with the opening lead of the ♦4.

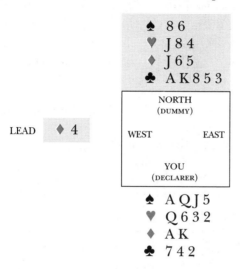

♠ 8 6
♥ J 8 4
♦ J 6 5
♣ A K 8 5 3

NORTH
(DUMMY)

LEAD   ♦ 4

WEST                    EAST

YOU
(DECLARER)

♠ A Q J 5
♥ Q 6 3 2
♦ A K
♣ 7 4 2

You have a sure trick in spades, two in diamonds, and two in clubs. You need four more. If the ♠K is on your right, you can get two extra tricks with the help of a repeated finesse. The clubs also provide an opportunity for two extra tricks through length, if the defenders' clubs divide as you might expect, 3–2. You've got a lot of work to do, so you'll have to be careful in the order in which you play your tricks.

You need two entries to dummy to take the repeated spade finesses. The ♣A and ♣K can be used for this purpose. At the same time, you want to develop the club suit by giving up a trick to the defenders. You can't afford to play both the ♣A and ♣K before giving up a trick in the suit because you'd be left with no entry to dummy's established clubs. Instead, you'll have to duck a club trick early, keeping at least one of your high clubs as an entry.

Having determined what you need to do, there are a couple of ways you can go about it. After winning the first trick with one of your high diamonds, you could give up a club trick right away by playing low clubs from both hands. You have to do that at some point, and it's usually best to take your losses early. The defenders will win this trick and presumably lead another diamond, establishing their winners in the suit by getting rid of your remaining high diamond.

Enough giving up tricks to the opponents. You now cross to the dummy with one of the high clubs. Assuming the clubs divide 3–2, you're in a position to take all four of your club tricks, but you can't afford to play any more clubs yet. While you're in dummy, lead a low spade and finesse your ♠J. If this works, things are looking up. Cross back to dummy with your last high club. Since you're in the dummy for the last time, take your two club winners. Finally, lead dummy's last spade, and take your second spade finesse. The ♠A will be your ninth trick.

On this next hand, you'll have to be even more careful about the order in which you play your cards. It's the difference between going down two tricks in your contract and making an overtrick. You're again in 3NT, this time with the lead of the ♥Q.

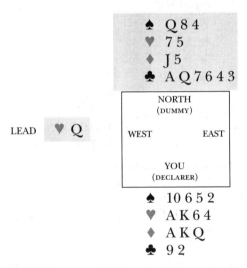

♠ Q 8 4
♥ 7 5
♦ J 5
♣ A Q 7 6 4 3

NORTH
(DUMMY)

LEAD ♥ Q

WEST      EAST

YOU
(DECLARER)

♠ 10 6 5 2
♥ A K 6 4
♦ A K Q
♣ 9 2

There are six top tricks: two hearts, three diamonds, and the ♣A. You might be able to set up an extra trick from the spade suit, but clubs look like the better choice, since you need three extra tricks. You can get one extra trick if the ♣K is favorably placed on your left. If the defenders' clubs are favorably divided, 3–2, you can get three more tricks from the suit by giving up a trick to the opponents.

The only challenge is that there's no entry to the dummy outside of the club suit itself. This requires careful thought about the order in which to play your cards. After winning the first heart trick, if you start by taking the club finesse and it's successful, you'll end up with only seven tricks. You can take your ♣A and give up a trick in the suit, but even when the defenders' clubs divide 3–2, you have no way to reach the established clubs.

The answer is to change the order in which you play the clubs. Instead of taking the finesse first and later giving up a club trick, consider the effect of playing a low club from both hands on the first round of the suit. When you regain the lead, you can play your last club and take the finesse. When this succeeds and clubs divide 3–2, you can play the ♣A and take all the rest of the club tricks. You end up with ten tricks: two hearts, three diamonds, and five clubs. Here's the complete hand:

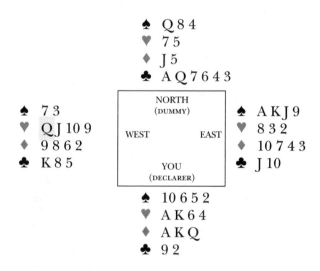

```
              ♠ Q 8 4
              ♥ 7 5
              ♦ J 5
              ♣ A Q 7 6 4 3
                  NORTH
                 (DUMMY)
♠ 7 3                          ♠ A K J 9
♥ Q J 10 9   WEST      EAST    ♥ 8 3 2
♦ 9 8 6 2                      ♦ 10 7 4 3
♣ K 8 5          YOU           ♣ J 10
              (DECLARER)
              ♠ 10 6 5 2
              ♥ A K 6 4
              ♦ A K Q
              ♣ 9 2
```

If East had held the ♣K, you wouldn't have enjoyed the hand very much. After ducking the first club and then losing the club finesse, you wouldn't even get a trick from your ♣A. You'd end up with five tricks, one fewer than the number with which you started. Your task, however, is to try to make the contract. Only by ducking the first round of clubs and finessing on the second round, do you give yourself a chance.

## Two-for-One

There are many hands on which you'll have more than one way to go about developing the extra tricks you need. Whenever possible, you want to give yourself more than one chance. This might require you to order your play carefully. On the following hand, you're in a contract of 3NT, with the opening lead of the ♦3. How can you give yourself two chances to make the contract?

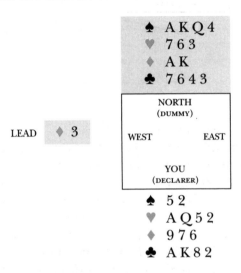

♠ A K Q 4
♥ 7 6 3
♦ A K
♣ 7 6 4 3

NORTH
(DUMMY)

LEAD ♦ 3

WEST          EAST

YOU
(DECLARER)

♠ 5 2
♥ A Q 5 2
♦ 9 7 6
♣ A K 8 2

You have eight sure tricks: three spades, one heart, two diamonds, and two clubs. Your one extra trick could come from a finesse in the heart suit, if the ♥K is favorably located on your right. It could also come from the club suit, if the defenders' five clubs divide 3–2.

After winning a diamond trick, suppose you decide to try the heart finesse first. You'll be fine if it works, but what if it loses? The defense will lead another diamond, and now it may be too late to establish a club winner, even if the clubs divide favorably. When you give up the club trick, the defenders may be able to take enough diamond tricks—along with their heart and club tricks—to defeat the contract. The complete hand might be something like this:

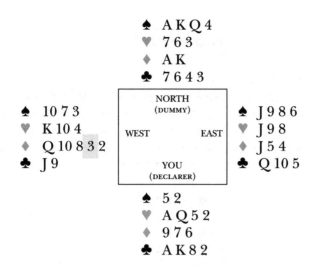

Instead, you should reverse the order in which you try for an extra trick. After winning the diamond trick, start with the club suit by playing the ♣A and ♣K. If both opponents follow suit, their clubs must be divided 3–2, and you can develop your extra trick for certain by playing another club. There's no need to risk the heart finesse. On the other hand, if one of the defenders fails to follow suit on the first or second round of clubs, you'll know the suit is breaking badly. You can now switch tactics and try the heart finesse. You'll be twice as successful if you always give yourself two chances to make the contract, rather than one.

## The Right Choice

Sometimes you'll have a choice of ways to develop the extra tricks you need, but you won't be able to combine your chances. If that's the situation, go with the choice that gives you the best chance of making the contract. In the following hand, you're in 3NT and have to decide what to do after the opening lead of the ♠4.

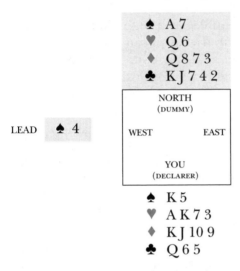

♠ A 7
♥ Q 6
♦ Q 8 7 3
♣ K J 7 4 2

NORTH
(DUMMY)

LEAD   ♠ 4        WEST          EAST

YOU
(DECLARER)

♠ K 5
♥ A K 7 3
♦ K J 10 9
♣ Q 6 5

There are five sure tricks: two spades and three hearts. The diamond suit can provide three additional tricks through promotion. The club suit can provide two tricks through promotion and might provide two more through length, if the defenders' clubs divide 3–2. Given enough time, you could certainly develop all the tricks you need. Unfortunately, the defense is also busy at work. The spade lead will drive out one of your high cards in the suit, and when you go about promoting one of your suits, the defenders can win their ace and drive out your remaining high card. If you let them back in, they'll be able to take enough spade tricks to defeat the contract.

At first glance, it might appear safer to promote extra winners in the diamond suit. Since you have all the high cards except the ace, you can promote three tricks for sure. You require four extra tricks, however, so playing diamonds after winning the first spade trick won't do the job. Instead, you'll have to start with the club suit. If you drive out the ♣A and the defenders' clubs divide 3–2, you can make the contract.

Technically, you have a good chance of making the contract even if the clubs divide badly. After winning the first spade trick in either hand, lead a low club toward one of your high cards. If the next player holds the singleton ♣A, it will appear, and you won't have to waste one of your high clubs. You'll take four club tricks even if the suit divided 4–1. Better yet, if the next player has the ♣A and doesn't play it, you'll play a high club and win the trick. Now that you've won a club trick, you can switch to diamonds and promote your three winners in that suit. You'll end up with nine tricks no matter how the minor suits divide.

The important point, however, is that choosing to play diamonds at trick two gives you no real chance of making the contract. Choosing clubs gives you an excellent chance of making the contract. Easy choice.

Try this next hand. The contract is 4♥, and the opening lead is the ♦10.

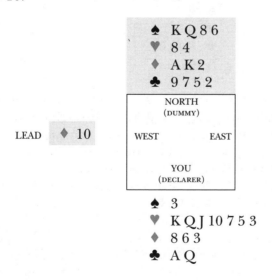

You have a spade loser, a heart loser, a diamond loser, and a club loser. One of them will have to go. You can't do anything about the losers in spades and hearts, but you could eliminate the club loser by taking the finesse, if the ♣K is favorably placed on your right.

That's a 50–50 chance. You also have the opportunity of discarding one of your losers by establishing an extra spade winner in dummy. Which suit do you go after?

There's only one correct choice. Leading one of your high spades after winning the first diamond trick practically guarantees the contract. You're certain of establishing your other spade as a winner, and unless the spades or diamonds divide very badly, you'll be able to discard your diamond loser on the spade. You could then try the club finesse for an overtrick.

If you were to try the club finesse first, you'd likely go down if the finesse lost. The defenders would lead another diamond, driving out your last high diamond in dummy, and it would be too late to promote a spade winner. You'd no longer have an entry left in the dummy to reach your winner. Make the choice that gives you the best chance of making the contract.

Here's a final example of making the right choice. The contract is 4♠, and the opening lead is the ♥4.

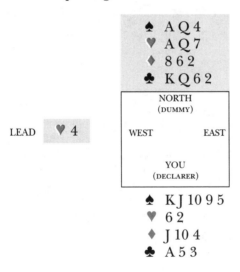

There are no losers in clubs or spades, but there's a heart loser and three diamond losers. To get rid of your extra loser, there are two choices. You can try the heart finesse, or you can hope the defenders' clubs divide 3–3 so that you can discard your heart loser on dummy's fourth club. What's it to be?

Here the decision is quite close. The heart finesse is a slight favorite. It will work half the time. You'd expect the six outstanding clubs to divide 4–2 or worse, more frequently than they'd divide exactly 3–3. I'd take the finesse, unless I had some indication from the auction that it was unlikely to work—for example, if the opponent on my right had opened the bidding, or overcalled in hearts.

Notice how the defenders, by leading a heart, took away your opportunity to combine chances. If they led a spade or a club, you could draw trump and then try the club suit. If the clubs failed to divide 3–3, you could fall back on the heart finesse. You have to make your choice right away. I hope you make the right one at the table!

## Summary

When using the checklist of techniques for creating winners and eliminating losers, look for opportunities to combine the techniques within a single suit and opportunities to combine your chances in more than one suit.

| | *Checklist* |
|---|---|
| ✓ | Promotion |
| ✓ | Length |
| ✓ | Finessing |
| ✓ | Trumping Losers |
| ✓ | Discarding Losers |

When you have a choice of suits to play, keep in mind the following principles:

- Try to give yourself more than one chance by combining your options in the right order.
- Go with the choice that gives you the best chance of making the contract.

# Practice Hands

## Hand 11.1

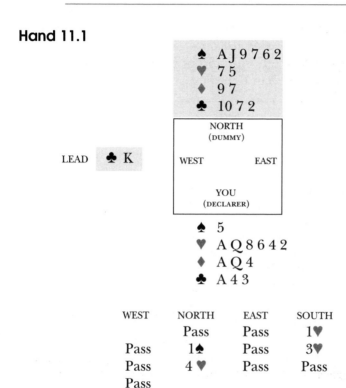

♠ A J 9 7 6 2
♥ 7 5
♦ 9 7
♣ 10 7 2

NORTH
(DUMMY)

LEAD ♣ K

WEST          EAST

YOU
(DECLARER)

♠ 5
♥ A Q 8 6 4 2
♦ A Q 4
♣ A 4 3

| WEST | NORTH | EAST | SOUTH |
|------|-------|------|-------|
|      | Pass  | Pass | 1♥    |
| Pass | 1♠    | Pass | 3♥    |
| Pass | 4 ♥   | Pass | Pass  |
| Pass |       |      |       |

Partner's raise to the game level has expressed a lot of confidence in your play as declarer. You'll need some luck to make your 4♥ contract, but can you justify partner's faith if the cards are favorably placed?

## Solution 11.1

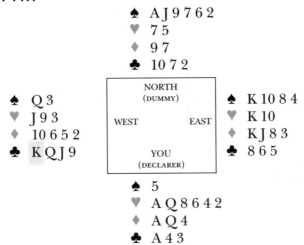

♠ AJ9762
♥ 75
♦ 97
♣ 1072

NORTH
(DUMMY)

WEST          EAST

YOU
(DECLARER)

♠ Q3
♥ J93
♦ 10652
♣ KQJ9

♠ K1084
♥ K10
♦ KJ83
♣ 865

♠ 5
♥ AQ8642
♦ AQ4
♣ A43

Assuming the defender's five trump are divided 3–2, you have two losers in the suit. You also have two diamond and two club losers. That's three too many. You can't use dummy's long spade suit because there's only one sure entry to dummy. So, there's nothing you can do about the club losers. You can avoid a heart loser with the help of a finesse. If East has the ♥K and the hearts divide 3–2, you can escape with one trump loser. Diamonds also offer possibilities. If East holds the ♦K, you can take a finesse to eliminate one loser. With dummy holding a doubleton, you can trump the other loser. You need to be lucky, but you have a further challenge to overcome. Dummy is short of entries.

Be careful in the order you play your tricks. After winning a trick with the ♣A, travel to dummy's ♠A. Now that you're in the dummy, lead a low diamond and take the finesse. When this succeeds, you're over the first hurdle. Play the ♦A and trump your remaining diamond in dummy. That's the second hurdle, and now you're back in dummy. Lead dummy's last heart, and take the finesse. When this works, you're almost there. Play the ♥A and another heart. When hearts divide 3–2, you've made the contract. Time to congratulate partner on the decision to raise to the game level. You had to take the diamond finesse before the heart finesse. If you finesse hearts first, there's no way back to dummy to take a diamond finesse. On this hand, you have to combine two finesses with trumping a loser in the dummy and suit establishment through length.

## Solution 11.2

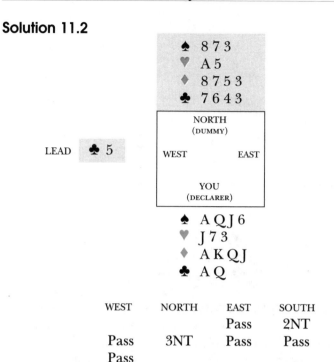

♠ 8 7 3
♥ A 5
♦ 8 7 5 3
♣ 7 6 4 3

NORTH
(DUMMY)

LEAD  ♣ 5

WEST          EAST

YOU
(DECLARER)

♠ A Q J 6
♥ J 7 3
♦ A K Q J
♣ A Q

| WEST | NORTH | EAST | SOUTH |
|------|-------|------|-------|
|      |       | Pass | 2NT   |
| Pass | 3NT   | Pass | Pass  |
| Pass |       |      |       |

You're in a contract of 3NT, and the opening lead is the ♣5. Does the spade finesse give you the best chance of making the contract?

## Solution 11.2

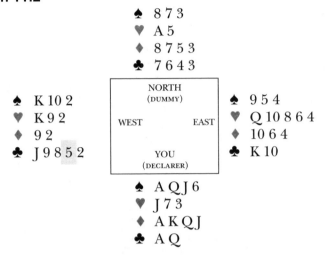

♠ 8 7 3
♥ A 5
♦ 8 7 5 3
♣ 7 6 4 3

NORTH
(DUMMY)

♠ K 10 2
♥ K 9 2
♦ 9 2
♣ J 9 8 5 2

WEST          EAST

♠ 9 5 4
♥ Q 10 8 6 4
♦ 10 6 4
♣ K 10

YOU
(DECLARER)

♠ A Q J 6
♥ J 7 3
♦ A K Q J
♣ A Q

Initially, you have a sure spade trick, a heart trick, four diamond tricks, and a club trick. If the defense had led something other than a club, you'd have to take a finesse in that suit for a second trick. After the opening club lead, however, they've done the work for you. No matter whether East produces the ♣K or a lower club on the first trick, you're going to get two club tricks. That brings your total to eight.

The spade suit is the only possibility for extra tricks. If the ♠K is on your right, you can travel to dummy using the ♥A and take the finesse. If it works, you have nine tricks. If it doesn't, you'll have promoted an extra winner in the suit. The only problem with this approach is that you have to use dummy's ♥A during all this. If the finesse loses, as it would on the actual hand, the defenders may now take four heart tricks, defeating the contract. You need only one extra trick from the spade suit, and you want to hold on to dummy's ♥A to stop the opponents from taking tricks in that suit. You can get an extra spade trick without any risk by simply playing the ♠A and then the ♠Q. You'll drive out the defenders' ♠K, promoting your ♠J into the one extra winner you need.

Simplicity pays off on this hand. If you forget about the spade finesse and use promotion to develop an extra trick, you make an overtrick when spades luckily divide 3–3. The last spade becomes a trick through length. If you cross to dummy's ♥A to try the finesse, you end up with an undertrick. West wins the ♠K and the defenders take four heart tricks.

## Hand 11.3

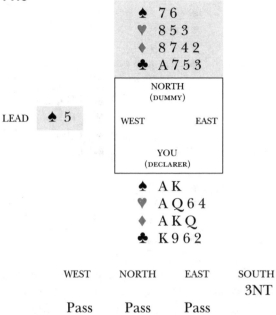

♠ 7 6
♥ 8 5 3
♦ 8 7 4 2
♣ A 7 5 3

NORTH
(DUMMY)

LEAD ♠ 5

WEST          EAST

YOU
(DECLARER)

♠ A K
♥ A Q 6 4
♦ A K Q
♣ K 9 6 2

| WEST | NORTH | EAST | SOUTH |
|------|-------|------|-------|
|      |       |      | 3NT   |
| Pass | Pass  | Pass |       |

With such a powerful hand, it would be a shame not to make your contract. There are lots of possibilities for taking the nine tricks you need in 3NT. How do you give yourself the best chance of succeeding after the opening lead of the ♠5?

## Solution 11.3

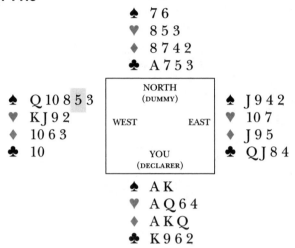

```
                    ♠ 7 6
                    ♥ 8 5 3
                    ♦ 8 7 4 2
                    ♣ A 7 5 3
                        NORTH
♠ Q 10 8 5 3        (DUMMY)         ♠ J 9 4 2
♥ K J 9 2      WEST         EAST     ♥ 10 7
♦ 10 6 3                             ♦ J 9 5
♣ 10                YOU              ♣ Q J 8 4
                  (DECLARER)
                    ♠ A K
                    ♥ A Q 6 4
                    ♦ A K Q
                    ♣ K 9 6 2
```

There are eight winners: two spades, a heart, three diamonds, and two clubs. One possibility is the heart finesse. That's a 50–50 proposition—either the ♥K is favorably located, or it isn't. If it isn't, you won't have time to set up an extra trick through length, even if hearts divide 3–3. You have to give up a second trick. By then the defenders will establish enough spade winners to defeat the contract. A second possibility is diamonds. The diamonds could divide 3–3 and you'd establish dummy's fourth diamond through length. You can reach the winner with the ♣A. That's an unlikely source for an extra trick because you expect the defenders' diamonds to be divided slightly unevenly, 4–2, rather than 3–3. The final chance comes in clubs. If the defenders' five clubs divide 3–2, as you might expect, you can establish a trick through length. The club suit is actually the best choice if you could try only one suit.

On this hand, you can combine chances. It might seem best to play the ♣K, then a club to dummy's ♣A. If clubs divide favorably, you give up a club trick and claim the contract. If they don't, you're in dummy and can try the heart finesse, falling back on your second chance. You can do better than that, however. After winning a spade trick, play the three top diamonds. If the suit divides 3–3, use dummy's club entry to get over to your ninth trick. If diamonds don't divide, try clubs, by playing the ♣K and ♣A. If that doesn't work, try the heart finesse. You give yourself three chances. On the actual hand, it's the most unlikely chance that comes home.

**Hand 11.4**

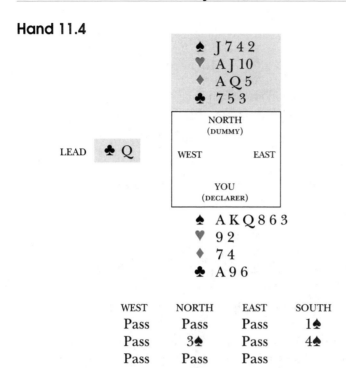

♠ J742
♥ AJ10
♦ AQ5
♣ 753

NORTH
(DUMMY)

LEAD ♣Q

WEST EAST

YOU
(DECLARER)

♠ AKQ863
♥ 92
♦ 74
♣ A96

| WEST | NORTH | EAST | SOUTH |
|------|-------|------|-------|
| Pass | Pass | Pass | 1♠ |
| Pass | 3♠ | Pass | 4♠ |
| Pass | Pass | Pass | |

You're in a contract of 4♠, and the opening lead is the ♣Q. You have one too many losers, but there are interesting possibilities in both hearts and diamonds. Which suit is the better choice?

## Solution 11.4

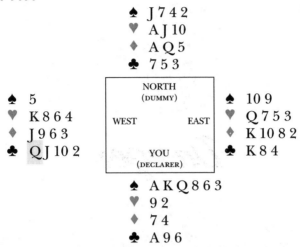

♠ J 7 4 2
♥ A J 10
♦ A Q 5
♣ 7 5 3

NORTH
(DUMMY)

♠ 5
♥ K 8 6 4
♦ J 9 6 3
♣ Q J 10 2

WEST          EAST

♠ 10 9
♥ Q 7 5 3
♦ K 10 8 2
♣ K 8 4

YOU
(DECLARER)

♠ A K Q 8 6 3
♥ 9 2
♦ 7 4
♣ A 9 6

There are four losers: one in hearts, one in diamonds, and two in clubs. Going down the checklist, the obvious way to eliminate a loser is through the diamond finesse. If West has the ♦K, you make the contract; if East has the ♦K . . . on to the next hand. The heart suit, however, provides a better chance of making the contract. You can make the contract if West holds the ♥K, or the ♥Q, or both the ♥K and ♥Q. After winning the first trick with the ♣A, draw trump, and play a low heart toward dummy. If West produces a high heart, win dummy's ♥A and drive out the defenders' remaining high heart and discard your diamond loser on dummy's promoted winner. If West produces a low heart, finesse dummy's ♥10—or ♥J. If this loses to the ♥K or ♥Q, it's still not over.

Suppose the defenders now take two club winners, ending in West's hand, and West leads a diamond. You have a choice. You can take the diamond finesse—a 50–50 chance—or you can win the ♦A, cross back with a trump, and lead your remaining heart toward dummy. If West produces another low heart, you repeat the finesse. As long as East didn't start with both the ♥K and ♥Q, the second finesse will succeed, and you can play the ♥A, discarding the diamond loser. Taking a repeated finesse in hearts is the best choice, since you make the contract about 75% of the time—when West holds either heart honor, or both heart honors. You lose only when East holds both the high hearts—about 25% of the time. That's better than the straight 50% chance in diamonds.

# Danger

"There was only one catch and that was Catch-22, which specified that a concern for one's own safety in the face of dangers that were real and immediate was the process of a rational mind."

—Joseph Heller,
*Catch-22* [1955]

You're the declarer and your focus is on developing extra winners and eliminating losers. While you're occupied with all this, the defenders are also keeping busy. They're trying to develop and take tricks and thinking of ways to stop you from getting your tricks.

The defenders have the advantage of the opening lead. They get the first opportunity to go about establishing and taking tricks. You'll have to keep them in mind when considering the order in which to play your cards.

## The Holdup

Suppose you've reached a contract of 3NT on the following hand, and the defenders start off by leading the ♠K.

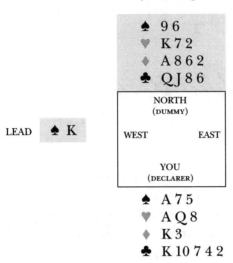

♠ 9 6
♥ K 7 2
♦ A 8 6 2
♣ Q J 8 6

NORTH
(DUMMY)

LEAD   ♠ K        WEST            EAST

YOU
(DECLARER)

♠ A 7 5
♥ A Q 8
♦ K 3
♣ K 10 7 4 2

There are six sure winners: a spade, three hearts, and two diamonds. The only source of extra winners is the club suit. You can develop four winners through promotion, more than enough to make your contract. Your plan seems quite straightforward. After winning a trick with the ♣A, you'll lead clubs, establishing the trick you need. Unfortunately, there's danger lurking in the form of the opponents.

The defenders are doing a bit of promotion themselves. They're planning to drive out your ♣A. When they regain the lead, they may be able to take enough spade tricks to defeat the contract. One of the disadvantages of playing in notrump is that, once the defenders start taking their winners, you have no way of stopping them. There's something you can do, however, to try to make it more difficult for them to take their winners.

You don't have to take your ♠A right away. You have a choice of winning the first trick, or ducking—letting the opponents win the trick. Maybe they'll switch to another suit—you wouldn't mind that! If they persist in leading spades, you can duck again. This is sometimes referred to as a *holdup play*—you hold up taking your winner. If they lead spades a third time, you have no choice but to win your ♠A. Now you'll have to go after the club suit, letting the defenders regain the lead. How has the holdup play helped you? This might be the complete hand:

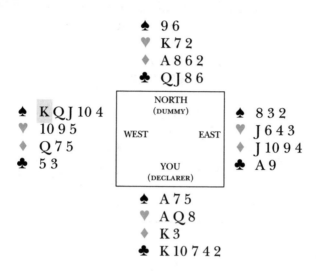

♠ 9 6
♥ K 7 2
♦ A 8 6 2
♣ Q J 8 6

NORTH
(DUMMY)

WEST        EAST

YOU
(DECLARER)

♠ K Q J 10 4
♥ 10 9 5
♦ Q 7 5
♣ 5 3

♠ 8 3 2
♥ J 6 4 3
♦ J 10 9 4
♣ A 9

♠ A 7 5
♥ A Q 8
♦ K 3
♣ K 10 7 4 2

When East wins a trick with the ♣A, East doesn't have any spades left—thanks to your holdup play. There's no link card left to West's hand. Whichever suit East leads back, you win and take the rest of the tricks.

Contrast this with what would happen if you won the first or second spade trick. On winning the ♣A, East has a spade left to lead over to West's winners, and the defenders take four spade tricks, along with the ♣A—enough to defeat the contract.

"Aha!" you might think. "What if West, rather than East, held the ♣A?" Then your holdup play would have been to no avail. There was nothing you could do. The defenders defeated the contract fairly and squarely. You can only sit back and congratulate them. Of course, you also deserve a pat on the back for giving the hand a good try.

"Aha, again! What if East still had a spade left after the holdup play?" Then the defenders' eight spades would originally have been divided 4–4, rather than 5–3. East would be able to lead the last spade, and the defenders would win the trick, but that would be all for them. They'd end up with three spade tricks and the ♣A. You'd still make the contract.

The holdup play is an attempt to create entry problems for the defenders by removing all the link cards in one defender's hand. It's commonly used in notrump contracts but can also be effective in a suit contract. Take a look at this hand. You've reached 4♥, and as usual the defense has got off to the best lead, the ♦K.

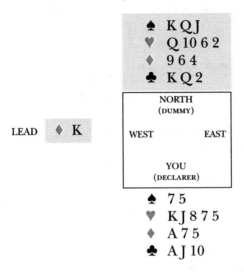

♠ K Q J
♥ Q 10 6 2
♦ 9 6 4
♣ K Q 2

NORTH
(DUMMY)

LEAD ♦ K

WEST　　　　EAST

YOU
(DECLARER)

♠ 7 5
♥ K J 8 7 5
♦ A 7 5
♣ A J 10

This looks like trouble. You have certain losers in spades and hearts, in addition to two losers in the diamond suit. The only glimmer of hope is that you can establish an extra winner in the spade suit through promotion. You could then discard one of your diamond losers. Unfortunately, the defenders are likely to take their two diamond winners as soon as you give them the lead with the ♣A.

It's a little difficult to foresee, but it's unlikely any harm can come from holding up your ♦A on the first round of the suit. You have to lose a diamond trick anyway—and isn't there something about taking your losses early? Maybe your left-hand opponent won't lead another diamond, and you'll get an opportunity to establish your extra spade winner.

Suppose, however, a second diamond is led. It wouldn't be a good idea to hold up again. Now you'd have four losers for sure, since you still have to lose the ♠A and ♥A. So, you win the second round of diamonds and lead a spade to promote the extra winner in that suit.

Your right-hand opponent wins this trick with the ♠A and starts to think. What's going on? Hopefully, your right-hand opponent has no more diamonds left. Perhaps this is the complete hand:

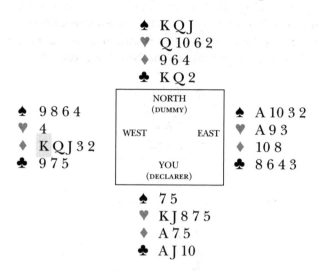

♠ K Q J
♥ Q 10 6 2
♦ 9 6 4
♣ K Q 2

NORTH
(DUMMY)

WEST          EAST

YOU
(DECLARER)

♠ 9 8 6 4
♥ 4
♦ K Q J 3 2
♣ 9 7 5

♠ A 10 3 2
♥ A 9 3
♦ 10 8
♣ 8 6 4 3

♠ 7 5
♥ K J 8 7 5
♦ A 7 5
♣ A J 10

Your holdup play is an unqualified success. East is helpless after winning the ♠A. There's no entry back to West's hand so that the defense can take another diamond trick. Whatever East leads back, the defenders can't stop you from discarding your diamond loser on dummy's extra spade winner.

You're a little lucky to find East with both the missing aces, but you still had to use the holdup play to give yourself a chance. In practice, you might even make the hand when West holds the ♥A. After winning the ♠A, East is unlikely to know that West holds the ♥A as an entry. East may lead a club, hoping West holds the ♣A. You can win this, take your discard on the spades, and then drive out the ♥A. It's too late for the defense to do you any harm. Your opponents will likely be shaking their heads, wondering how they could have found the way to take their tricks.

You usually use the holdup play when you hold the ace of the opponents' suit, but sometimes a king might become the winner you need. Look at this hand. You're back in your favorite contract of 3NT, and the opening lead is the ♦5.

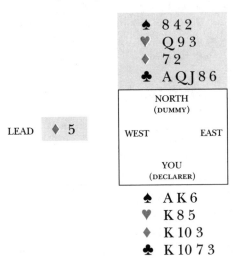

You start with two spade tricks and five club tricks. You're going to get one diamond trick after the opening lead. If the ♦A is played on your right, your ♦K becomes a winner. If a lower diamond is played, such as the ♦J or ♦Q, you'll be able to win a trick with your ♦K immediately. Your ninth trick can come from promotion in the heart suit, through driving out the defenders' ♥A. The only danger is that the defenders may be able to take enough diamond tricks to defeat you when they get the lead with the ♥A.

A lot depends on what diamond is played to the first trick by your right-hand opponent. If it's the ♦A, your ♦K is now a winner. Assuming another diamond is led, you don't have to play your ♦K right away. You can hold up until the third round of the suit. This gives you the extra chance that the defender winning a trick with the ♥A won't have any diamonds left. This might be the complete hand:

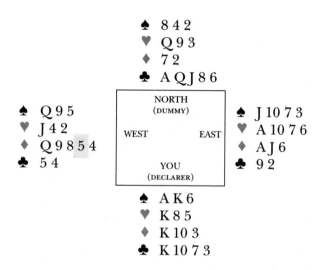

East wins the first trick with the ♦A and leads back the ♦J. You hold up your ♦K. East leads another diamond and you win the ♦K. West's last two diamonds are winners, but there's no way to reach them. When you lead a heart to promote a trick, East can win the ♥A but can't prevent you from taking nine tricks: two spades, one heart, one diamond, and five clubs.

Be careful when holding up. The situation would be different if East had played the ♦J or ♦Q on the first trick:

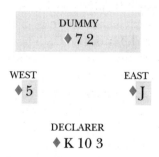

Your ♦K isn't a sure winner unless you take it right away. If you don't take it, you may never get a trick with it. The complete layout of the diamond suit might be something like this:

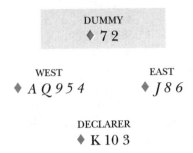

DUMMY
♦ 7 2

| WEST | EAST |
|------|------|
| ♦ A Q 9 5 4 | ♦ J 8 6 |

DECLARER
♦ K 10 3

If you let East win the first trick with the ♦J, East will lead back a diamond, and you'll lose all five tricks in the suit. Instead, you'll have to win the first diamond trick and hope the defenders can't take enough tricks to defeat you when they get in with the ♥A.

You also don't want to hold up in one suit if there's more danger elsewhere. Consider this hand. The opening lead is the ♥2 against your 3NT contract.

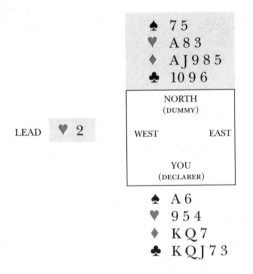

♠ 7 5
♥ A 8 3
♦ A J 9 8 5
♣ 10 9 6

NORTH
(DUMMY)

LEAD ♥ 2     WEST       EAST

YOU
(DECLARER)

♠ A 6
♥ 9 5 4
♦ K Q 7
♣ K Q J 7 3

You have a spade trick, a heart trick, and five diamond tricks. You're going to have to develop the rest of the tricks you need from the club suit, by driving out the defender's ♣A. Looking at the heart suit by itself, it may seem like a good idea to use the holdup play, so that when the defenders get in with the ♣A, they can't take too many heart tricks. If you let the defenders win the first heart trick, however, they may decide to switch to spades. You have even more trouble in that suit, if the defenders drive out your ♠A. Better to win the first trick right away with the ♥A and lead clubs. Hopefully, the opponents won't be able to take enough heart tricks to defeat you when they win a trick with the ♣A.

## Dangerous Opponents

You may feel that both your opponents are hazardous to the health of your contract. Sometimes, however, one opponent is more dangerous than the other. To see what this means, take a look at the following hand. The contract is 3NT, and the opening lead is the ♥K.

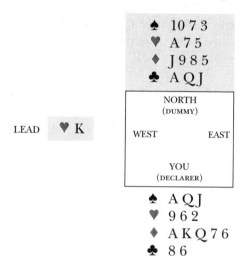

```
              ♠ 10 7 3
              ♥ A 7 5
              ♦ J 9 8 5
              ♣ A Q J
              NORTH
              (DUMMY)
LEAD  ♥ K   WEST        EAST
              YOU
              (DECLARER)
              ♠ A Q J
              ♥ 9 6 2
              ♦ A K Q 7 6
              ♣ 8 6
```

You start with eight tricks: one spade, one heart, five diamonds, and one club. There are lots of places your ninth trick can come from. You could simply promote an extra trick in spades, or you could try the spade finesse, hoping the ♠K is on your right. Similarly, you could promote a trick in clubs or try the club finesse. The only danger is your opponents. They've attacked your weakest suit. It looks like time for the holdup play.

You duck the first trick, letting the ♥K win. The ♥Q is led, and you duck this trick also. Another heart is led, forcing you to play your ♥A, and on this trick, your right-hand opponent discards a low diamond. Which opponent is dangerous?

In this situation, you can't afford to let the opponent on your left gain the lead. The defenders' hearts were originally divided 5–2, with the five-card suit on your left. Your left-hand opponent has become the *dangerous opponent*. On winning a trick in another suit, your dangerous opponent could take the rest of the established heart winners and defeat your contract. On the other hand, the opponent on your right can do you no harm upon gaining the lead. You can afford to lose a trick to your opponent on the right—the *safe opponent*. Thanks to your holdup play, your right-hand opponent has no hearts left to lead.

How do you take advantage of this "good news, bad news" situation? You can't afford to develop your ninth trick through promotion. If the dangerous opponent wins the trick, it's all over. You can, however, take the club finesse with impunity. You don't care whether it wins or loses. If it wins, you have your nine tricks. If it loses, you still have your nine tricks because you'll have promoted an extra trick in the suit.

You couldn't take the spade finesse with the same assurance. If the spade finesse lost, it would lose to the very opponent you want to avoid—the dangerous one. You take the club finesse to avoid the dangerous opponent.

It's important to recognize which of your opponents is the dangerous one. In this next hand, the contract is 4♥, and the opening lead is the ♠2.

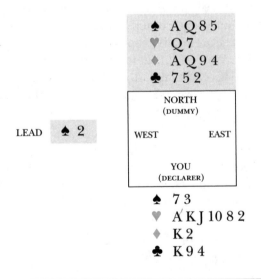

You have four potential losers: a spade loser and three club losers. There are several possibilities for eliminating your extra loser. You could try the spade finesse; you could try the club finesse, by leading toward your ♦Q; or you could discard one of your losers on the ♣K. Should you start with the spade finesse?

Not on this hand. Your right-hand opponent is the dangerous one. To see why, here's the complete hand:

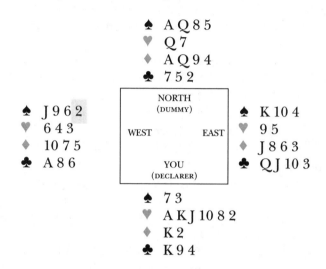

♠ A Q 8 5
♥ Q 7
♦ A Q 9 4
♣ 7 5 2

NORTH (DUMMY)
WEST     EAST
YOU (DECLARER)

♠ J 9 6 2
♥ 6 4 3
♦ 10 7 5
♣ A 8 6

♠ K 10 4
♥ 9 5
♦ J 8 6 3
♣ Q J 10 3

♠ 7 3
♥ A K J 10 8 2
♦ K 2
♣ K 9 4

If you play the ♠Q on the first trick, East will win the ♠K and may now lead the ♣Q. Your ♣K is trapped. You can't prevent the defenders from taking three club tricks, to defeat the contract. East is dangerous because East can potentially trap your ♣K. Even though it's West who holds the ♣A, West isn't the dangerous opponent. If West has the lead, the defenders can't take more than one club trick without giving you a trick with your ♣K. Sometimes it's the defender with the high cards that's dangerous; sometimes it's the defender without the high cards.

On the actual hand, simply win the first trick with dummy's ♠A, draw trump, and take your three diamond winners, discarding a loser from your hand. With ten tricks in the bag, you can try the club finesse for an eleventh. Even though it doesn't work, you're satisfied. You never gave the dangerous opponent a chance.

## Losing Control

It's nice to have a trump suit to prevent the opponents from taking all their winners, but there's always the danger that you'll run out of trump. Once all the trump are gone, it's like playing in notrump: if the defenders get the lead, they can take all their established tricks. You have to manage your trump suit wisely. Here's an example. The contract is 4♠, and the opening lead is the ♥K.

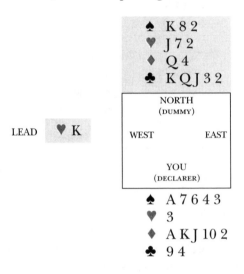

♠ K 8 2
♥ J 7 2
♦ Q 4
♣ K Q J 3 2

|  | NORTH (DUMMY) |  |
|---|---|---|
| LEAD ♥ K | WEST | EAST |
|  | YOU (DECLARER) |  |

♠ A 7 6 4 3
♥ 3
♦ A K J 10 2
♣ 9 4

Provided the spades divide 3–2, you have only one spade loser. You also have a heart loser and a club loser. It appears that your contract is quite safe. There's still some danger, however, if you aren't careful in your handling of the trump suit.

The defenders win the first heart trick and lead another high heart. You have to trump this in your hand. You're down to four trump in your hand. When you don't have too many losers, it's a good idea to draw trump. You don't want the defenders to be able to ruff one of your diamond winners with a low trump. You play a spade to dummy's ♠K and a spade back to your ♠A. Both opponents follow suit. So far, so good. The defenders' trump have divided 3–2. What now?

Suppose you decide to lead a third round of trump, to get rid of the defenders' last trump. On winning this trick with the high trump, the defender leads yet another heart. You have one trump left and are able to win this trick, but that's your last trump. You can take your five diamond tricks, but when it comes time to establish a club trick through promotion, it's too late. The defender winning the ♣A leads a final heart, and you have no trump left to stop them from winning the trick. Instead of one heart loser, you end up with two. Here's the entire hand.

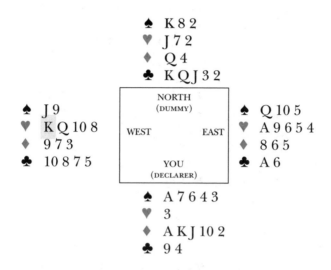

The problem you ran into on this hand is that you *lost control* of the trump suit. You didn't have a trump left when you needed one. You could have avoided this through a change to the order in which you played your cards. After trumping the second round of hearts and taking your ♣K and ♠A, there was no need to lead another round of trump. There was only one trump outstanding in the defenders' hands, and it was the high trump. The defenders are entitled to this trick—you counted it among your losers—but there's no reason to use up two of your low trump to get rid of the defenders' high trump.

Instead, once the trump divide 3–2, simply go about your other business. You can take your diamond winners. You don't mind if they ruff one of your winners with the high trump. It's their trick anyway, and you'll still have two trump left in your hand to stop their heart winners. If they don't trump one of your diamond winners, you can lead a club to promote a winner in that suit. They can win the ♣A and may play the high spade to extract two of your trump. The difference is that you still have one trump left. If they lead another heart, you trump it and take your club winner to make the contract.

Here's another example of maintaining control in the trump suit. This time you're in 4♥, and the defense starts off by leading a high diamond.

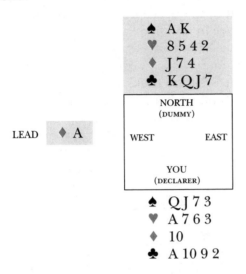

♠ A K
♥ 8 5 4 2
♦ J 7 4
♣ K Q J 7

NORTH
(DUMMY)

LEAD ♦ A

WEST      EAST

YOU
(DECLARER)

♠ Q J 7 3
♥ A 7 6 3
♦ 10
♣ A 10 9 2

Once again, you should be okay if the defenders' trump are divided 3–2. You'll have two heart losers and a diamond loser. Still, you'll have to manage the trump suit carefully to avoid any danger.

Suppose the defense starts off with two rounds of diamonds. You trump the second round, leaving you with three trump in your hand. You need to draw some trump before trying to take your winners in the other suits. Otherwise, a defender might trump one of your winners with a low trump, and you'd still have two more trump tricks to lose.

If you play your ♥A and lead a second heart, you may run into trouble even though the trump divide nicely, 3–2. The defender with the third high trump might decide to play it, drawing the last trump from your hand. You still have a trump left in the dummy, but it won't prevent the defenders from taking a second diamond trick. You have to follow suit with the diamond in the dummy, and you have no trump left in your hand.

To solve this dilemma, you have to change the order in which you play your cards. After trumping the second diamond, instead of playing the ♥A followed by a low heart, start by playing a low heart from both hands, ducking the trick to the opponents. They're entitled to two trump tricks; you're just taking your losses early. If they lead another diamond after winning the trump trick, you can ruff with the low trump still in your hand. Now you play the ♥A, drawing a second round of trump. If both opponents follow suit, their trump have divided 3–2, and you're in fine shape. You don't need to worry about the last trump in the defenders' hands. It's their trick to take whenever they want. You merely start taking your winners. Other than the trump trick, the rest of the tricks are yours.

Lest you get the impression that you never draw the defenders' high trump, we'll finish with a hand in which it's important to get rid of their trump. The contract is 4♠, and the opening lead is the ♦Q.

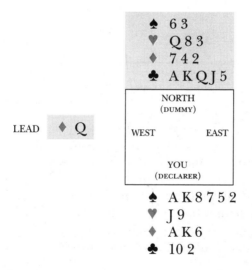

♠ 6 3
♥ Q 8 3
♦ 7 4 2
♣ A K Q J 5

NORTH
(DUMMY)

LEAD ♦ Q

WEST          EAST

YOU
(DECLARER)

♠ A K 8 7 5 2
♥ J 9
♦ A K 6
♣ 10 2

If the defenders' five spades divide 3–2, you have only one loser in that suit. You also have two losers in hearts and one loser in diamonds. Your plan is to discard one or more of your losers on dummy's extra club winners. There's no hurry to do this because not all your losers are quick. You can start by playing two rounds of trump. When they divide 3–2, your contract appears safe. There's only one high trump outstanding.

Suppose you leave that trump in the defender's hand and start to take your club winners. That will be fine if both opponents keep following suit as you play your clubs. You'll be able to discard your diamond loser and perhaps one or both of your heart losers. However, you're putting the contract at risk. If the defender with the high trump has only one club, the second round of clubs can be ruffed. Now you have no way to reach dummy's winners. You'll end up with both your heart losers and a diamond loser, to go along with the trump loser.

Instead, play the third round of trump, getting rid of the defenders' high trump. There's no longer any danger. The defenders can take two heart tricks, but that's all. When you regain the lead, you can safely take your club winners, discarding the diamond loser from your hand.

Careful management of the trump suit can help keep you out of danger.

## Summary

As part of the FUN of playing the hand, you need to "Note the order" in which you should play your cards. Whenever possible, try to order your play to minimize any danger from the opponents. Some things to look for are:

- Use the holdup play to make it more difficult for the opponents to take their tricks.
- Avoid giving up the lead to the dangerous opponent.
- Manage the trump suit to maintain control of the hand.

## Practice Hands

### Hand 12.1

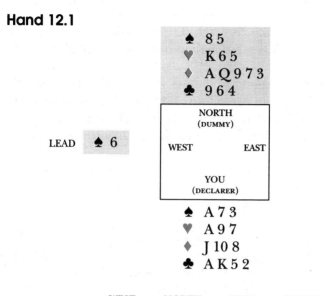

♠ 8 5
♥ K 6 5
♦ A Q 9 7 3
♣ 9 6 4

NORTH
(DUMMY)

LEAD ♣ 6

WEST        EAST

YOU
(DECLARER)

♠ A 7 3
♥ A 9 7
♦ J 10 8
♣ A K 5 2

| WEST | NORTH | EAST | SOUTH |
|------|-------|------|-------|
|      | Pass  | Pass | 1NT   |
| Pass | 3NT   | Pass | Pass  |
| Pass |       |      |       |

West leads the ♣6 against your contract of 3NT. How do you plan to take nine tricks? Is there any danger?

## Solution 12.1

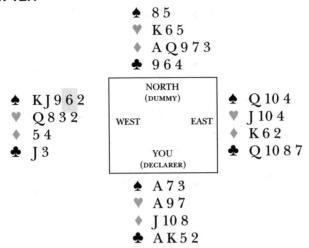

```
              ♠ 8 5
              ♥ K 6 5
              ♦ A Q 9 7 3
              ♣ 9 6 4
                   NORTH
♠ K J 9 6 2       (DUMMY)        ♠ Q 10 4
♥ Q 8 3 2    WEST        EAST    ♥ J 10 4
♦ 5 4                            ♦ K 6 2
♣ J 3              YOU           ♣ Q 10 8 7
                (DECLARER)
              ♠ A 7 3
              ♥ A 9 7
              ♦ J 10 8
              ♣ A K 5 2
```

There are six sure tricks: one spade, two hearts, one diamond, and two clubs. The extra tricks can come from the diamond suit by driving out the opponents' ♦K. You may even be able to take all five diamond tricks using the finesse, if West holds the ♦K.

The danger comes from the spade suit. The opponents are about to drive out your only high card in the suit. Since you may have to let the opponents win a trick with the ♦K, you don't want them to be in a position to take enough tricks from the spade suit to defeat the contract.

You can reduce the danger considerably by using the holdup play. Let the opponents win the first spade trick and the second. Wait until the third round to take the ♠A—being careful to discard a low heart or club from the dummy. Now take the diamond finesse by leading a high diamond from your hand and playing a low diamond from dummy, unless the ♦K appears from West. On the actual hand, the finesse loses to East's ♦K, but you don't mind. East isn't the dangerous opponent. Because of your holdup play, East has no spades left to lead. Whatever suit East leads back, you win and take your nine winners.

Notice what would happen if you won the first or second spade trick. When the diamond finesse lost, East would still have a spade to lead. The defenders would take four spade tricks and the ♦K to defeat the contract.

**Hand 12.2**

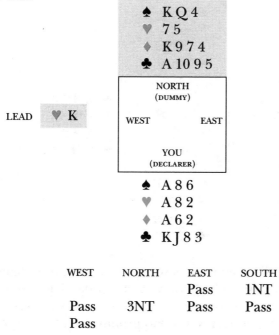

♠ K Q 4
♥ 7 5
♦ K 9 7 4
♣ A 10 9 5

NORTH
(DUMMY)

LEAD ♥ K

WEST            EAST

YOU
(DECLARER)

♠ A 8 6
♥ A 8 2
♦ A 6 2
♣ K J 8 3

| WEST | NORTH | EAST | SOUTH |
|------|-------|------|-------|
|      |       | Pass | 1NT   |
| Pass | 3NT   | Pass | Pass  |
| Pass |       |      |       |

You're in a contract of 3NT, and the opening lead is the ♥K. What's the danger? How do you plan to avoid it?

## Solution 12.2

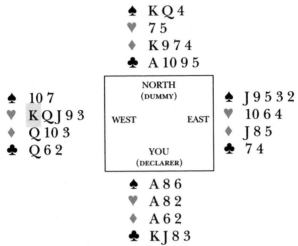

| | ♠ K Q 4 |
| | ♥ 7 5 |
| | ♦ K 9 7 4 |
| | ♣ A 10 9 5 |

NORTH (DUMMY)

WEST ♠ 10 7 ♥ K Q J 9 3 ♦ Q 10 3 ♣ Q 6 2

EAST ♠ J 9 5 3 2 ♥ 10 6 4 ♦ J 8 5 ♣ 7 4

YOU (DECLARER)

| | ♠ A 8 6 |
| | ♥ A 8 2 |
| | ♦ A 6 2 |
| | ♣ K J 8 3 |

You have eight tricks on top: three spades, a heart, two diamonds, and two clubs. An extra trick could come from diamonds—if the diamonds divide exactly 3–3—or from clubs. The club suit is more promising. You can get a ninth trick through promotion, by simply driving out the ♣Q, or you can take a club finesse for the missing ♣Q. If it wins, you have at least nine tricks; if it loses, you still have nine tricks.

The only danger is the heart suit. From the opening lead, it looks as though West has the length in the suit. Your first step to reduce the danger is to use the holdup play. Duck the first two heart tricks, waiting until the third round to take the ♥A. If West started with five or more hearts, West becomes a dangerous opponent. The next step is to avoid giving up the lead to the dangerous opponent. It's not a good idea to play the ♣A and ♣K, then give up a trick to the ♣Q if it hasn't appeared. If West wins the trick, you may be defeated. It's also not a good idea to play a low club to dummy's ♣A and a low club back to your ♣J, taking the finesse. If the finesse loses to West's ♣Q, as on the actual hand, West defeats you by taking two more heart tricks. The club suit offers the possibility of a two-way finesse. Instead of hoping the ♣Q is in East's hand, you can hope it's with West. After winning the ♥A, play the ♣K and then the ♣J. If West doesn't play the ♣Q, take the finesse. You don't care if it wins or loses. If East wins, the contract is in no danger. On the actual hand, the finesse works, and you're rewarded with an overtrick.

**Hand 12.3**

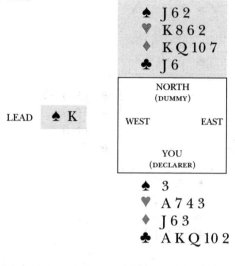

♠ J 6 2
♥ K 8 6 2
♦ K Q 10 7
♣ J 6

NORTH
(DUMMY)

LEAD  ♠ K

WEST          EAST

YOU
(DECLARER)

♠ 3
♥ A 7 4 3
♦ J 6 3
♣ A K Q 10 2

| WEST | NORTH | EAST | SOUTH |
|------|-------|------|-------|
|      |       |      | 1♣    |
| Pass | 1♦    | Pass | 1♥    |
| Pass | 3♥    | Pass | 4♥    |
| Pass | Pass  | Pass |       |

You've reached 4♥, and the defense has started with the ♠K. As long as the defenders' trump are divided 3–2, is there any danger? How do you plan to handle the trump suit?

## Solution 12.3

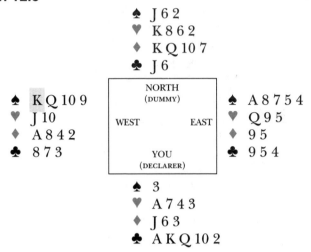

```
              ♠ J 6 2
              ♥ K 8 6 2
              ♦ K Q 10 7
              ♣ J 6
                  NORTH
 ♠ K Q 10 9      (DUMMY)        ♠ A 8 7 5 4
 ♥ J 10                          ♥ Q 9 5
 ♦ A 8 4 2    WEST      EAST     ♦ 9 5
 ♣ 8 7 3                          ♣ 9 5 4
                  YOU
              (DECLARER)
              ♠ 3
              ♥ A 7 4 3
              ♦ J 6 3
              ♣ A K Q 10 2
```

If the trump divide 3–2, you have only one loser in that suit. You also have a spade loser and a diamond loser. You can afford three losers, so the contract appears safe. You only need to be careful in managing the trump suit.

Suppose the defenders start by playing two high spades. You trump the second round and can begin by playing the ♥A and ♥K, drawing two rounds of trump. That gets rid of four low trump in the defenders' hands, leaving only one high trump outstanding. You can't afford to play another round of trump. If you do, the defenders will win this trick and be able to take another spade winner, since you have no trump left in your hand.

Instead, start playing your club winners, eventually discarding dummy's last spade. If the defender with the outstanding trump still hasn't ruffed one of your winners, turn your attention to the diamond suit, driving out the ♦A. The defenders still have a trump winner, but that's all.

You could also make the contract by ducking a heart completely at the second trick, giving up a trump trick early. That's a bit more complicated, but you maintain control of the trump suit and can draw trump when you regain the lead. Just as long as you're the one in control, not the opponents.

**Hand 12.4**

♠ K 10 9 3
♥ 7 5 3
♦ A Q J 8
♣ K 5

|  | NORTH (DUMMY) |  |
|---|---|---|
| LEAD ♣ Q | WEST | EAST |
|  | YOU (DECLARER) |  |

♠ A J 8 6 5
♥ K 6 2
♦ K 5 2
♣ A 7 .

| WEST | NORTH | EAST | SOUTH |
|---|---|---|---|
| Pass | 1♦ | Pass | 1♠ |
| Pass | 2♠ | Pass | 4♠ |
| Pass | Pass | Pass | |

You're in a contract of 4♠, and the opening lead is the ♣Q. Is there a dangerous opponent? Will you follow the guideline of "eight ever, nine never" when playing the trump suit, or do you have other ideas?

## Solution 12.4

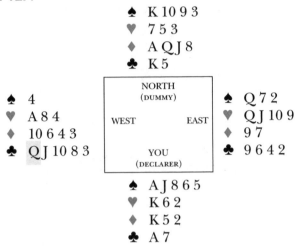

```
              ♠ K 10 9 3
              ♥ 7 5 3
              ♦ A Q J 8
              ♣ K 5
                    NORTH
    ♠ 4           (DUMMY)        ♠ Q 7 2
    ♥ A 8 4    WEST      EAST    ♥ Q J 10 9
    ♦ 10 6 4 3                   ♦ 9 7
    ♣ Q J 10 8 3    YOU          ♣ 9 6 4 2
                  (DECLARER)
              ♠ A J 8 6 5
              ♥ K 6 2
              ♦ K 5 2
              ♣ A 7
```

There's a potential loser in spades and three in hearts. With nine spades in the combined hands, you could play the ♠A and ♠K, hoping the ♠Q falls. You also have the possibility of taking a spade finesse in either direction, depending on which opponent you think holds the ♠Q. In hearts, you can lead toward the ♥K, and you can also discard a loser on dummy's extra diamond winner. Is there a dangerous opponent? Yes, East. If East gains the lead before you've done something about the heart losers, the defenders may take three tricks when the ♥A is unfavorably placed. West isn't dangerous. The defense can take only one quick heart trick with West on lead.

With nine combined spades, you usually play the ♠A and ♠K. Having identified East as dangerous, however, you don't want to risk letting East win a trick with the ♠Q. After winning the club trick, play dummy's ♠K. Take a spade finesse against East by playing a low spade to the ♠J. On the actual hand, this is spectacularly successful. The finesse wins, and you draw the last trump. You then take four diamond winners, discarding a heart loser. Even with the ♥A unfavorably placed, you end up with eleven tricks. What if West held the ♠Q? The finesse would lose, but the contract would be safe. With all the trump gone, you can discard a heart loser on dummy's extra diamond winner. You end up with only ten tricks, but that's all you need. On the actual hand, the contract is defeated if you play the ♠A and ♠K. When the ♠Q doesn't fall and you try to take the diamond winners, East trumps and leads the ♥Q, trapping your ♥K.

# 𝓘𝓵𝓵𝓾𝓼𝓲𝓸𝓷𝓼

*"The eye may see for the hand, but not for the mind."*

—HENRY DAVID THOREAU

Which of these two lines is longer?

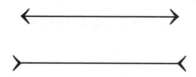

Yes, they're the same length—it's an optical illusion that the bottom line appears longer. Things aren't always what they seem, and this can happen when you're playing a hand of bridge. Some winning plays seem to defy common sense. You may have the number of tricks you need, but you might need a change in perception to get them.

## Count Your Winners and Losers

Compare the following two suit combinations:

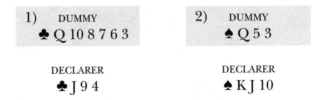

1)  DUMMY
  ♣ Q 10 8 7 6 3

2)  DUMMY
  ♠ Q 5 3

DECLARER
♣ J 9 4

DECLARER
♠ K J 10

Which combination would you prefer when playing in a notrump contract? Although you're missing the two highest cards in the first combination, you can develop four tricks through promotion. In the second combination, you're missing only one high card but can develop only two tricks through promotion. Which is better? Let's look at both suits within the context of a complete hand. The contract is 3NT, and the opening lead is the ♥4.

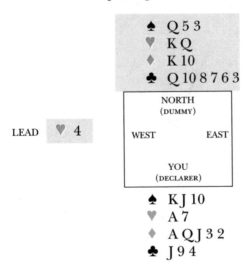

♠ Q 5 3
♥ K Q
♦ K 10
♣ Q 10 8 7 6 3

NORTH
(DUMMY)

LEAD ♥ 4

WEST          EAST

YOU
(DECLARER)

♠ K J 10
♥ A 7
♦ A Q J 3 2
♣ J 9 4

You have two sure tricks in hearts and five in diamonds. You could develop four more tricks from the club suit through promotion. That would be more than enough, but it wouldn't be a good idea to lead clubs after winning the first heart trick. You'll lose the race. You have to let the defenders in twice while promoting the club winners.

By then, they'll have established enough tricks in hearts to defeat the contract.

Instead, lead a spade after winning the first heart trick. You can promote only two extra tricks from the spade suit, but that's all you need. You have to let the defenders win only one trick while promoting your spade winners, so you'll still have a high card left in the heart suit. You'll take two spade tricks, two heart tricks, and five diamond tricks.

Would the spade combination always be the better suit to play in a notrump contract? Let's change the hand slightly.

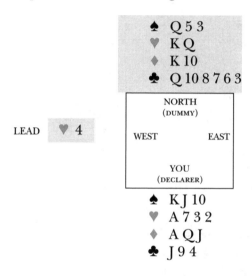

You're still in 3NT, with the same lead, but now you have only six sure tricks: three hearts and three diamonds. Two extra tricks from the spade suit won't be enough. After winning the first heart trick, you should immediately lead a club, to drive out one of the defenders' high cards. They can lead another heart, but you win and drive out the other high club. You'll end up with three heart tricks, three diamond tricks, and four club tricks.

This time, you make an overtrick by going after the club suit. If you'd gone after the spade suit, you might be defeated if the defenders can establish enough tricks before you have time to develop a club winner.

Don't be distracted by the appearance of the suits themselves. How you play each suit will depend on the nature of the complete hand.

## Choose the Right Tactic

Familiar-looking suit combinations must sometimes be handled in an unfamiliar manner. You need to keep an open mind. How would you plan to play the following combination?

DUMMY
♥ K 9

WEST          EAST
♥ ?           ♥ ?

DECLARER
♥ 8 6 3

Having learned all about finesses, the natural instinct is to lead a low heart from your hand toward dummy's ♥K, hoping that West holds the ♥A. There are times, however, when playing the suit that way may be an illusion. Consider the following hand. The contract is 2♠, and the opening lead is the ♣K.

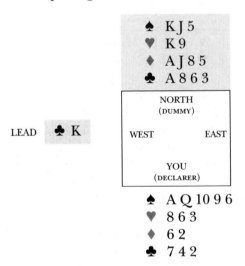

♠ K J 5
♥ K 9
♦ A J 8 5
♣ A 8 6 3

NORTH
(DUMMY)

LEAD   ♣ K      WEST          EAST

YOU
(DECLARER)

♠ A Q 10 9 6
♥ 8 6 3
♦ 6 2
♣ 7 4 2

You can afford five losers, but you have six: three hearts, one diamond, and two clubs. You can't do much about the diamond and club losers, but there are several possibilities for eliminating a heart loser. One possibility is the heart finesse. If the ♥A is on your left, leading a low heart toward dummy will establish the ♥K as a winner. Since you have more hearts than dummy, you could also plan to trump one of your heart losers in the dummy. A final possibility is to try to establish an extra winner using dummy's club suit. If the defenders' clubs are divided exactly 3–3, dummy's fourth club will become a winner, and you can use it to discard one of your other losers.

Suppose you follow your natural instincts, and after winning a trick with dummy's ♣A, you travel to your hand using a trump so that you can lead a low heart toward dummy's ♥K. You probably won't make the contract if all four hands look something like this:

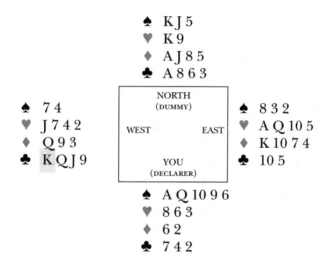

♠ KJ5
♥ K9
♦ AJ85
♣ A863

NORTH
(DUMMY)

♠ 74
♥ J742
♦ Q93
♣ KQJ9

WEST          EAST

♠ 832
♥ AQ105
♦ K1074
♣ 105

YOU
(DECLARER)

♠ AQ1096
♥ 863
♦ 62
♣ 742

When you play dummy's ♥K, your finesse will lose to East's ♥A. Looking at the singleton heart left in dummy, East might return a spade. Since you already used up one of dummy's spades to travel to your hand for the finesse, there's now only one trump left in dummy. If you lead another heart, planning to trump your last heart loser in the dummy, East can win and lead another spade. You no longer have any trump left in dummy with which to ruff your loser. You lose three heart tricks, a diamond trick, and two club tricks.

Unlucky, you might think, but the presence of dummy's ♥K created an optical illusion. Suppose you had to play the same 2♠ contract, without the ♥K in the dummy.

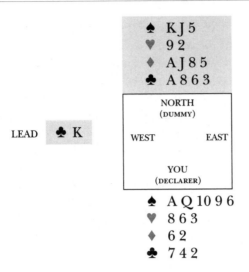

♠ K J 5
♥ 8 6 3
♦ 6 2
♣ 7 4 2

Three fewer points to work with, but you'll probably have an easier time making the hand. Without the possibility of the heart finesse, you have little option but to trump a heart loser in the dummy. After winning a trick with dummy's ♣A, you'd lead a heart. The defenders can win this and lead a trump, but you win and lead another heart. The defenders can lead another trump, but you can win the trick in your hand and lead your last heart, trumping with dummy's last spade. You lose two heart tricks, one diamond trick, and two club tricks. No problem.

It's a lot easier now to see the solution to the original hand. After winning the ♣A, lead a low heart from dummy right away, even though you have the ♥K in the dummy. It may go against your instincts, but the ♥K is only clouding your vision.

Now consider this combination of cards:

Ideally, you'd like to lead from dummy and take a finesse, hoping East holds the ♦K. But not all hands are ideal. Suppose you're in a contract of 3NT on the following hand, and the defenders start off with the ♥Q.

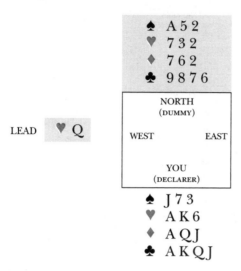

♠ A 5 2
♥ 7 3 2
♦ 7 6 2
♣ 9 8 7 6

NORTH
(DUMMY)

LEAD ♥ Q

WEST           EAST

YOU
(DECLARER)

♠ J 7 3
♥ A K 6
♦ A Q J
♣ A K Q J

You start with eight tricks: one spade, two hearts, one diamond, and four clubs. You need only one more. There's lots of potential in the diamond suit to create an extra trick, and on the surface, it might not seem like a bad idea to cross to dummy with the ♠A and take the diamond finesse. If it wins, you have nine tricks; if it loses, you still have nine tricks, since you've promoted a second diamond winner in your hand. This line of play, however, might not be too successful if this is the complete hand:

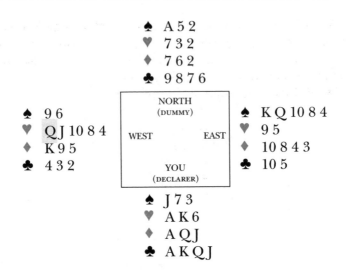

When you lead a spade to dummy's ♠A and take the diamond finesse, West wins the trick with the ♦K. West might now decide to lead a spade, rather than a heart, and East will take the next four spade tricks, defeating the contract.

There was no need to put the contract at risk by taking the diamond finesse. Needing only two tricks from the diamond suit, forget about the finesse. After winning the first heart trick, play the ♦A, followed by the ♦Q. The ♦J is promoted into your ninth trick, and you still have the ♠A in the dummy. Don't let dummy's spade entry, and the familiar looking combination of cards in the diamond suit, lead you astray.

The following combinations of cards probably look familiar:

In the first combination, if you needed an extra trick, you'd lead a low heart from dummy and finesse the ♥Q, hoping the ♥K is on your right. In the second combination, you have a two-way finesse for the missing ♣Q: if you think it's on your right, you could play the ♣A and lead a low club toward your hand, finessing the ♣J; if you think it's on your left, you could play the ♣K and then lead the ♣J, hoping to trap the queen.

If you put the two combinations together in the same hand, however, you might get your extra trick by taking no finesses! Your contract is 6♠, and the opening lead is the ♦10.

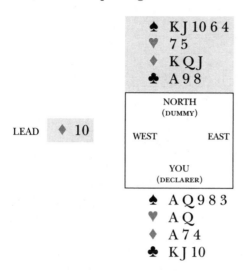

♠ KJ10 6 4
♥ 7 5
♦ KQJ
♣ A 9 8

NORTH
(DUMMY)

LEAD ♦ 10

WEST          EAST

YOU
(DECLARER)

♠ A Q 9 8 3
♥ A Q
♦ A 7 4
♣ K J 10

You have a potential loser in the heart suit and a potential loser in the club suit. One of them has to disappear, if you're to make the slam contract. There's the possibility of the heart finesse, and if that doesn't work, there's the possibility of finding the ♣Q. You'd be pretty unlucky not to make the contract.

But you don't have to rely on luck. You have a sure thing. You can make the opponents find the ♣Q for you! You remove all their other options. Start by winning the first diamond trick and drawing all their trump—since they have only three trump between them, the ♠A and ♠K will probably take care of that. Now take your two remaining diamond winners, and play the ♥A followed by the ♥Q. You don't need to try the club finesse because you don't care which opponent has the ♥K. The cards you have left in the two hands look something like this:

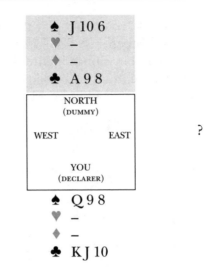

♠ J 10 6
♥ —
♦ —
♣ A 9 8

NORTH
(DUMMY)

?          WEST          EAST          ?

YOU
(DECLARER)

♠ Q 9 8
♥ —
♦ —
♣ K J 10

You still don't know which opponent holds the ♣Q, but you don't care. Whichever opponent won a trick with the ♥K has to lead. If it's West and West leads a club, you play a low club from dummy and win three club tricks whether or not East plays the ♣Q. If East has the lead, it's the same thing. If East leads a club, you play the ♣10 or ♣J, and you're assured of three club tricks whether or not West produces the ♣Q. You've trapped the defenders into doing your work for you. It won't do them any good to lead a heart or a diamond. You could then trump in the dummy, and discard the club loser from your hand on the same trick—that was the reason for eliminating all their trump and all the hearts and diamonds from your two hands.

This type of play is called a *throw-in* or *endplay* because you "throw" one of the opponents into the lead at an inopportune time for the defenders, usually toward the end of the hand. There are many variations on this theme, but the point is that you don't always take a finesse just because it's there. Sometimes, it's better to refuse the finesse. It all depends on the context of the whole hand.

## Breaking the Rules

The general principles you've seen throughout this book are guidelines, not rules. There will always be exceptions to statements such as, "eight ever, nine never" or "trump your losers in the dummy." As declarer, you have to be imaginative and flexible—learning when to apply the guidelines and when to step outside them.

Let's finish off with a couple of examples. In this next hand, you're in a contract of 3NT, and the opening lead is the ♠4.

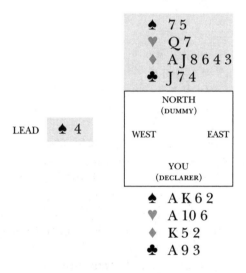

```
                    ♠ 7 5
                    ♥ Q 7
                    ♦ A J 8 6 4 3
                    ♣ J 7 4
                    ┌─────────────────────┐
                    │      NORTH          │
                    │     (DUMMY)         │
                    │                     │
  LEAD    ♠ 4       │ WEST          EAST  │
                    │                     │
                    │      YOU            │
                    │   (DECLARER)        │
                    └─────────────────────┘
                    ♠ A K 6 2
                    ♥ A 10 6
                    ♦ K 5 2
                    ♣ A 9 3
```

There are six sure tricks: two spades, one heart, two diamonds, and one club. The diamond suit is the obvious place to look for extra tricks. You're missing the ♦Q but have nine diamonds between the two hands. The guideline in this situation is "eight ever, nine never." With nine cards, it's usually better to play the ace and king, hoping the queen will fall, rather than taking the finesse. If the diamonds divide 2–2, you'll end up with four extra tricks, more than enough to make the contract. If they divide 3–1, you can still establish three extra tricks, which is all you need.

After winning the spade trick, suppose you play the ♦K, and both opponents follow suit, but the ♦Q doesn't appear. You now lead a low diamond toward dummy, and the opponent on your left plays the ♦10—still no ♦Q. Do you play the ♦A, or do you take the finesse?

If you routinely adhere to the guideline and play dummy's ♦A,
you won't make the contract if this is the complete layout:

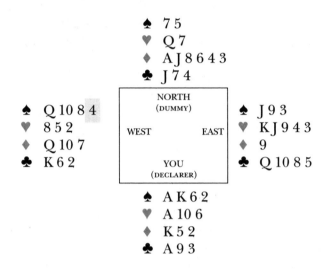

      ♠ 7 5
      ♥ Q 7
      ♦ A J 8 6 4 3
      ♣ J 7 4

        NORTH
♠ Q 10 8 4   (DUMMY)   ♠ J 9 3
♥ 8 5 2  WEST    EAST ♥ K J 9 4 3
♦ Q 10 7         ♦ 9
♣ K 6 2    YOU   ♣ Q 10 8 5
      (DECLARER)

      ♠ A K 6 2
      ♥ A 10 6
      ♦ K 5 2
      ♣ A 9 3

East discards on the second round of diamonds. You can give up
a diamond trick to West's ♦Q, establishing dummy's remaining diamonds as winners, but you have no way to reach them.

On this hand, you need to ignore the guideline and take the finesse. That guarantees your contract, whether it wins or loses. If it
wins, you'll take ten tricks; if it were to lose to East's doubleton ♦Q,
you'd take nine tricks.

From experience, I know some declarers will be more concerned
about partner's reaction if they lose the finesse to East's doubleton
queen than if they make the contract. If the diamonds divide 3–1,
they can always say, "Sorry, I was only following the rule of eight ever,
nine never." They don't want to feel partner's eyes on them if they
take a losing finesse, especially when they could have followed the
guideline and made an overtrick.

Don't automatically follow the guidelines, and don't be concerned
with what partner might say when the hand is over. Focus on making
the contract. If you give it a reasonable effort, you don't owe apolo-
gies to anyone—even yourself.

This last contract requires some imagination. You're in 6♠, and the opening lead is the ♥K.

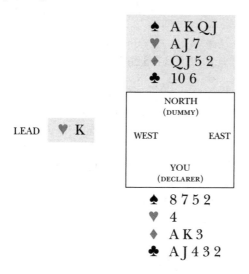

♠ A K Q J
♥ A J 7
♦ Q J 5 2
♣ 10 6

NORTH
(DUMMY)

LEAD ♥ K

WEST            EAST

YOU
(DECLARER)

♠ 8 7 5 2
♥ 4
♦ A K 3
♣ A J 4 3 2

You can afford only one loser in your small slam contract. As long as the defenders' spades don't divide 5–0, you have no spade losers. You also have no losers in hearts or diamonds. You do, however, have four potential club losers. You can plan to discard one of your club losers on dummy's extra diamond winner, but that still leaves you with three losers in the suit.

Dummy has only two clubs, so in situations like this you usually consider trumping your extra losers in the dummy. That's not going to work on this hand. If you trump two club losers in the dummy, you'll have to use two of dummy's high spades. When it comes time to draw trump, you'll now have a trump loser, even if the defenders' spades divide 3–2. What can you do? The contract seems impossible to make.

The solution appears rather magical when you first see it. You'll actually get to discard two of your losers on dummy's trump! This is done as follows. After winning the first trick with dummy's ♥A, instead of looking to trump losers from your hand in the dummy, you reverse the process, and trump two of dummy's losers in your hand. You lead a heart and trump it with one of your spades. You cross back to dummy with a trump, lead dummy's last heart, and trump it in your hand. That leaves you with one trump in your hand and three high trump in dummy. You go back to dummy with your last trump, and then play dummy's two remaining high trump. This draws any remaining trump in the defenders' hands, and since you have no trump left in your hand, you can discard two of your club losers. You now take your four diamond tricks, discarding another club from your hand, and take your ♣A. You're left with one losing club in your hand, but that's it.

Essentially, you took one heart trick, four diamond tricks, one club trick, and six trump tricks—dummy's four high trump plus the two ruffs in your hand. Playing a hand in this fashion—where you trump dummy's losers in your hand, rather than your losers in dummy's hand—is called a *dummy reversal*. The reason for this is apparent if you turn the hand upside-down: making your hand the dummy and partner's hand the declarer. Now it would look like this:

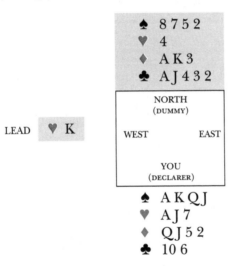

♠ 8 7 5 2
♥ 4
♦ A K 3
♣ A J 4 3 2

NORTH
(DUMMY)

LEAD  ♥ K

WEST          EAST

YOU
(DECLARER)

♠ A K Q J
♥ A J 7
♦ Q J 5 2
♣ 10 6

If you were counting losers in this hand, you'd have two heart losers and one club loser. You'd plan to trump your two heart losers in dummy, draw trump and take all the rest of the tricks except for the club loser at the end. It's amazing how straightforward the hand becomes when you look at it from a different perspective.

The ability to be flexible as declarer and look at the hand from more than one perspective will be a great asset when you're having FUN playing bridge. There's more to the game than meets the eye!

## Summary

Don't get drawn in by illusions. The way you play a particular suit has to be put in the context of the entire hand. If a hand seems confusing, change your perspective, and look at the hand from another point of view. What if the high card were a low card, or dummy's hand and declarer's hand were switched? Most of all, have FUN when you get to play a contract:

- <u>F</u>ocus on the target
- <u>U</u>se the checklist
- <u>N</u>ote the order

As you're looking for ways to create extra winners and eliminate losers:

- Develop the suits that will give you the number of tricks you need.

- Play each suit to give you the tricks you need; not necessarily the maximum number of tricks.

- Be flexible and imaginative, looking beyond the guidelines where appropriate.

## Practice Hands

### Hand 13.1

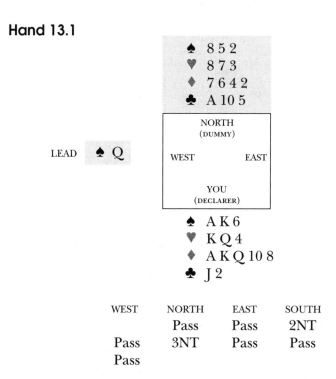

♠ 8 5 2
♥ 8 7 3
♦ 7 6 4 2
♣ A 10 5

NORTH
(DUMMY)

LEAD    ♠ Q     WEST          EAST

YOU
(DECLARER)

♠ A K 6
♥ K Q 4
♦ A K Q 10 8
♣ J 2

| WEST | NORTH | EAST | SOUTH |
|------|-------|------|-------|
|      | Pass  | Pass | 2NT   |
| Pass | 3NT   | Pass | Pass  |
| Pass |       |      |       |

West leads the ♠Q against your contract of 3NT. How do you plan to plan to play the heart suit? Is there anything that can go wrong in the diamond suit?

## Solution 13.1

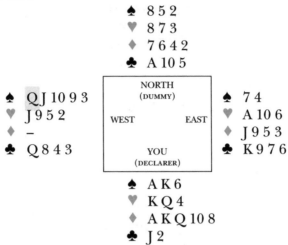

$\spadesuit$ 8 5 2
$\heartsuit$ 8 7 3
$\diamondsuit$ 7 6 4 2
$\clubsuit$ A 10 5

NORTH
(DUMMY)

$\spadesuit$ Q J 10 9 3
$\heartsuit$ J 9 5 2
$\diamondsuit$ –
$\clubsuit$ Q 8 4 3

WEST          EAST

$\spadesuit$ 7 4
$\heartsuit$ A 10 6
$\diamondsuit$ J 9 5 3
$\clubsuit$ K 9 7 6

YOU
(DECLARER)

$\spadesuit$ A K 6
$\heartsuit$ K Q 4
$\diamondsuit$ A K Q 10 8
$\clubsuit$ J 2

There are six sure tricks: two spades, three diamonds, and a club. You expect to get two extra tricks from diamonds, if the suit divides 2–2 or 3–1. Even if diamonds divide 4–0, you can get at least one extra trick—and perhaps take all five if East holds all of the diamonds. Since you're expecting two extra tricks from diamonds most of the time, you need only one trick from hearts. Looking at the hearts in isolation, you'd like to lead twice from dummy toward your hand, hoping the $\heartsuit$A is on your right. That way, you might get two tricks. Since you need only one trick from the suit, however, you can get it through promotion.

After winning a spade trick, lead the $\heartsuit$K to drive out the $\heartsuit$A, promoting your $\heartsuit$Q. If East wins and leads another spade, you win and start going about taking your tricks. You have a small setback when West discards on the first round of diamonds, but you can recover by playing a club to dummy's $\clubsuit$A and taking the finesse against East's $\diamondsuit$J. Technically, you should play a high diamond before promoting the heart trick. You get the bad news about the 4–0 break, but know how to handle it. Although the $\heartsuit$A is favorably located, the contract can be defeated if you cross to dummy with the $\clubsuit$A to lead a heart toward your hand. East can win the $\heartsuit$A, play a low club to West's $\clubsuit$Q, and get three more club tricks when West leads another club. Even if East plays a low heart and lets you win the first heart trick, you'll still be defeated when diamonds break badly, since you no longer have an entry to dummy to take the finesse.

## Hand 13.2

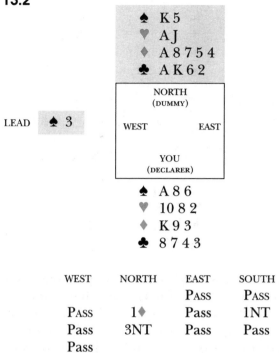

♠ K 5
♥ A J
♦ A 8 7 5 4
♣ A K 6 2

NORTH
(DUMMY)

LEAD ♠ 3

WEST          EAST

YOU
(DECLARER)

♠ A 8 6
♥ 10 8 2
♦ K 9 3
♣ 8 7 4 3

| WEST | NORTH | EAST | SOUTH |
|------|-------|------|-------|
|      |       | PASS | PASS  |
| PASS | 1♦    | Pass | 1NT   |
| Pass | 3NT   | Pass | Pass  |
| Pass |       |      |       |

You're in a contract of 3NT, and the opening lead is the ♠3. You have eight combined cards in both diamonds and clubs. Which suit do you plan to play first?

## Solution 13.2

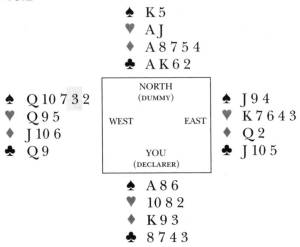

♠ K 5
♥ A J
♦ A 8 7 5 4
♣ A K 6 2

NORTH
(DUMMY)

WEST                    EAST

YOU
(DECLARER)

♠ Q 10 7 3 2
♥ Q 9 5
♦ J 10 6
♣ Q 9

♠ J 9 4
♥ K 7 6 4 3
♦ Q 2
♣ J 10 5

♠ A 8 6
♥ 10 8 2
♦ K 9 3
♣ 8 7 4 3

You have seven sure tricks to start with: two spades, one heart, two diamonds, and two clubs. Using the checklist for developing extra tricks, the only hope appears to be the length in clubs and diamonds. You have eight combined cards in clubs. If the defenders' clubs divide 3–2, as you might expect, you can develop one trick through length by giving up a trick to the defenders. In diamonds, you also have eight combined cards and can develop two extra tricks through length by giving up a trick to the defenders if the missing diamonds divide 3–2.

Developing extra tricks in both clubs and diamonds requires the defenders' cards in the suit to be divided 3–2 and involves giving up one trick to the defenders. There's a difference, however. You get two extra tricks from the diamond suit and only one extra trick from the club suit. Since you need two more tricks, play diamonds, rather than clubs, after winning a spade trick.

You don't have time to develop extra tricks in both clubs and diamonds. By the time you have let the defenders in twice, they'll likely have developed enough tricks to defeat you.

## Hand 13.3

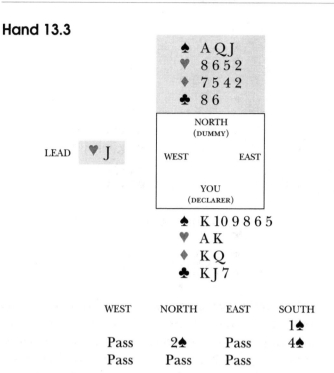

♠ A Q J
♥ 8 6 5 2
♦ 7 5 4 2
♣ 8 6

NORTH
(DUMMY)

LEAD ♥ J

WEST       EAST

YOU
(DECLARER)

♠ K 10 9 8 6 5
♥ A K
♦ K Q
♣ K J 7

| WEST | NORTH | EAST | SOUTH |
|------|-------|------|-------|
|      |       |      | 1♠    |
| Pass | 2♠    | Pass | 4♠    |
| Pass | Pass  | Pass |       |

You've reached 4♠, and the defense has started with the ♥J. What do you plan to do after winning the first trick?

## Solution 13.3

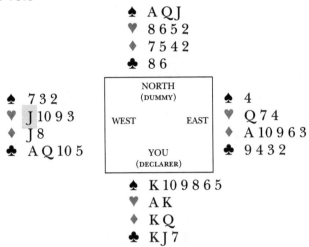

```
                    ♠ A Q J
                    ♥ 8 6 5 2
                    ♦ 7 5 4 2
                    ♣ 8 6
              ┌─────────────────────┐
              │      NORTH           │
  ♠ 7 3 2     │     (DUMMY)          │   ♠ 4
  ♥ J 10 9 3  │  WEST        EAST    │   ♥ Q 7 4
  ♦ J 8       │                      │   ♦ A 10 9 6 3
  ♣ A Q 10 5  │      YOU             │   ♣ 9 4 3 2
              │    (DECLARER)        │
              └─────────────────────┘
                    ♠ K 10 9 8 6 5
                    ♥ A K
                    ♦ K Q
                    ♣ K J 7
```

You have a diamond and three club losers—one too many. There's nothing you can do about the diamond loser, but there are lots of possibilities for eliminating a club loser. The natural instinct is to make use of the ♣K and ♣J. You could cross to dummy with a trump and lead a club toward your hand. If East follows with a low club, you finesse the ♣J, hoping the ♣Q is on your right. If that doesn't work, you travel back to dummy and lead a club toward your ♣K, hoping East has the ♣A. Even if that doesn't work, you have the possibility of trumping the last club loser in the dummy. Unfortunately, on the actual hand, none of those chances succeed. After winning a heart trick, if you lead a spade to dummy and then a club to your ♣J, West wins and leads a trump. You win this in dummy and lead a club to the ♣K, but West wins the ♣A and leads another spade. You now have no spades left in dummy and must still lose a diamond trick and another club trick.

As you might have suspected, the ♣K and ♣J were given to make the hand more difficult—beware the Trojan horse. If you had three low clubs, you'd win the first heart trick and immediately lead a club. The defense could lead a trump, but you'd win and give up a second club trick. Even if the defenders lead another trump, you could win and lead the last club, ruffing it in dummy. Don't let the ♣K and ♣J deflect you from trumping a club loser in dummy. After winning the first heart trick, lead a club from your hand. Nothing can stop you now.

# Hand 13.4

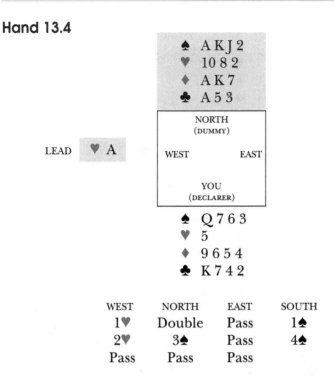

♠ A K J 2
♥ 10 8 2
♦ A K 7
♣ A 5 3

NORTH
(DUMMY)

LEAD   ♥ A

WEST      EAST

YOU
(DECLARER)

♠ Q 7 6 3
♥ 5
♦ 9 6 5 4
♣ K 7 4 2

| WEST | NORTH | EAST | SOUTH |
|------|--------|------|-------|
| 1♥ | Double | Pass | 1♠ |
| 2♥ | 3♠ | Pass | 4♠ |
| Pass | Pass | Pass | |

You're in a contract of 4♠, and the opening lead is the ♥A. How do you plan to get rid of all the losers in your hand?

## Solution 13.4

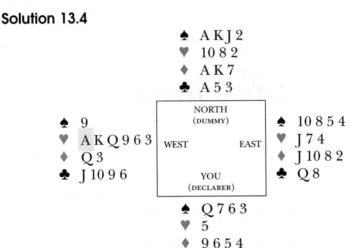

♠ A K J 2
♥ 10 8 2
♦ A K 7
♣ A 5 3

NORTH
(DUMMY)

♠ 9
♥ A K Q 9 6 3
♦ Q 3
♣ J 10 9 6

WEST          EAST

♠ 10 8 5 4
♥ J 7 4
♦ J 10 8 2
♣ Q 8

YOU
(DECLARER)

♠ Q 7 6 3
♥ 5
♦ 9 6 5 4
♣ K 7 4 2

There are no losers in spades, provided the defenders' trump divide no worse than 4–1. You have a heart loser, two diamond losers, and two club losers. You can hope the defenders' diamonds and clubs both divide 3–3—in which case you'd have only one loser in each suit. You could also consider trumping both a diamond loser and a club loser in the dummy.

A much simpler solution appears if you consider how to play the hand from the other side of the table. Dummy's hand contains three heart losers, a diamond loser, and a club loser. By trumping two of dummy's heart losers in your hand, you should end up with enough tricks.

Suppose West continues with a second high heart after winning the first trick. Trump this in your hand, cross to one of dummy's high cards in the minor suits, and lead dummy's last heart, trumping in your hand. Play the ♠Q and a low spade over to dummy. Then draw the rest of the trump. On the last two high trump from dummy, discard two losers from your hand. Take the rest of your winners, and there you go. You get six trump tricks—four high trump plus the two ruffs in your hand—plus two diamond tricks and two club tricks.

You make the contract, despite the fact that the trump suit divided 4–1 and neither minor suit divided 3–3. You've played the hand as a dummy reversal. It would have been a lot easier with partner as declarer. Turn the hand upside-down and try it.

# Glossary

**behind**   The position at the table relative to the player on one's right. A player's cards are said to be behind, or over, those held by the player on the right.

**blocked suit**   A suit with no link cards in the opposite hand.

**break**   The division between the defenders of the cards held in a specific suit. For example, five cards in the defenders' hands could break 3-2.

**count**   Keep track of the number of cards that have been played in each suit.

**cover**   Play a higher-ranking card than the previous card played to a trick.

**crossruff**   Ruff both dummy's losers in declarer's hand and declarer's losers in the dummy during the play of the hand.

**dangerous opponent**   The opponent who could defeat the contract upon gaining the lead.

**discarding a loser**   Throwing away a loser from declarer's hand on an extra winner in the dummy.

**drawing trump**   Playing the trump suit to remove the trump cards held by the opponents.

**ducking**   Playing low cards from both hands to concede a trick to the opponents that could have been won.

**dummy reversal**   Play of the hand in which dummy's losers are trumped in declarer's hand.

**endplay**   Giving a trick to an opponent in an attempt to gain one or more tricks through having the opponent lead to the next trick. Same as throw-in.

**entry**   A card providing a means to win a trick in a specific hand.

**finesse**   An attempt to win a trick with a card when the defenders hold one or more higher-ranking cards in the suit.

**holdup play**  Declining to take a winner at the first opportunity, usually with the intention of removing the link cards from one opponent's hand.

**in front of**  The position at the table relative to the player on one's left. A player's cards are said to be in front of those held by the player on the left.

**length**  The number of cards held in a suit; development of a card into a potential winner by removing all cards held by the opponents in the suit.

**link card**  A card which can be led to a winner (entry) in the opposite hand.

**long side**  The hand containing the majority of cards in a particular suit.

**loser**  A trick which will potentially be lost by declarer during the play.

**losing control**  As declarer, having no trump left in a suit contract to prevent the defenders from taking enough winners to defeat the contract.

**over**  The position at the table relative to the player on one's right. A player's cards are said to be over, or in front of, those held by the player on the right.

**overruff**  Play a higher-ranking trump to a trick than one already played. Same as overtrump.

**overtrump**  Play a higher-ranking trump to a trick than one already played. Same as overruff.

**promotion**  Developing a card into a potential winner by driving out any higher-ranking cards held by the opponents.

**quick loser**  A trick that could be lost by declarer as soon as the defenders have the lead.

**repeated finesse**  A finesse that must be taken more than once.

**ruffing**  Playing a trump to a trick when holding no cards in the suit led. Same as trumping.

**ruffing finesse**  A combination of ruffing a loser and taking a finesse on the same trick.

**safe opponent**  Opponent who could not defeat the contract upon gaining the lead.

**short side**  The hand containing the fewer cards in a specific suit.

**slow loser**  A trick that will potentially be lost by declarer.

**splitting honors**  The play of one of two or more touching high cards by the second player to a trick.

**stranded**   Winners which cannot be taken because there is no entry to the hand containing them.

**sure trick**   A trick which can be taken without giving up the lead to the opponents.

**throw-in**   Giving a trick to an opponent in an attempt to gain one or more tricks through having the opponent lead to the next trick. Same as endplay.

**trumping**   Playing a trump to a trick when holding no cards in the suit led. Same as ruffing.

**trumping a loser**   Playing a trump from dummy on a potential loser in declarer's hand.

**two-way finesse**   A finesse that can be taken against either opponent.

**winner**   A card held by one of the players that will win a trick when it is played.

# Bridge America

Join Bridge America and receive *Bridge America's Better Bridge* magazine. This bi-monthly magazine, edited by Audrey Grant, keeps you up-to-date on everything you need to know to play better bridge. There are articles on a wide variety of topics including play, defense, bidding conventions, famous hands, bridge etiquette, and bridge history.

With your annual membership to Bridge America, you receive a unique deck of E-Z Deal Cards and Companion Booklet which lets you deal and play 20 specially prepared hands. Each year hands cover a different theme, such as "The ten most common mistakes and how to correct them" or "Famous hands from the history of bridge." In addition, Bridge America members receive special discounts on top-rated bridge products.

To join Bridge America, send your name and address along with a check for $30 (US) or $35 (Can.) to Bridge America, 2990 Airways Blvd., Memphis, TN 38116-3847. Or, you can join immediately by calling 1-888-66BRIDGE (1-888-662-7434).

## Bridge Workshops, Seminars, and Festivals

For information on bridge workshops, seminars, and festivals with Audrey Grant call Marilyn Albright: 514-488-0688

## Bridge Supplies

Randy Baron produces a full-color catalog of bridge supplies, including a selection of cards and other specialties. The American Contract Bridge League also has a catalog offering bridge supplies.

Baron-Barclay Bridge Supplies
3600 Chamberlain Lane, Suite 230
Louisville, KY 40241
1-800-274-2221; 502-426-0410; FAX: 502-426-2044

The American Contract Bridge League
Order Department—The Bridge Source
2990 Airways Blvd.
Memphis, TN 38116-3847
1-800-264-2743; FAX: 901-398-7754

Other titles in
# The Better Bridge Series
## by Audrey Grant

From one of the world's foremost bridge teachers comes *Bidding*.
*Bidding* teaches, in clear language, everything you need to know
about the most widely accepted bidding methods. Valuing Your Hand,
Opening the Bidding, and Competitive Bidding are all explained in
easy-to-understand chapters. Exercises and full answers
are also provided. These essential elements will help improve your
bidding practices. You will:

❏ Read about the secrets of hand evaluation so that you can dramati-
cally improve your game;

❏ Learn how to describe your hand to your partner so that the partnership can find its way to the best contract;

❏ Discover new concepts to keep the bidding conversation straightforward.

## BIDDING: The Better Bridge Series
$19.95   ISBN 0-13-080119-4

You'll be defending half the time in any game, so *Defense* is a must for
your bridge library. Soon you'll feel as if you've developed X-ray vision
as you are introduced to ways of visualizing the cards held by your partner. Defense skills, the cornerstone of bridge success, can be honed and
polished with the help of this useful and valuable book. Including:

❏ Learn how to use ten defensive guidelines that have passed the test
of time;

❏ Discover ways to think about defense that go beyond the opening lead;

❏ Find out how to describe your hand to a partner through the cards
you play.

## DEFENSE: The Better Bridge Series
$19.95   ISBN 0-13-080118-6

Let Audrey Grant teach you how to make the most of your bridge
game with her tried-and-true methods for playing for maximum enjoy-
ment and success. Achieve maximum bridge expertise with the help of
this well-written and comprehensive series. Audrey will have you
playing like a professional before you know it! Suitable for novice
players as well as those wishing to perfect their game - these books are
the key to bridge success.

**Available at leading bookstores everywhere.**